The Moral of the Story

Literature, Values, and American Education

The Moral of the Story

Literature, Values, and American Education

Susan Resneck Parr
Department of English
Ithaca College

Teachers College, Columbia University
New York and London   1982

Published by Teachers College Press, 1234 Amsterdam Avenue, New York, N.Y. 10027

Copyright © 1982 by Teachers College, Columbia University

Library of Congress Cataloging in Publication Data

Parr, Susan Resneck.
  The moral of the story.

  Bibliography: p. 221
  Includes index.
  1. Literature and morals.   2.   Literature—Study
and teaching.   3.   Moral education.   4.   Literature,
Modern—History and criticism—Addresses, essays,
lectures.   I.   Title.
PN49.P29   807'.1073   82-751
                                     AACR2

ISBN 0-8077-2669-9 (cloth)
ISBN 0-8077-2716-4 (paper)

Permissions

Some of this work has been previously published and is reprinted here by permission, as follows:

   Parts of Chapter I appeared in slightly different form in my essay "Ethics in Undergraduate Nonethics Courses," in *Ethics Teaching in Higher Education,* ed. Daniel Callahan and Sissela Bok (New York: Plenum Publishing Corp., 1980).
   Portions of Chapter XI originally appeared in my article "Individual Responsibility in *The Great Gatsby,*" *The Virginia Quarterly Review,* 57, no. 4 (Autumn 1981), 662–80.
   Part of Chapter XVI has appeared in my article "Everything Green Looked Black: *Catch-22* as an Inverted Eden," *Notes on Modern American Literature,* 4, no. 4 (Fall 1980), 7–10.
   Quotations from Ralph Ellison's *Invisible Man* that are reprinted in Chapter XV are Copyright © 1947, 1948, 1952 by Ralph Ellison, reprinted by permission of Random House, Inc.

Manufactured in the United States of America

87   86   85   84   83   82   1   2   3   4   5   6

For Alexandra

[Alice] had quite forgotten the Duchess by this time, and was a little startled when she heard her voice close to her ear. "You're thinking about something, my dear, and that makes you forget to talk. I ca'n't tell you just now what the moral of that is, but I shall remember it in a bit."

"Perhaps it hasn't one, " Alice ventured to remark.

"Tut, tut, child!" said the Duchess. "Everything's got a moral, if only you can find it."

—Lewis Carroll
Alice's Adventures in Wonderland

Contents

Contents

Foreword

Every high school teacher of English and every college teacher of undergraduate literature courses could profit from reading, and using, this book. That is a large generalization but, I think, a responsible one. What Professor Parr proposes is at once highly traditional and highly novel: that teachers should arouse in their students an alert, sensitive, undogmatic awareness of the moral issues and values expressed in literature, specifically in fiction. Some prospective readers of this book might assume from its title and subtitle that the approach the author advocates must of necessity be stuffy, "old-fashioned," manipulative, repressive, but such is not at all the case. She does not want us teachers to indoctrinate our students, to force them backward into the role of rigid, censorious moralists; rather, she wants us to urge them forward into becoming truly educated persons.

Quite rightly she has been troubled that present generations of American high school and college students "tend to be morally apathetic, now-oriented, and alienated from learning," and in her first chapter she carefully searches out the causes of this sickness of the spirit that too many young people—and too many older people as well—are not even aware they suffer from. She does not wish, however, to blame the victims but to find a cure. Certainly part of the blame lies with us teachers, since for various reasons we have not sufficiently confronted our students with the problems, moral in the largest sense, that fiction embodies always implicitly, sometimes explicitly.

Fiction writers might be defined, in fact, as persons concerned to put into story form the moral problems faced by individuals within their society and by the society itself; writers use their fictions to analyze such problems, to dramatize them, often to propose or imply solutions, sometimes "optimistic," sometimes "pessimistic." These problems may be presented—to take representative authors and works discussed in this book—through one of the many modes of realism as in William Faulkner's "Dry September" or F. Scott Fitzgerald's *The Great Gatsby,* or in highly symbolic form as in Joseph Conrad's *Heart of Darkness* or Ralph Ellison's *Invisible Man,* or even in fable as in Franz Kafka's *The Metamorphosis.* Even fiction writers more interested in immediate large sales of their books than in future critical fame have some sort of vision of what is right and wrong with the world which they tell their stories about, however simplistic the vision and the telling may be.

What Professor Parr urges us to try to effect in our students through this approach to literature is a more aware, more sensitive, more compassionate, yet also clear-minded, informed, realistic understanding of themselves and other human beings. In her second chapter she puts her purpose eloquently.

> Although my own hope is that students become more aware, more caring, and more committed to responsible choice, I am not advocating that teachers argue for a particular code of behavior or a particular set of values. Rather, I think that we as teachers serve our students best if we can engage them in the learning process, teach them to understand and express the complexities of all that they study, bring them to recognize the value of individual moral choice, and give them a sense that they are part of a larger human community.

Fortunately she is not satisfied merely to assert theoretically; she demonstrates practically. The largest part of this book is composed of extended discussions of sixteen novels and short stories that are among the most frequently taught in college-preparatory high school courses and in introductory literature courses in college. From my own teaching experience I know that the author's presentation will be immediately useful in the classroom. First, she briefly summarizes the central issues of the work being examined. Second, she provides two sets of questions, one set focusing on significant general issues raised by the work, the other listing "Questions for Discussions, Papers, Exams." Third, and most importantly, she analyzes each work at length and in detail, showing how patterns of development emerge from the text and coalesce into patterns of meaning. Having myself taught eight of these works, some of them several times, and having read the others, some of them several times, I confidently affirm that her suggested readings are perceptive and are clearly and persuasively set forth. There is a strong, penetrating mind at work here, one that raises basic issues and questions and suggests solutions and answers, but not one that seeks to enforce its own conclusions. When Professor Parr states her own views, as she often forthrightly does, it is with the purpose of encouraging others, both teachers and students, to state their own.

I began these remarks by asserting the value of this book for teachers of literature. I conclude by asserting its value for other teachers, teachers in other areas of the humanities, in the social sciences, even in the physical and biological sciences, these last, I have found, often being more aware of the humanities than we in the humanities are of the sciences. Indeed, I would recommend this book to non-teachers as well—to doctors, lawyers, electricians, filing clerks, airplane pilots, assembly line workers, filling station attendants, bankers, businessmen, politicians (especially politicians)—in short, to anyone. If all literate American citizens read this book and the fictions it discusses with such insight, I expect our nation would be, not merely a good place for many to live in, but a better place for all of us to live in. Still, one should not ask for too much, and anyway I distrust large claims. I'll settle—for now, at least—for having just all teachers of literature read and use *The Moral of the Story*.

—Walter B. Rideout
Harry Hayden Clark Professor of English
The University of Wisconsin-Madison
January 30, 1982

Preface

THE IMPETUS FOR THIS BOOK is my perception, shared by other teachers and verified by national surveys and tests, that the post-Vietnam, post-Watergate generations of American high school and college students tend to be morally apathetic, now-oriented, and alienated from learning.[1] Many of these students are simply indifferent to questions of morals and values. Others tend to be unreflective about the complexities of such questions. Yet others reject such concerns as irrelevant, believing that individual choice, moral and otherwise, is futile. In addition, many students leave our schools with little if any understanding of the power of cultural, social, political, religious, and familial values to shape perception and choice. Of this group, some naïvely assume that they are self-created and fully able to design their lives. Others, with equally limited understanding of the complex ways in which values influence perception and choice, genuinely believe that individuals, alone or in groups, can do little or nothing to alter their lives or affect their worlds.

But whether they perceive themselves to be truly powerful or totally powerless, many of these students concern themselves primarily with the immediate and the personal without taking the next step into a consciousness of the implications of their actions or into responsibility. For many of them, the past often seems lifeless, the future beyond their ability to affect, and genuine communication between people elusive. Not surprisingly, they value subjective responses rather than informed, critical judgments and choices. They also tend to be indifferent to matters of context, values, the future, and the tools of analysis and communication. Such students embody what many social critics of the 1970s have dubbed meism or the new narcissism.[2]

Such attitudes and beliefs have led increasing numbers of students to define their schooling primarily in vocational terms. Favoring pre-professional training over humanistic study, many of these students assume that a liberal education will have little pertinence to either their immediate or their future lives.[3] At the same time, the growing need for remedial courses has shifted the emphasis of many high school and freshman-sophomore college programs from general education to work in basic skills.[4] This shift has meant that many students do not elect the very courses which they may need most; that is, courses which encourage them to see themselves as part of an ongoing culture, which communicate to them the complexities of the human experience, and which demonstrate that a concern with moral choice is not merely a meaningless or academic exercise.

I am not blaming the victim. Given the fact that most of these students were children during the Vietnam conflict, Watergate, and the horrifying assassinations of political figures in the sixties, their desire to distance themselves from all but their own lives may be understandable. In addition, it is possible that the very complexity of the choices facing them is itself leading to alienation and apathy. Like computers that have been overloaded, many of these students may simply shut down.

But whatever the causes, the alienation and apathy exist, and the educational system has done little to address them. Nevertheless, as bleak as this assessment seems, I am optimistic that the educational system can do much to revitalize itself and address these problems. Even though I recognize that the schools themselves in great measure have contributed both to student attitudes and to the crisis in knowledge and literacy, I am convinced that individual teachers can and do motivate students to learn and to care. I make this argument largely because I have come to believe that what appears to be moral callousness on the part of students is much more frequently the product of a mixture of unreflectiveness, limited knowledge, and the notion that questions of morals, values, and responsibility are not pertinent to education. In contrast, my own experience tells me that when students become engaged in the moral and values questions inherent in the material that they study and when they believe that responsible choices are possible, they are likely as well to become engaged in all aspects of their learning.

What I am advocating is simply this: that those of us who teach must address, directly and within our regular courses, these problems of moral apathy, now-orientation, and alienation from learning. In particular, we need to incorporate, routinely and reflectively, in all our courses a focus on the moral and values dimensions of that which we teach. Although much of this book will concentrate on how literary works give life to the complexities of moral and values questions, the approach I am suggesting throughout is applicable to almost all disciplines. In fact, I believe that this book will be of use not only to literature teachers but to others—such as historians, philosophers, political scientists, and sociologists—whose courses might well benefit from a literary component that critically explores morals and values.

The first chapter of this book elaborates on many of the ideas outlined in this preface. It focuses on the problems of student ignorance, illiteracy, now-orientation, and moral apathy. It examines why these problems need to be redressed. It also argues that the educational system, albeit an outgrowth of the larger American culture, nevertheless to a great extent has been responsible for these problems and therefore can contribute to their remedy.

The next chapter introduces the discussion of the literature and outlines the values, assumptions, and educational goals of that discussion. Here, I also make reference to certain nonliterary works that stimulated my own thinking about morals and values and that often helped clarify my ideas. The remainder of the book consists of a series of chapters devoted to exploring the moral and values dimensions of specific literary works and an Appendix suggesting model courses centered around the books discussed. Most of these works fall into the category of classics typically taught in introductory level college courses and college-preparatory high school courses. The majority of them are by American writers, but Tolstoy, Conrad, Kafka, and Camus are also represented. I have also included several works by women writers that have been recently rediscovered, which will enrich courses in which they are taught. All the books were chosen because they dramatize in some way the complexities of such issues as consciousness, freedom, choice, responsibility, and the search for meaning and self-realization.

I am indebted to several institutions and a great many people for their help with this book. Princeton University, where I was a visiting associate professor and then a visiting fellow in 1979–80, provided me an opportunity to develop my ideas and begin writing. In particular, I want to thank A. Walton Litz, whose interest and support has meant a great deal. Ithaca College, my home institution, has contributed to the writing of this book in significant ways. By naming me a Dana Scholar, the college released me from some of my teaching duties as I was completing the manuscript. My colleagues provided intellectual companionship. In this regard, I am especially grateful to Thomas C.

Longin, Dean of Humanities and Sciences. It is he who encouraged me to write the book and then, as it evolved, became its most effective critic. His friendship is one I shall always cherish. The Institute for Educational Affairs provided substantial grant support so that I could teach less and write more. Given our different approaches to education, I want to credit and thank them for funding my work. I also wish to thank Daniel Callahan and the Hastings Center, Institute of Society, Ethics, and the Life Sciences. Their Teaching of Ethics project gave me a context in which to explore my concerns.

I am also grateful to a number of other friends, colleagues, and members of my family. Phyllis Janowitz has been my most consistent and thorough reader and a wonderful friend throughout the writing of this book. Jan Beyea has contributed an important combination of rigorous criticism and friendship. Karen Brazell, Doreet Hopp, D. Bob Gowin, John Marmora, William Scoones, Jean Smith, and my parents, Elliott and Dory Resneck, all have been thoughtful readers and perceptive critics. In addition, my parents have been for me an example of how to live in the world. George Bonham has been a wonderful resource person and sounding board. Dennis Thompson gave me invaluable help in the beginning stages of my writing. Thomas M. Rotell, Director of Teachers College Press, has from our first meeting been a genuine support because of his confidence in the book and his very helpful counsel. Walter B. Rideout, a model of what a mentor can be, has helped me throughout my career. To Michael Hopp, I am grateful for the title. Donna Freedline, who typed the manuscript, deserves special thanks for her care and her help. Pat Andrews, Daniel Boylen, D. Lydia Bronte, Holly Clemans, Mary Beth Norton, Gary Parr, Alice Pempel, Joel Savishinsky, Niki Zaloom, my sister, Brenda Resneck, and my sister and brother-in-law, Linda and Richard DiStefano, have all contributed to my writing in less tangible but equally important ways.

I am, of course, deeply indebted to my students over the past sixteen years. Their responsiveness to ideas and their enthusiasm about learning when they are given the opportunity, the tools, and the encouragement to think for themselves have given me hope and inspired me to write.

Most of all, I want to thank my ten-year-old daughter Alexandra (Sasha) for her patience, her love, and for being who she is. In the most essential of ways, it is for her that I have written this book.

Ithaca, New York
May, 1982

The Moral
of the
Story

Literature, Values,
and American Education

CHAPTER

I

Values and American Education

A FEW WEEKS BEFORE the American Olympic Committee voted to support an American boycott of the 1981 Moscow games, I met a group of young women who were in training for the competition. All were in their early to mid-twenties, and all were graduates of or on leave from highly reputable Eastern colleges. Not unexpectedly, to a woman they were unhappy that their efforts and self-discipline of the last few years might not bring them Olympic glory. The others at this social gathering, for the most part academics a generation or two older than the athletes, were sympathetic to the disappointment but generally supported the concept of a boycott. The athletes rejected most of the reasons offered. The boycott would not, they insisted, prompt Russia to withdraw troops from Afghanistan nor would it affect future Soviet policies. As participants in the game, they argued, they might informally and personally be able to educate the Soviet citizenry, an opportunity they believed the boycott would deny them. They were also emphatic that because they had paid for their own training, the United States government had no right to limit their freedom and to negate their individual rights.

The proponents of the boycott were as persistent, asserting that the United States had a moral obligation to protest the invasion of Afghanistan, regardless of whether it might alter Soviet policy. It was, they explained, a matter of standing up for certain principles. Others pointed out that it was highly unlikely that the Olympians would have

1

any genuine access to the Russian people. Eventually, I asked the question that had been nagging me: Would the athletes have participated in the 1936 Berlin Olympics? The response was not what I had anticipated. I had expected to be told either that our participation in those Olympics had been desirable because of Jesse Owens' victory or that the analogy was a faulty one because the Soviet action was not the equivalent of the Hitlerian evils. To my dismay, however, these college-educated and unquestionably intelligent young women explained that they could not really answer my question because they did not know much about the Berlin Olympics.

Nor was this the first time I had been confronted with people of this age willing to make complex value judgments and moral choices without knowledge of historical precedent or cultural context. In one of the more striking examples, I was similarly distressed by student ignorance of Nazism. During a classroom discussion, a number of my students, all juniors and seniors, attacked Joseph Heller for not advocating pacifism at the end of *Catch-22*. They were unhappy that Yossarian, the novel's hero, needed to justify his desertion from the American army. Most had glossed over the details of Yossarian's argument that his action was not irresponsible. They simply did not perceive the importance of his rationale that he had already flown far more than the standard number of missions, that the war in Germany had already been won, that the war in Japan was nearly over, and that his continued participation would not serve America but only those who were exploiting the war for personal profit. These students saw desertion as the best choice under all circumstances.

I probed more deeply and it soon became evident that these students and a great many others in the class were unaware of or unmoved by the horrors of the Holocaust and the realities of World War II. They did not see Hitler as a genuine threat to freedom, and many were startled to learn that Paris had fallen to Nazi troops and that London had been under siege. Rather, they equated American action in World War II with American involvement in Vietnam, attributing both primarily to economic motives. Although all could talk about the six million Jews whom the Nazis murdered, many of them did so in what seemed to be a detached way, as though they were discussing a scene in a novel or a historical fact that was the equivalent of any other fact they had studied in school.

Nor did any student challenge Yossarian's refusal to deal seriously with the conflict his choice embodied, that between individual morality and social order. They were instead content with the flippancy of Yossarian's response that if all people thought only of themselves,

"Then I'd certainly be a damned fool to feel any other way, wouldn't I?"[1]

Because so many of these students, like the athletes, had been willing to adopt a stance without being fully informed and without being reflective about the complexities of the issues, I devoted the rest of the session to a discussion of the nature of Hitler's design and Nazi actions. I also pointed out the larger philosophical implications of Yossarian's choice of desertion. The few students who were extremely knowledgeable about the historical events took an active part, and the tenor of the discussion changed. By the end of the hour, many in the class became actively engaged in considering the moral complexities of Yossarian's attempt to reach the neutral and socialist Sweden and of his rationale for his choice.

I wish to emphasize that in neither case was my concern rooted in the specifics of the students' positions but rather in their ability to make judgments so easily with so little knowledge of history and so little attention to the larger moral implications of their choices. I also worried about their indifference to issues beyond the immediate and the personal, their belief that the individual's primary obligation is to self, and their conviction that attempts at moral action are futile.

For the athletes, these attitudes took form in their argument that because the American government had not financed their training, they owed nothing to the government. Moreover, because they had so little confidence that the boycott would bring immediate and tangible results, the athletes resented the personal sacrifice that it would require. With *Catch-22*, the focus was slightly different. In that discussion, the prevailing belief was that the established system was so powerful and corrupt that individuals could not affect it and should therefore make choices in terms of self-interest. But to make this argument, the students had to overlook evidence in the novel to the contrary. For example, they ignored the fact that Yossarian's earlier refusal to fly more missions *had* influenced others to protest the corruption and the injustice. They also minimized Yossarian's willingness to risk his own life in an attempt to take responsibility for the only remaining innocent in the novel, Nately's whore's kid sister.

Values, Perception, and Choice

The conviction that individuals can make no impact on the world is especially worrisome because it is often self-fulfilling. Cynicism about moral action is likely to lead to moral apathy and to an abdication of individual responsibility. As significantly, these attitudes affect the ways in which people actually perceive what they read, hear, and personally experience. In my own classes, I frequently recognize that a belief that individuals are morally impotent leads my students to disregard or misperceive evidence suggesting otherwise. In other words, preconceptions shape not only my students' interpretive response to the course material but, on an even more basic level, what in the material they consciously attend to.

Such has been the case when I have taught Heller's *Something Happened* in junior-senior seminars, first at Ithaca College and then at Princeton University. In both classes, a few students, although far from the majority, saw as positive Robert Slocum's decision to conform totally to a dehumanizing corporate structure and to deny his conscience and his consciousness. He was gaining peace, they argued. But to make their judgments, the students ignored the textual evidence that Slocum's peace was itself dehumanizing. Specifically, they overlooked the fact that his equilibrium was founded on his ability to repress both his sense of responsibility for having killed his son and his memories of the boy. Other students, who were distressed by Slocum for those reasons, nevertheless found acceptable his achieving a better relationship with his wife and his teenage daughter. Once again, the pattern was to dismiss the means Slocum employed to gain his goals; that he lied and that he bought his new relationships. Unable to give his wife and daughter love or communication, Slocum gained their favor by buying his wife a new house and his daughter a new car.

But what seems most significant is that all of these students and many others in the class believed that Slocum really had no other alternatives. Even those who were appalled at his choices explained that they shared his sense of impotence and his belief that he could do nothing to effect change or to assert his own humanity. They tended to assume that Heller too was condoning Slocum's actions. Heller might not like his protagonist, the discussion went, but he does not really expect people to be otherwise, given the power of society. In other words, many of the students had not considered the possibility that Heller might be dramatizing the devastation wrought by moral abdication.

The same sense of individual impotence shaped the responses of another class of mine to Lina Wertmüller's provocative film *Seven Beauties*. Although the film horrified most of my students, they accepted as both understandable and inevitable the protagonist's decision to attempt to survive a Nazi concentration camp regardless of the cost to his own humanity and to the lives of others. They condoned his metaphorical and his literal prostitution. They even condoned his decision to murder a friend so that he himself could live. Almost everyone in the class argued that the protagonist, Pasqualino, had no other options. As a product of an immoral and perverted world, several insisted, he could not be expected to be better than that world. The students did not recognize that the film might be condemning Pasqualino for his failure to say no to evil; nor did they perceive that Wertmüller might be arguing that other options, however difficult or dangerous, might be better ones.

In this case, their prior attitudes seemed literally to affect what the students saw on the screen. Of the approximately thirty juniors and seniors in the class, not one recalled a final moment in the film which suggested that Wertmüller was condemning Pasqualino's choices. It was not that they did not understand the scene; it was that they did not remember even seeing it. In that episode, Pasqualino has just returned home to discover that his girlfriend and his sisters have become prostitutes. The discovery has several ironies. Before the war, Pasqualino had been so devoted to preserving what he saw as his family's honor and name that he had murdered the man who had corrupted one of his sisters. It was this act that had eventually led to his incarceration in the concentration camp, to his own prostitution, and to his sacrificing his friend. Now, home and free, Pasqualino observes his image in a two-tiered mirror. His mother stands behind him, celebrating the fact that he is still alive. At that instant, the camera moves in for a close-up and in the process, Pasqualino's face disappears, replaced on the screen by the slat between the two sides of the mirror. He may be alive, the moment implies, but the price of his survival is that his life now has little meaning.

Others in higher education have reported a similar fatalism and a similar willingness on the part of students to assume that there are only limited options. After showing the film *Battle of Algiers,* Cornell history professor John Weiss was surprised that many of his students so easily accepted the film's stance—that the Algerians had no choice other than terrorism. Because history had happened in a certain way, these students believed that way was inevitable.[2]

Richard Hunt, professor of government at Harvard, has labeled this phenomenon a "no fault" view of history. After teaching a course called "Moral Dilemmas in a Repressive Society: Nazi Germany," Hunt concluded that his students held "depressingly fatalistic conclusions about major moral dilemmas facing the German people at their particular time and place in history." Hunt was especially concerned that "clearly some of the trends of our time seem to be running toward a no-fault, guilt-free society. One might say the virtues of responsible choice, paying the penalty, taking the consequences all appear at low ebb today."[3]

Meism, Moral Apathy, and Ignorance

In the past several years, statistical evidence has emerged to support the view that students are now-oriented, morally apathetic, and convinced that they are essentially powerless. There is also evidence to suggest that students of the late seventies and early eighties are less knowledgeable than their predecessors. Arthur Levine, for instance, has come to these conclusions after analyzing national surveys of student attitudes conducted in 1969, 1976, 1978, and 1979 by the Carnegie Commission and the Carnegie Council on Policy Studies in Higher Education. In his discussion of these surveys and others, *When Dreams and Heroes Died,* Levine contrasts students of the late seventies with their counterparts a decade earlier. His conclusion is that the later generation is, among other things, "self-concerned and me-oriented," "disenchanted with politics," "career-oriented," "competitive," and "interested in material success."[4] Levine stresses the statistical finding that "91 percent of the students say they are optimistic about themselves, but only 41 percent are optimistic about the country."[5] This disparity, he argues, supports the contention that the students' me-orientation stems from a "lifeboat mentality."[6] Levine also notes that in 1976, 49 percent of the students surveyed "agree that individuals can do little or nothing to bring about change in our society."[7] In summary, Levine insists:

> There is a sense among today's undergraduates that they are passengers on a sinking ship, a Titanic if you will, called the United States or the world. Fatalism and fear of becoming one of the victims is widespread. And there is a growing belief among college students that if they are being forced to ride on a doomed vessel, they owe it to themselves to make the trip as lavish as possible and go first class. This attitude permeates their educational, social, and political lives.[8]

The Council on Learning and the Educational Testing Service, after testing students for "global understanding," have arrived at the equally dismal view that today's students seem to possess "a limited, parochial view of the world." They have also concluded that students lack substantial knowledge of international affairs and, as significantly, that this lack of knowledge "would appear to be related to the general lack of interest in other nations and world issues."[9] But as the eval-

6

uators of the survey report, "the most dismaying result was that education majors, the teachers of tomorrow, were the lowest scorers on the knowledge test."[10]

Such national surveys also reveal that students do seem to separate questions of morals and values from their education. Again and again, students define the knowledge they seek as vocational. For example, in 1979, three-quarters of the incoming freshmen surveyed cited their hope of obtaining a "better job" as one of their major reasons for going to college.[11] As a result, students increasingly devalue humanities courses, the very place where they would be most apt to consider the complexities of moral and values questions. Instead, in 1976, "At least one out of every three students believe that the humanities are of value only to students planning to teach (33 percent); that they are irrelevant to the student's own interests (33 percent); and more practically, that they are useless in preparing for a job (32 percent)."[12]

Enrollment patterns and surveys of college presidents and personnel officers verify that students are acting on these convictions. Increasingly, students are taking more professional and preprofessional courses and fewer courses in both the humanities and the social sciences.[13] It is especially telling in this regard, that between 1969 and 1979 the number of college freshmen who told questioners that they thought it important or essential that they develop a philosophy of life shrank from 82 percent to 53 percent.[14]

Faculties also commonly complain that their students lack knowledge of and interest in both the distant and the recent past, in literature, and in other cultures. For example, high school teachers and college professors alike, from a variety of different locations, have reported to me their worry that most of their students are unfamiliar with the Bible, the source of so much Western thought and art. Their students are equally uninformed about such recent phenomena as the civil rights movement, the Vietnam war, and, except in the simplest terms, the Watergate scandal.[15] A class of my own college freshmen and sophomores explained to me in 1976 that Vietnam was a war of importance and interest only to my generation and not to theirs. Whether or not noted biologist Erwin Chargaff is right that "Ours is about the most ignorant age that can be imagined,"[16] other measures— such as declining college board scores and the increasingly simplistic level at which textbooks are being written—must be viewed with concern.[17]

Some disclaimers do seem in order here. To begin with, attempts to generalize about one's own era and to distinguish between past and present almost certainly carry with them biases of their own. Typically, adults are nostalgic about their own youth and critical of those younger than they. Indeed, Princeton philosopher Walter Kaufmann was probably right that the perception that the past was better is itself likely to be oversimplistic, uninformed, and, ironically, indicative of the need for humanistic study. As Kaufmann put it:

> I do not mean to praise the past at the expense of the present as if there had been more reflection on goals in my youth. Those who complain that the salt used to be saltier (i.e., "that things used to be good") may be suspected of having lost their taste and of being old. And those who believe that past ages were not sick ought to study the humanities.[18]

Secondly, a variety of social, political, and psychological factors have affected student attitudes, beliefs, and knowledge. For example, the country's movement toward mass education at the secondary and college levels has changed the nature of the student population. That an increasing percentage of college-bound and college-going students are female, members of minority groups, and over the age of twenty-five is certain to have had an impact on student interests, motivations, objectives, and academic preparation. The economic recession of the seventies has also influenced student thought. In contrast to their socially concerned and politically active predecessors in the sixties, this later generation of students does not have the assurance that if it dropped out it could tune back in if it so chose.

Television, as the most significant purveyor and creator of popular American culture, is also likely to be responsible for certain attitudes, beliefs, and goals. Television may well condition its viewers, often at very young ages, to be passive observers rather than active participants. The fantasy world of easy solutions that television frequently creates may also lead young people to assume that individual sacrifice is unnecessary. At the other extreme, the violent world that television regularly dramatizes may further encourage individuals to become more self-concerned than they might otherwise be.

It is also likely that television has replaced for at least some students the far richer common culture to be gained by reading. This lack of a shared culture itself is felt in the classroom in subtle and important ways. Because so many students are unfamiliar with the Bible, mythology, history, and literature, teachers cannot draw on these sources to illustrate certain abstract concepts. In turn, when students lack a ready understanding of these concepts, they may not recognize either the complexities inherent in many of their own experiences or the possibilities of alternative choices and actions.

The Responsibility of the Schools

The question of assigning responsibility is often difficult. In the case of the educational system, it is even more complicated because schools both are the product of and contributors to the larger culture. On the one hand, the structure, the content, and the goals of a great many courses and programs reflect whatever anti-intellectualism, moral apathy, and now-orientation exist in American society. On the other hand, the educational system contributed to those attitudes. In fact, I would contend that the educational experience itself encourages students to oversimplify the complexities of the moral choices that the modern world and their personal lives occasion. It also often devalues informed choice in favor of a more personal, subjective response.

To begin with, many teachers, like their students, see questions of morals and values as distinct from knowledge. Many academicians focus on facts and skills alone. Those who confuse any overt attention to morals and values with indoctrination tend to avoid issues with any ethical component, insisting that teaching ought to be value-free. Those committed to teaching the so-called basics shy away from morals and values, generally perceiving such concerns to be frills or luxuries for which they have neither the time nor the energy. Those influenced by either positivism or relativism, although for differing reasons, are also likely to avoid morals and values questions. The former are wary of issues that offer no measurable solutions, whereas the latter, deeming values to be matters of personal preference, often judge ethical problems unworthy of classroom attention. In fact, many humanists and social scientists have adopted both a value-free stance and pseudoscientific methods. For instance, advocates of such critical schools as New Criticism, behaviorism, structuralism, and metaethics typically stress the quantitative rather than the qualitative and concern themselves with questions of form rather than meaning. But whatever their reasons, the message that such teachers give to their students is that morals and values have no pertinence to education and may even be trivial issues.

College faculties especially tend to ignore moral and values questions because higher education usually rewards the scholar with expertise in a narrow field and devalues the generalist.[19] The departmental structure further encourages specialization. Because departments make the initial recommendations for tenure and promotion, they generally approve of research and teaching within the boundaries of their own disciplines. In fact, faculty members often distrust those whose interests cross territorial lines, arguing that interdisciplinary concerns detract from the work they deem the most important: the knowledge and methodology of their own disciplines. Professional journals and foundations perpetuate these biases, further discouraging a broader approach that might consider the complexities of moral choice, the power of values, and the relationship between knowledge, morals, and values. Specifically, journals seldom publish and foundations seldom fund work on pedagogical, interdisciplinary, or moral issues.

Nor do colleges integrate for their students the disparate areas of knowledge to which they are exposed. Students typically design their own course of study, with little guidance outside their majors. Whatever its merits, this elective system has the obvious disadvantage of allowing students to select courses unreflectively and to concentrate on studies related only to their special interests.

In contrast, teachers who do concern themselves with morals and values all too often do so without an accompanying emphasis on the need for reflection, critical analysis, and informed choice. Stressing the personal and the subjective, they often use the material of their disciplines as a springboard for student discussions of personal experiences. For example, the increasingly popular values-clarification movement consistently asks students to determine how they feel—not what they think, know, or need to know—about such value-laden issues as integration and the draft. Professing to be value-free, values clarification instead embodies a series of values antithetical to informed, critical choice. By encouraging students to identify and to judge their own values in the context of the immediate and the personal, values-clarification exercises suggest that history, literature, philosophy, and the study of other cultures are irrelevant to the development of a personal value system or to acts of individual choice. By emphasizing the personal and the immediate, the values-clarification approach similarly devalues the vast reservoir of historical, literary, and philosophical exploration of the complexities facing individuals who must choose between self and others, who must balance personal obligations with societal ones, and who strive for self-realization in the context of their culture, their community, and their family.[20]

Ironically, the proliferation of ethics courses on college campuses inspired by Watergate may further reinforce the sense that there is and should be a split between knowledge and moral choice. Such courses generally are electives, issue-oriented, applied rather than theoretical, and "aimed explicitly at preprofessional students."[21] Other ethics courses tend to be located in philosophy or religion departments or in special values programs. Despite their appeal, such courses generally reach only a self-selected audience of students already interested in morals and values. Valuable as these courses are, it may well be that the rest of the student population is even more in need of considering ethical issues. Moreover, compartmentalizing moral concerns into separate courses may trivialize those concerns, suggesting to students and faculties alike that ethics are important only in a professional, purely intellectual, or religious context.

There are also those who want schools to teach a certain set of values. For example, the eighties have brought with them the so-called Moral Majority, whose devotees argue that the values of Christianity and capitalism should be taught as moral absolutes. Attacking what they have labeled as secular humanism, parent groups holding this view have begun to insist that education be stripped of any critical deliberation of morals and values questions.[22]

The reasons for such diverse approaches to the educational process and to educational goals are themselves illuminating. Indeed, the history of the educational system suggests that it has been the product of some of the same problems it is now perpetuating: unreflectiveness, now-orientation, lack of confidence in the efficacy of individual and group action, and the compartmentalization of knowledge and moral issues. Certainly, educators as a group have failed and continue to fail to confront actively and fully the goals of the educational system as a whole and the complexities of contemporary education in particular.[23] Instead, discussions about such matters often have an unreflective, ritualistic quality.

Year after year, in most colleges, faculties perform their own variations on a ritual drama. The same play is staged regularly with great seriousness and the best intentions. Although the play allows improvisations, the basic script was written long ago, and time and place seem to alter it only slightly. Occasionally, an actor or two retires or does not have his or her contract renewed. Those parts then are assumed by newly hired, usually younger players. These new actors often seem like clones of the old, so generally their presence changes nothing at all. Sometimes they bring a new intensity or a new timidity to the roles, which, to the relief of the veterans, usually becomes muted within a year or two. The most excitement occurs when, for political and personal reasons external to the play itself, characters exchange roles. For example, the faculty member who has been a self-serving Iago for years suddenly begins to sound like a naïve Othello, and Othello, in dismay at being usurped, plays Iago with a vengeance. The play's title: *The Annual Review of the Curriculum.*

Faculties typically address at least some if not all of the following questions: Should students be required to take courses in certain specified areas? If so, how many courses, in what areas, and which students? Should the goal of introductory courses be breadth or depth? Should more interdisciplinary courses be offered? Is team-teaching productive? What should be done about students who need remedial work? Should remedial reading, writing, and math courses be given for credit? Should students be required to take composition courses? foreign languages? more science? How can non-English teachers be encouraged to stress the importance of clear and logical writing in their classes?

At the end of the discussions, there usually is a vote, which either preserves the status quo or adjusts the existing system slightly. But for the most part, the content, the goals, and the assumptions behind individual courses and the larger curriculum remain unquestioned.[24] In other words, few people really question the departmental structure and few wish to question genuinely, critically, and thoroughly their function, their objectives, or their methodology.

Many of the same issues dominate discussions about primary- and secondary-school programs, discussions that are frequently as ritualized as those on college campuses. The difference is that faculty members are seldom involved. Rather, the players are state boards of regents appointed by elected officials, elected local school boards, and administrators chosen by those boards. Because power is directly tied to electoral politics, elementary and secondary education often is more immediately affected by external social and political factors than is higher education. In the sixties and the seventies, for example, busing, the attack on schools as oppressive institutions, and a wide range of new social attitudes all have had an impact on school policies. Controversies about such previously debated issues as tracking, community versus centralized control, open classrooms, the place of basic skills in the curriculum, the separation of church and state, sex education courses, and censorship of course content have been newly inflamed.

In her study of the New York public school system, *The Great School Wars,* Diane Ravitch verifies that many of the same concerns have characterized school debates over the past century. Ravitch also demonstrates just how much the substance, the form, and the administration of elementary and secondary education are tied to political, economic, and social factors but not to specifically educational ones. As she concludes, "While the language of the school wars relates to educational issues, the underlying context will continue to reflect fundamental value clashes among discordant ethnic, cultural, racial, and religious groups."[25] In other words, although educational debates typically reflect a community's values, the debaters often do not reflect on these values.

The history of American education has also been characterized by confusion about whether schools should provide students with vocational or professional training, should prepare them for citizenship in American society, or should offer learning for its own sake.[26] In addition, the revolution in social values in the sixties led schools to focus more directly on students' personal and psychological development and to assume social service functions once left to families, communities, and religious institutions. Each approach was tied to larger social attitudes and trends. For example, the more pragmatic concern with skills and vocational training seems an outgrowth of a certain anti-intellectual strain in American life and the country's commitment to mass education. The concern with citizenship apparently came with the secularization of the schools. The concern with student development accompanied the increase in the number of working parents, the breakdown of the nuclear family, changing sexual mores, and the increased involvement of teenagers with drugs and alcohol. All three approaches were also tied to a traditional but almost certainly exaggerated confidence in the schools.

External considerations, far more often than an educational vision, seem to have shaped and continue to shape curricular offerings, methodology, and goals. But whatever the cause, little attention has been paid to creating curricula that integrate morals, values, personal development, and knowledge. When students in the late sixties demanded relevance, the response was an immediate and unreflective proliferation of electives focusing on the contemporary. As a result, in many high school and college English departments, the classics have been abandoned in favor of science fiction, fantasy, detective novels, popular fiction, the media, and what at least one program designates as "Interpersonal and Intrapersonal Relations." In many history and social studies courses, students similarly focus on contemporary events without ever gaining an understanding of the larger context or of their own cultural values. Although many such courses are effective and desirable, they have become substitutes for, rather than additions to, a carefully designed program of study. Their effect, moreover, has been to further encourage the now-orientation of many students.

In the seventies, economic considerations began, in even more serious ways than in the past, to influence the educational experience. Some schools, desperate to maintain an economically feasible faculty-student ratio, easily pandered to popular tastes at the expense of educational ideals.[27] They simultaneously began to eliminate courses and programs that were considered frills. Because many of these so-called frills were in the arts, languages, and interdisciplinary studies, a growing number of students are now being denied access to courses that might broaden their historical and cultural awareness. Moreover, some courses that had been developed in response to popular demand have faltered when student interest moved elsewhere, even though some of them—such as environmental studies, women's studies, and black studies—fulfilled legitimate curricular needs. Frequently, these courses have either become institutionalized as tokens that have little effect on the curriculum as a whole or they have been eliminated altogether.

Even textbooks have become victim to economic concerns rather than educational ones. As Frances FitzGerald documented in her study of American history textbooks, *America Revised,* the textbook industry, not educators, determines the content and the viewpoint of most high school texts. The result has been that publishers, desiring to reach the broadest market possible while satisfying various special-interest groups, have eliminated anything that might be controversial. In Fitz-Gerald's words, the textbooks now represent "a kind of lowest common denominator of American tastes."[28] Teachers have aided this process by failing to judge individually and critically the material they use in their own classes. Instead, they typically give over to committees the authority to select their textbooks.[29]

Despite such problems in the American educational system, I do not agree with Ivan Illich and others that societies should be de-schooled. In part, I see deschooling as an impractical, unworkable alternative. Although I do share many of Illich's criticisms of the values schools currently embody and inculcate, I am also skeptical about his premise that once societies are deschooled, individuals will take control of their lives and their learning.[30] But perhaps most importantly, whatever its flaws, the educational system has an intact structure that has the power, the facilities, and the resources to accomplish immense good.

Moral Dilemmas of the Modern Age

Although I am aware of the paradox inherent in asking the education-al system to become an antidote to the culture out of which it has grown and which it has helped create or, at least, helped perpetuate, I am convinced that the attempt is necessary. Specifically, the modern age is demanding far more complex individual and social choices than has any previous age in history. Certainly, the abundance of new and increasingly difficult moral dilemmas created by modern technologies, by instantaneous communication and information flow, by nuclear power, by advances in medical and biochemical research, and by rapidly changing social mores demand that the greatest number of people possible be informed, reflective, possess analytical skills, be able to distinguish between the factual and value components of a problem, and be committed to making the best choices possible.

Many of these problems in the broadest sense are not new. The question of the effect of science and technology on the safety and quality of life, the conflict between new and traditional moral codes, and the need to balance individual freedom with the social good all are age-old dilemmas. What is unique is that their consequences are more far-reaching and potentially significant than in the past. Nuclear weapons, for instance, have the capability for destruction far greater than any previous weaponry. The devastation to both human life and the environment from a serious nuclear accident would be far more catastrophic than other forms of industrial accidents.

It is also important that many current moral dilemmas confront laypeople and not only experts or specialists. As Love Canal and the problem of nuclear wastes so painfully reveal, such problems no longer concern only industry and government. According to the nuclear physicist and environmentalist Jan Beyea, the decisions that need to be made ultimately concern questions, not of technology, but of public policy, with moral and political implications. As Beyea explains it, the public will have to decide what constitutes acceptable risk and to whom. People will have to balance the question of their own safety, that of others, and that of future generations against their economic well-being, their personal convenience, and the demands of American foreign policy. Eventually, they will have to make choices and take actions that will affect life on this earth in ten thousand years, a time span most people find irrelevant.[31] But despite such complexities, many people see nuclear energy as an either/or problem, and so they line up on one side or the other, often with a great deal of emotion. They are embracing a simplistic solution to a problem that has no easy answers.

Advances in medical and biochemical research similarly present dilemmas that are complex, emotional, and demanding of informed moral choices. Like the energy problem, they tend to frustrate massive numbers of people because there seem to be no clear-cut right or wrong answers. For instance, the choices now made available by safe and simple abortions, the decisions that unfavorable results from amniocentesis may present for prospective parents, the reality of test-tube babies, and the tormenting questions that a Karen Quinlan exemplifies all raise exceedingly difficult questions that require the careful integration of knowledge, moral judgment, and caring.

The truth is that few people are prepared to make such choices. Indeed, although the choices that need to be made depend on an understanding of precedent, thoughtfulness about the future, and a willingness of individuals to take responsibility, contemporary culture devalues those very qualities. The culture that most people, especially students, share today is the rapidly changing popular culture created by television, film, and music. The episodic quality of those media and the speed at which they change reinforce the notion that only the present and the personal have importance. And so, at a time when people most need to understand the context out of which current dilemmas have grown, need to think about the future implications of their choices, and need to recognize the differences between fact and value, they seem increasingly incapable of, or indifferent to, doing so. Unhappily, school curricula often reinforce this now-orientation.

In the following chapters, I will suggest an approach that will allow those of us who teach to use literature to engage our students in the complexities of the moral dimensions of their learning and their lives. In addition, I hope we can convince our students that they do have the ability, as individuals and as parts of groups, to assume responsibility for themselves and others. Although there is no certainty that such efforts in the classroom will succeed, it is certain that, without the conviction that they can positively affect their worlds, most people will simply not try to do so.

CHAPTER

II

Literature, Values, and Moral Choice

ANY ATTEMPTS TO INCLUDE a moral and values component within a conventional course invariably raise a series of questions that do not arise when education is more narrowly defined. What criteria should be used to define morality? Who should decide what values should be taught? What qualifications should teachers have? What safeguards are there to protect students from instructors who proselytize for a personal set of values that others might deem immoral or amoral? And in the end, are there any assurances that the classroom experience will influence students' choices, that it will make them more moral?[1]

On the face of it, such questions seem formidable but only because they assume that the educational objective is to alter student conduct in some specific ways. And although my own hope is that students become more aware, more caring, and more committed to responsible choice, I am not advocating that teachers argue for a particular code of behavior or a particular set of values. Rather, I think that we as teachers serve our students best if we can engage them in the learning process, teach them to understand and express the complexities of all that they study, bring them to recognize the value of individual moral choice, and give them a sense that they are part of a larger human community. If we are successful in these ways, then the questions about the appropriateness of a classroom focus on morals and values—however valid and interesting they may be philosophically, politically, or practically—lose their pertinence. In particular, a critical examination of moral and values questions should give students the means by which they can resist indoctrination and manipulation.

To be even more specific, the approach I am advocating is rooted in the notion that education should have as its goal more than the mere transmittal of a body of knowledge or training in particular skills. It should also be defined as more than a socializing or therapeutic experience. Rather, teachers should endeavor to teach students to think critically and logically, to garner evidence in support of their ideas, and to express themselves clearly. I also believe that we should encourage our students to think about what they learn in terms of their own lives and the lives of others.

Humanities, social science, and many science courses should have the additional goal of teaching students to recognize, analyze, understand the importance of, become engaged in, and articulate their conclusions about the nature and complexities of the human experience as it is presented in the material that they study. Because moral and values questions are inevitably at the core of the human experience, it is important that students learn to confront—deliberately, reflectively, and with caring—such questions.

Consciousness, Belief, and Choice

First, I believe that, given the possibilities of genuine freedom, moral choice is predicated on consciousness and a belief in free will. Without consciousness, individuals will not recognize the moral implications of their actions. Without a belief in freedom, they will not see themselves as accountable for their actions. Instead, they are likely to transfer responsibility for their conduct to people, institutions, and forces external to themselves. It is true that consciousness often causes torment and that freedom brings with it the burdens of responsibility. Nevertheless, history and literature are replete with devastating examples of the dangers, to individuals and societies alike, of unreflective abdications of individual and social responsibility. And so, I am convinced that, paradoxical as it may seem, the more humans recognize and understand the difficulties of consciousness and responsibility, the more aware and responsible they are likely to become. Similarly, I am convinced that the more people recognize and understand the limitations, both real and perceived, on their own freedom, the more freedom they are likely to achieve.

Second, I believe that literary study is an especially effective way to engage students in the complexities of such matters as consciousness, freedom, choice, and responsibility. Again and again, regardless of time and place, literature gives life to the problems of being human. It dramatizes how people—given their cultural values, their individual aspirations and talents, and their perceptions of the possibilities for freedom and self-realization—define themselves, make choices, and act. Literature also often encourages students to consider difficult moral problems that they might otherwise choose to ignore.

Finally, literature has the ability to break into the sense of individual isolation that so often induces moral apathy and meism. By giving students an awareness that they are part of the larger human community, it reassures them that they alone do not carry the burden of certain thoughts, ideas, and feelings. By demonstrating to them that the dilemmas of their own lives have precedents, it further reassures them that they alone need not reinvent whatever metaphorical wheels their lives require. By leading them to empathize with others, it brings them the first step toward assuming responsibility for others. By creating for some of them an aesthetic sense, literature may also help students understand that life beyond the immediate and the personal has richness and value.

I hope that by exploring the power of values and the complexities of moral choice within the literature they read, students will be better able to recognize and understand the possibilities for responsible action and self-realization within their own lives. I also hope that by seeing themselves as part of a rich, ongoing culture they will decide that moral choice is not only desirable but also possible within their own worlds.

There is quite obviously no guarantee that a focus on morals and values within the classroom will have such a salutary effect on student attitudes, beliefs, and choices any more than there are guarantees that any classroom experience will fulfill its goals. Nevertheless, those of us who teach always do so with no small leap of faith. Typically, we operate on the hope that our efforts to communicate will be heard, understood, analyzed, appreciated, and integrated into our students' lives in some productive and meaningful ways. Sometimes that meaning will be practical, sometimes intellectual, sometimes aesthetic, and in some very special circumstances all three. But whether we are focusing on a specialized topic, teaching skills, or exploring morals and values, in the end we will be truly successful if we give our students the tools with which they can independently come to terms with not only our course materials, but their own values and assumptions about the world and about that which their own lives offer them.

Moral and Values Questions to Be Explored

Each chapter that follows focuses on the nature and thematic function of the moral and values dimensions of particular literary works. Because each novel and short story is unique, the emphasis of each chapter is different. Indeed, the diversity of the literature itself laid to rest my initial fear that the discussion of the fiction might become formulaic. Happily, writers as rich, complex, and moving as Tolstoy, Hawthorne, Chopin, Kafka, Ellison, and the others defy easy categorization and one-dimensional interpretations.

Nevertheless, certain preoccupations emerge repeatedly. Each work, to varying degrees, explores matters of consciousness, freedom, choice, responsibility, and the possibilities for self-realization. Some of the works focus on characters confronted with moral dilemmas. Others dramatize the power of social values to influence perception and choice. But ultimately, most of the works raise many of the same questions. Thus, early in each chapter I outline the moral and values questions that I think are most crucial to the particular work. I also suggest some specific questions to be asked about each text that would be appropriate for class discussions, examinations, and papers. In my own subsequent discussions, I generally do not attempt to provide answers to these questions. Rather, I offer them as a means of focusing the attention of teachers and students alike on the problems and issues that the literature raises.

As I tried to formulate these questions, I recognized that on some level almost everything I have ever read had influenced my thought. To acknowledge, even to remember, all such influences would of course be unrealistic. Thus, as I list these questions, I have instead referred to a series of contemporary social critics, psychologists, and philosophers who especially helped me to clarify my own thoughts and to understand the complexities of the problems I was addressing. They all are also accessible, intellectually as well as practically, to the nonspecialist. Specifically, the recurring questions that teachers may themselves wish to consider and, when appropriate, raise in their own classes are these:

1. How much freedom do individuals really have? What forces—be they environmental or hereditary, economic, social, or instinctual—limit that freedom? What factors enhance it? How does context affect it?
2. How much freedom do people really want? In this regard, take into account Erich Fromm's argument that individuals often pre-

fer to "escape from freedom" rather than to risk the "moral aloneness" and the uncertainty that freedom brings.[2] Also, consider Jean-Paul Sartre's belief that individuals flee freedom because it condemns them to the anguish of making choices and to the burdens of responsibility.[3]

3. Assuming some measure of individual autonomy, to what degree and under what circumstances should people assume responsibility for others? To what degree can they assume responsibility for themselves?

4. Thoreau insists that when there is a conflict between the law and the right, individuals should defy the law and embrace the right and that when there is a conflict between social or personal expedience and justice, the individual should choose justice.[4] But if human beings no longer accept unquestionably those values offered them by society, religion, and the family, how do they decide what is moral and what is not? Specifically, what criteria should people use when faced with conflicts between their personal sense of morality and social customs and laws? with conflicts between their personal sense of morality and the demands of social, professional, or familial roles they reject? with the need to choose between self-interest and the social good?

5. Under what circumstances is it desirable for people to strip away the cultural myths and personal illusions that may have shaped their lives? On the other hand, what are the dangers to individuals and societies when such myths and illusions are denied? To put it another way, is consciousness a blessing or a curse? Does consciousness bring with it a sense of possibility for self-realization and social change? In addition, what are the dangers to individuals and societies of a lack of consciousness? For example, to what extent does unreflectiveness allow tyranny and injustice? In contrast, might not an awareness of the constraints on individual freedom cause a sense of powerlessness, a lack of identity, and feelings of frustration or even torment that might lead to violence, as Rollo May argues?[5] In thinking about these questions, consider Michael Novak's view that individuals embrace the myths of their culture and define themselves in terms of social structures, rules, roles, and institutions rather than risk what Novak calls "the experience of nothingness."[6]

6. What sort of person seems able to develop an ethical sense even when estranged from cultural myths and laws? What sort of person seems to need an externally imposed value system? Here it might be useful to think about Stanley Milgram's experiments, from which he concluded that most people readily submit to

authority and the pressures to conform rather than to follow an individual sense of right and wrong.[7]

7. What prompts certain individuals to take an existential leap of faith into meaning and responsible action? What prompts them to confer value and meaning, in Novak's terms, on "the fact of choice and the existence of a desire to question"?[8] What prompts them to develop what Victor Frankl calls a "will-to-meaning"?[9] What leads some individuals to believe in their own free will and to value consciousness, moral choice, and responsible action?

8. Are human beings inherently evil or potentially good? On the one hand, Freud argues that societies are necessary to protect people from one another; that is, to restrain, socialize, and transform irrational impulses into something positive for individuals and society.[10] On the other hand, Niebuhr believes that it is societies which induce immoral action, transforming essentially moral individuals into groups that act immorally.[11]

9. How does a society find an appropriate balance between the individual's right to adhere to the dictates of conscience and society's need for order? What are the possible implications to the social order of many individuals choosing, whether it be unilaterally or collectively, to follow the dictates of their own consciences? On the other hand, what are the implications for individual freedom and perhaps for justice if such a right is denied?

10. What are the advantages and limitations of symbolic protest?

11. How effective is art as social protest? Would Thoreau's refusal to pay his poll tax have affected history had he not also written "Civil Disobedience"? In this regard, think about the position of some of Ralph Ellison's critics who attack *Invisible Man* because it does not offer specific political solutions to social problems.

12. How much do such factors as race, gender, and class affect individual freedom?

13. What has been the effect of technology on individual freedom? How much has industrialization and bureaucratization been responsible for conformity, and how much is the desire to conform an instinctual rather than a learned response? Here it might be illuminating to read Richard L. Rubenstein's argument that the Holocaust was an inevitable result of the dehumanizing tendencies of the modern age, tendencies that grew out of industrialization and the power of bureaucracies.[12]

14. If a society is unjust, are such escapes as exile, insanity, suicide, or violence ever positive choices? In this regard, who decides what is acceptable behavior? Who decides what is sane behavior? Here,

consider R. D. Laing's view that insanity may be a sane response to an insane world.[13]

15. What factors lead people to dehumanize one another? What factors lead to violence?[14]

16. What are the advantages and what are the dangers for individuals who choose to live outside society's boundaries, constraints, and protections?

Content, Structure, and Approach

None of these questions offers easy answers, and different writers adopt different stances in regard to them. For example, Tolstoy's *Death of Ivan Ilych* offers religious faith as the answer to death; Kafka's *The Metamorphosis* treats religion in this context ironically; Camus's *The Stranger* overtly rejects such belief. Ellison's invisible man eventually triumphs over negative social values, assuming responsibility for himself and others, while Chopin's Edna fails in her effort to do so. Huck Finn does not achieve consciousness of society's corruption but acts with instinctive morality. Camus's Meursault becomes acutely aware of social injustice but never develops what the prosecutor in the novel calls a "moral sense." Yossarian in *Catch-22* and Esther in *The Bell Jar* in contrast come to consciousness and assume responsibility, while the governess in *Turn of the Screw* and McLendon in Faulkner's "Dry September" deflect responsibility from themselves to forces outside themselves. Several of the works also explore but do not come to conclusions about moral and values questions. *Turn of the Screw* and *Heart of Darkness*, for instance, preserve many ambiguities, in great part because their narrators may be unreliable. In such instances, the moral and value judgments are left to the reader.

In my own discussion, I seek no definitive answers to moral and values questions. Rather, I hope that students, through the literature, come to recognize how values shape perceptions and how, in turn, perceptions define choices and influence actions. To this end, I discuss only works that I have taught with some success, works that have in fact stimulated students to think about the power of values and the complexities of matters of freedom, responsibility, choice, consciousness, and self-realization.

Although I hope that the students do become more reflective about their own values and more engaged in the choices that their own lives offer, within the chapters to follow I do not directly relate the literature to contemporary social problems. For instance, I do not suggest that students consider wife and child abuse when they read "Barn Burning" or that they debate busing when they read *Invisible Man* or that they contemplate the problems of single parenting when they read *The Scarlet Letter*. Although it is quite obviously appropriate and desirable for teachers and students alike to allude to analogous contemporary problems when it will illuminate the literature or enliven the discussions, nevertheless, I am convinced that the emphasis should be on the literature itself and not on the immediate and the personal.[15] Once again, I believe that what our students need most is to understand their place in a rich, ongoing culture, to develop the critical skills with which they can recognize and confront value problems and moral dilemmas of all sorts, and, most of all, to believe that individual and social acts of responsibility do make a difference.

To these ends, I would also encourage teachers to ground each of the literary works they and their students study in the historical context and philosophical tradition out of which it grew. Because my own emphasis has been on the more universal implications of the moral and values questions as each author presents them, I have not provided this information in any detail. I do, however, see it as another important way of illuminating the material and introducing students to the value of understanding their own heritage and the heritage of others.

For clarity and convenience, I first tried to design a series of model courses centered around such topics as "Search for Self," "Individual versus Society," and "Responsibility." But as I attempted to assign books to courses, I felt much like Sisyphus, condemned eternally to push his rock up the mountain. Each time I thought I had finalized a syllabus, another arrangement or another course topic presented itself. Did *The Scarlet Letter* really belong best in the course on responsibility? Or was it better placed in "Search for Meaning" or "Individual versus Society"? Or better yet, should it begin a course entitled "Civilization versus Wilderness" or one called "Images of Women"? Similarly, Conrad's *Heart of Darkness* and Ellison's *Invisible Man* seemed appropriate for almost all those courses, while *Invisible Man* would fit as well in a course on black literature and *Heart of Darkness* would be effective in a course on madness. More themes emerged. Topics about freedom, consciousness, and cultural myths all seemed possibilities. In the end, I abandoned the idea of structuring the book around model courses.

Whimsy took over. I began to fantasize that the book might be published as a series of self-contained chapters. Much like those learning exercises for children consisting of cardboard pictures that can be arranged and rearranged to make new stories, the book would allow the mixing and matching of chapters. After all, I told myself, one of my assumptions throughout is that it is desirable for all of us to see the world in new ways and to understand and appreciate the interconnectedness of so many of its aspects. I abandoned the idea as impractical.

Instead, I have arranged the books in chronological order. I have also included an Appendix in which I do suggest possible course topics and syllabi drawing on the books I discuss and others. My ultimate hope, however, is that teachers will design courses appropriate to their students' needs, interests, and academic level, and that this book will primarily have suggested to them an approach to teaching and to literature which they can apply to whatever courses they design, to whatever books or other material they teach.

CHAPTER

III

The Scarlet Letter (1880)

by Nathaniel Hawthorne

NATHANIEL HAWTHORNE's *The Scarlet Letter* depends upon the reader's understanding of two very different value systems: the sort of absolute moral code that New England Puritans in the seventeenth century embraced unhesitatingly and a more relativistic contemporary approach to morality in which the individual substitutes personal judgment for that of the church and community. It is in the tension between these two value systems that much of the drama of *The Scarlet Letter* lies.

On the one side, Hawthorne explores the power and nature of the moral absolutism of Puritanism. Rooted in religious convictions, Puritanism came to define social standards and to govern individual behavior. Its ministers had immense political power. On the other side, Hawthorne demonstrates how compelling and humanizing freedom from Puritanic rigidity and repression could be. But even as he judges harshly the life-denying qualities of Puritanism, he suggests the dangers of relativism and of an individual approach to moral choice. And even as he points to the dangers of a system of governance in which the religious, the social, and the political are merged, he dramatizes how life away from society can corrupt.

The village and the forest become Hawthorne's metaphors for the two value systems. Here especially, Hawthorne reveals his ambivalences about absolutism and relativism. He portrays the positive and negative aspects alike of life within and without society's literal and figurative boundaries. The inhabitants of the village seem for the most part to be without flexibility, joy, or compassion. The men wear "sad-colored garments" and "gray, steeple-crowned hats."[1] As they wait for Hester to leave the jail, there is a "grim rigidity that petrified the bearded physiognomies of these good people" (p. 77). The women, too, with only one exception, are unforgiving. In contrast, the forest is associated with love, with natural beauty, and with the genuine communication that Hester and Arthur find possible there. Nevertheless, it is in the forest, away from social restrictions, that sin with its own devastating consequences can govern.

The real action of the novel occurs after Hester and Arthur's adultery, after Pearl's birth, and after Hester's imprisonment. Hester is already wearing the Scarlet A when the novel opens. Significantly, the choices she and Arthur now face are far more complex than their adultery had been. In that instance, both believed their action to be sinful, and both accepted society's judgment as legitimate. Their later choices, especially Hester's, are less clearly defined in terms of the prevailing moral code.

In many ways, Hester's choices are the most difficult. Unlike Dimmesdale, she has come to question "human institutions, and whatever priests and legislators had established" (p. 217). Given her new "estranged point of view," Hester's dilemmas are rooted in a conflict of personal values rather than social or religious ones. She needs to choose between protecting the man she loves and acting on her newly formed, personal commitment to truth (p. 211). She must decide whether to identify Dimmesdale as Pearl's father and whether to name Chillingworth as her husband. In her allegiance to Dimmesdale, she does neither for seven years. Later, however, she questions her silence, seeing it as a deception that was responsible for Dimmesdale's anguish and Chillingworth's moral and physical decline.

Arthur's torment may be as great as Hester's, but his motives are less altruistic and his thought less critical of Puritan tenets. He does not see his choice as one of "principle, nor even purpose." Indeed, with the exception of his moment of passion for Hester, Dimmesdale never goes "beyond the scope of generally received laws" (p. 217). Ultimately, his dilemma has more to do with his role in the community than it does with the question of right and wrong. After Pearl's birth, Dimmesdale continues to play the public role of sainted minister rather than acknowledge that he was Hester's lover and Pearl's father. He even uses his religious beliefs to rationalize his failure of courage, promising Pearl that the three of them will stand together "at the great judgment day" but that "the daylight of this world shall not see our meeting!" (p. 173). His pain then comes not from a conflict of values but from the hypocrisy of his position in the community.

After Hester tempts the minister with the prospect of a new beginning in exile, he grapples with the question of his own responsibility in new ways. Believing himself "divinely inspired" by Heaven (p. 240), he rewrites his Election Day Sermon in order to reaffirm his commitment to God and the community. Because he is convinced of "the relation between the Deity and the communities of mankind" and implicitly sees New England as a new Eden, Dimmesdale decides he must publicly confess his own sins (pp. 262–63). He is no longer able to escape into the rationalization that he would take responsibility on judgment day. Nor is he able to exile himself with Hester and Pearl.

Chillingworth, in his obsession for revenge, has moved beyond the realm of choice. Because he acknowledges his responsibility for Hester's marital unhappiness, he forgives her for betraying their marriage vows. Instead, he focuses his wish for vengeance on Dimmesdale. In so doing, he becomes almost an exemplum of the power of evil. He loses all his earlier moral sense, becomes satanic in action and appearance, and eventually commits what Dimmesdale identifies as the greatest sin of all. He violates, "in cold blood, the sanctity of the human heart" (p. 212).

The Scarlet Letter also focuses on the relationship of values to perceptions. In numerous instances, individual preconceptions shape that which characters believe they see. For instance, those who come to admire Hester begin to think of the Scarlet A as signifying "Able" rather than adultress (p. 180). Many of those who idealize Dimmesdale insist that his dying confession was symbolic, while yet others assert that it had not occurred at all. In contrast, Hester, Dimmesdale, and Chillingworth all interpret the minister's confession as his triumph over Chillingworth's satanic scheme, indeed as the triumph of good over evil.

Moral and Values Questions

General Questions: Guide to Reading

1. What are the advantages and disadvantages of a system of governance that unites the secular and the religious?
2. What effect does an absolute moral code have on individual choice and on individual responsibility? In particular, what is the cost in terms of freedom and self-realization to the individual who fully embraces an external system of values? What are the dangers to those who strip away such values?

3. Under what circumstances and to what degree is it appropriate for individuals to defy social convention or civil law or both? What criteria should such people use in such circumstances?
4. What are the advantages and what are the dangers of life away from society's boundaries, restraints, and protections?
5. Are there circumstances in which it might be moral for an individual to conceal the truth? What criteria should an individual use when trying to choose between deception and honesty?

Questions for Discussions, Papers, Exams

1. In terms of *The Scarlet Letter,* discuss the negative and positive aspects of life within society and within the forest. Does Hawthorne seem to take a stance that life within society is better or worse than life away from its confines?
2. Discuss Hester's evolution in relationship to the power of social values. Does Hawthorne present her estrangement from human institutions and conventions as positive or negative? Does Hester ever fully escape them?
3. Discuss the function of Dimmesdale's moral transformation after he plans to exile himself from New England with Hester and Pearl.
4. Compare Hester's attitudes toward social and religious values with Dimmesdale's.
5. What is the function of Dimmesdale's Election Day Sermon and his subsequent public confession?
6. Discuss Pearl's evolution. In this regard, consider especially Hawthorne's attitudes toward love.
7. Hawthorne repeatedly satirizes Puritan society. Discuss his presentation of Puritanism, describing specifically what he rejects.
8. The word *chill* appears often in the novel. Discuss its function.
9. Chillingworth is described in terms of being satanic and snakelike. Discuss the function of these associations. How does his "sin," that he "violated, in cold blood, the sanctity of the human heart" (p. 212), compare with Hester and Arthur's act of adultery?

Religion and Law

Hawthorne stresses the religious basis for the law and for social conventions in the Puritan community. He specifically notes that the

Puritans are "a people amongst whom religion and law were almost identical" (p. 77). Similarly, he characterizes the age as a "period when the forms of authority were felt to possess the sacredness of divine institutions" (p. 91). This fusion of the religious and the civil resulted in a special harshness against those who did not conform. As Hawthorne explains, because religion and law "were so thoroughly interfused" in the Puritan character, "the mildest and the severest acts of public discipline were alike made venerable and awful" (p. 77).

Hester, for example, suffers not only imprisonment and the scarlet letter for her adultery, but she is also in danger of losing custody of Pearl. The authorities of the community, governmental and religious together, "cherishing the more rigid order of principles in religion and government," use religious convictions as the basis for their argument that mother and child be separated:

> On the supposition that Pearl, as already hinted, was of demon origin, these good people not unreasonably argued that a Christian interest in the mother's soul required them to remove such a stumbling-block from her path. If the child, on the other hand, were really capable of moral and religious growth, and possessed the elements of ultimate salvation, then surely, it would enjoy all the fairer prospect of these advantages by being transferred to wiser and better guardianship than Hester Prynne's. [p. 123]

Concerned that Pearl receive "Christian nurture as befits a child her age" (p. 134), the governor meets with Dimmesdale and "the venerable pastor, John Wilson" (p. 131), to decide Pearl's fate. Only Dimmesdale's argument that Pearl is both God's blessing for Hester and the means of her retribution dissuades the governor from separating mother and child. Had Dimmesdale not intervened, however, Hester would have had no judicial recourse. In other words, religious considerations dictated events.

The alliance of church and state in Dimmesdale's mind causes him much psychological torment. Although he sees himself as having transgressed both religious and social law out of his passion for Hester, he is caught by his "dread of public exposure" (p. 173). Society's expectations for its ministers bring additional burdens to him:

> At the head of the social system, as the clergymen of that day stood, he was only the more trammelled by its regulations, its principles, even its prejudices. As a priest, the framework of his order inevitably hemmed him in. [p. 218]

Hawthorne is also explicit that the priesthood brings with it "the almost worshipping respect of the community" as well as the possibility of genuine political power. Although Dimmesdale seems to have no earthly ambitions or desire for such power, he nevertheless is victim of his role in his need for social approval.

In contrast, Hester's role as social outcast brings her the freedom to separate the social and the moral from the religious. She gains a critical stance on "human institutions, and whatever priests and legislators had established" (p. 217). Her seven years of wearing the scarlet letter have allowed her to break away from social opinion so that "the world's law was no law for her mind" (p. 182).

Hawthorne explicitly contrasts Hester's freedom with Dimmesdale's lack of it:

> Hester Prynne, with a mind of native courage and activity, and for so long a period not merely estranged, but outlawed, from society, had habituated herself to such latitude of speculation as was altogether foreign to the clergy-man. She had wandered, without rule of guidance, in a moral wilderness. [p. 217]

The "freedom of speculation" that she had assumed may have been common in Europe, but, Hawthorne argues, such emancipated thought was not tolerated in New England. In fact, such freedom was "held to be a deadlier crime than that stigmatized by the scarlet letter" (p. 183). Fortunately, Hester is so isolated and private that the community is ignorant of her thoughts.

Although Hester never abandons her own personal faith, she does believe that she and Dimmesdale have sufficiently repented for their sins and should receive peace because of their good works (p. 209). She also believes that their love "had a consecration of its own" which justified it (p. 212). But most importantly, Hester has committed herself to truth. As she tells Arthur, "Truth was the one virtue which I might have held fast, and did hold fast through all extremity; save when thy good,—thy life,—thy fame,—were put in question!" Her deception in that instance was her failure to tell Dimmesdale that Chillingworth was her husband. Eventually, this silence leads her to an even deeper commitment to truth, for she comes to believe, "a lie is never good, even though death threaten on the other side!" (p. 211).

Such values allow Hester to decide that she, Arthur, and Pearl should exile themselves from New England and find a new life of their own either in Europe or in the wilderness. She insists to Dimmesdale that his life still holds value and the possibility of happiness. She entreats him, "Preach! Write! Act! Do anything, save to lie down and die!" (p. 214). Then, to symbolize her freedom from the social and religious conventions that had stigmatized her, Hester takes off the scarlet letter and releases her abundant and luxurious hair from its confining cap. It is a moment of radiance and happiness for her that revives her womanhood (p. 220).

Dimmesdale, however, is unable to escape the Puritan values. Because he has never questioned them on his own, he cannot free himself from their power. Although he momentarily agrees to go to Europe with Hester and Pearl, calling Hester "my better angel" (p. 219), Dimmesdale sees such freedom negatively. Still unable to separate the social from the religious, he believes his rebellion against society to be antireligious as well. His confusion is apparent. On the one hand, contemplating exile makes him feel exhilarated, like "a prisoner just escaped from the dungeon of his own heart." On the other hand, that freedom brings him to a "wild, free atmosphere of an *unredeemed, unchristianized, lawless region*" (p. 219, my emphasis).

Dimmesdale becomes further frightened when his plan of exile seems to change his inner self. As Hawthorne describes that transformation:

> In truth, nothing short of a total change of dynasty and moral code, in that interior kingdom, was adequate to account for the impulses now communicated to the unfortunate and startled minister. At every step he was incited to do some strange, wild, wicked thing or other, with a sense that it would be at once involuntary and intentional; in spite of himself, yet growing out of a profounder self than that which opposed the impulse. [p. 233]

Such impulses worry Dimmesdale, and he wonders whether he has either become mad or given himself over to evil (p. 236). He thus chooses to reembrace his old values and in the process distances himself from his bond with Hester. As he marches in the Election Day procession, Hester realizes that he is no longer accessible to her. As she watches him, she asks herself:

> And was this the man? She hardly knew him now! He, moving proudly past, enveloped, as it were, in the rich music, with the procession of majestic and venerable fathers; he so unattainable in his wordly position, and still more so in that far vista of his unsympathizing thoughts, through which she now beheld him. [p. 253]

With his sermon, Dimmesdale acknowledges once more his conviction that religious tenets and social law should be one. He argues in his sermon for "the relation between the Deity and the communities of mankind, with a special reference to the New England which they were here planting in the wilderness" (p. 261). And when he finally confesses his adultery, he reaffirms his belief that he has sinned against both divine and human law. He seeks judgments from both realms. He also directly rejects Hester's hope that their suffering and their good works have redeemed them from their sin. She asks him for the reassurance that they will "spend our immortal life together," arguing, "Surely, surely, we have ransomed one another, with all this woe!" (p. 269). Dimmesdale refuses to hold out any such hope. His dying words embrace Puritan ideology as he tells Hester, with "tremulous solemnity":

> The law we broke!—the sin here so awfully revealed! let these alone be in thy thoughts! I fear! I fear! It may be, that when we forgot our God,—when we violated our reverence each for the other's soul,—it was henceforth vain to hope that we could meet hereafter, in an everlasting and pure reunion.[p. 269]

For Dimmesdale, God's mercy lies in his suffering and his ability "to die this death of triumphant ignominy before the people!" (p. 269).

The Forest versus the Marketplace

Hester explicitly teaches Pearl that different behaviors are possible in and appropriate to the forest and the marketplace. For example, when Pearl asks her mother about their meeting with Dimmesdale in the forest, Hester admonishes the child, "Hold thy peace, dear little Pearl! . . . We must not always talk in the market-place of what happens to us in the forest" (p. 254). She explains to the child that although Dimmesdale kissed her in the forest, "Kisses are not to be given in the marketplace" (p. 254). Nevertheless, Hester feels both despair and some anger at how differently Dimmesdale behaves toward her in the different realms. In the "dim forest, with its little dell of solitude, and love, and anguish," she and Arthur had "mingled their sad and passionate talk with the melancholy murmur of the brook." In contrast, the depth of their understanding in the forest seems a "delusion" to her in the marketplace (p. 253).

The forest, then, is the place where Hester and Arthur are able to express and experience love. It also seems a place of freedom and genuine life. Only in the forest is Hester able to recover her womanhood again (p. 220). Only there can Pearl roam freely and happily. Moreover, it is only in the forest that Dimmesdale can admit his pain, his need, and his hypocrisy to Hester, that Pearl can chide the minister for his failure to acknowledge her publicly, and that Hester can admit both her anguish over Chillingworth and her love for Dimmesdale.

Nature itself seems to reaffirm such love, communication, and honesty. Freed from the constraints of human law and a commitment to a "higher truth," nature responds sympathetically to Hester and Arthur's reunion:

> Such was the sympathy of Nature—that wild, heathen Nature of the forest, never subjugated by human law, nor illumined by higher truth—with the bliss of these two spirits! Love, whether newly born, or aroused from a death-like slumber, must always create a sunshine, filling the heart so full of radiance, that it overflows upon the outward world. Had the forest still kept its gloom, it would have been bright in Hester's eyes, and bright in Arthur Dimmesdale's!
> [pp. 220–21]

The world of the marketplace is repressive and gloomy in contrast. The prison is described as "the black flower of civilized society" (p. 76), while the "grim and grisly presence of the town-beadle . . . prefigured and represented in his aspect the whole dismal severity of the Puritanic code of law" (pp. 79–80).

Even the children's games reveal the community's harshness, for in addition to "playing at going to church," the children also play at "scourging Quakers; or taking scalps in a sham-fight with the Indians, or scaring one another with freaks of imitative witchcraft" (p. 117).

The community's attitudes and values are equally repressive. The children are "the most intolerant brood that ever lived" (p. 118). The governor seems "so rigid and severe, and frostbitten with more than autumnal age" (p. 131). Servants are whipped for being sluggish, and children are whipped for being undutiful. Those who embrace something other than the accepted religious ideology are apt "to be scourged out of the town" (p. 77). An Indian who had been drinking and was rowdy might be driven with whips into the forest. Those who were judged witches were hanged. Indeed, this community seems to function "because it imagined and hoped so little" (p. 91).

On the other hand, Hawthorne also suggests the dangers of life away from society. Once Dimmesdale has separated himself from society by agreeing to exile, he becomes tempted to behave in ways he would never before have considered. He desires to tell an elderly deacon of the church "certain blasphemous suggestions . . . respecting the communion-supper" (p. 233). He wishes to reveal to "the eldest female member of his church" an argument from the Bible "against the immortality of the human soul," a piece of information he is sure would have "caused this aged sister to drop down dead, at once" (p. 234). He is tempted to corrupt a young girl committed to the spiritual life (p. 235). He considers teaching "some very wicked words to a knot of little Puritan children" (p. 235), and he contemplates sharing "a few improper jests" with a drunken soldier (p. 236). Dimmesdale is so horrified by these impulses that he wonders:

> Am I mad? or am I given over utterly to the fiend? Did I make a contract with him in the forest and sign it with my blood? And does he now summon me to its fulfillment, suggesting the performance of every wickedness which his most foul imagination can conceive? [p. 236]

Hawthorne also suggests that sin, once performed, taints the sinner forever. Actions that are possible in the forest may indeed damn the individual. For example, despite Hester's commitment to truth and the years of good work she performed subsequent to her adultery, Hawthorne insists that she is tainted. As she stands upon the scaffold, he contrasts her sin with "Divine Maternity":

> Here, there was the taint of deepest sin in the most sacred quality of human life, working such effect, that the world was only the darker for this woman's beauty, and the more lost for the infant that she had borne. [p. 83]

Years later, Hester herself comes to accept her limitations because of the adultery. She has long "recognized the impossibility that any mission of divine and mysterious truth should be confided to a woman stained with sin, bowed down with shame, or even burdened with a life-long sorrow" (p. 275). In contrast, Hawthorne asserts that the role of redeeming woman could only belong to one who conforms to Puritan values:

> The angel and the apostle of the coming revelation must be a woman, indeed, but lofty, pure, and beautiful; and wise, moreover, not through dusky grief, but the ethereal medium of joy; and showing how sacred love should make us happy, by the truest test of a life successful to such an end! [p. 275]

Hawthorne is therefore explicit that what Hester and Dimmesdale learn in the forest may at times be dangerous. Even though the scarlet letter brought Hester knowledge and a freedom of thought denied most women, it also brings her "Shame, Despair, Solitude!" As significantly, her suffering teaches her a mixed lesson, making her "strong," but also teaching her "much amiss" (p. 217).

Dimmesdale's last experience with Hester in the forest also has positive and negative connotations. It so transforms him that his earlier "self was gone!" In its place:

> Another man had returned out of the forest; a wiser one; with a knowledge of hidden mysteries which the simplicity of the former never could have reached. A bitter kind of knowledge that! [p. 238]

In other words, although life in the forest brings knowledge and liberation, it also brings the dangers of sin. In contrast, life in society may be repressive, but it is also protective. As Hawthorne explains of Dimmesdale, "it would always be essential to his peace to feel the pressure of a faith about him, supporting, while it confined him within its iron framework" (p. 145).

Chill versus Life

Chillingworth's sin is, in Dimmesdale's words, that "he has violated, in cold blood, the sanctity of a human heart" (p. 212). The older man is repeatedly associated with the word *chill* itself. He had wronged Hester by marrying her because his life was "lonely and chill, and without a household fire." As he explains it to her, by betraying her "budding youth into a false and unnatural relation with [his] decay," he has denied Hester a warmth and life that should have been hers (p. 100). He brings the same "chill" into Dimmesdale's life.

Chillingworth is also associated with the snake and therefore with Satan. When he first learns that Hester has betrayed him, "A writhing horror twisted itself across his features, like a snake gliding swiftly over them" (p. 88). When he first sees the Scarlet *A* on Dimmesdale's breast, he dances a satanic dance of joy.

Hawthorne also suggests that a moral decline such as Chillingworth's has physical manifestations. Chillingworth becomes nearly deformed as he gives himself over to his obsession for revenge. Dimmesdale, too, declines physically under the pressure of his secret sin. He "grew emaciated" and "his voice, though still rich and sweet, had a certain melancholy prophecy of decay in it" (p. 142). In time, Dimmesdale grows even more pale, more thin, and his voice becomes "more tremulous than before" (p. 143). His congregation fears that he is dying. As Chillingworth notes, there is "a strange sympathy betwixt soul and body" (p. 158). Some in the community even believe that the *A* on Dimmesdale's breast may have been "the effect of the ever active tooth of remorse, gnawing from the inmost heart outwardly, and at last manifesting Heaven's dreadful judgment by the visible presence of the letter" (p. 270).

In contrast, Hawthorne often glorifies life and warmth. When Dimmesdale first stands with Hester and Pearl on the scaffold, even though it is in darkness and initially unobserved by others, he gains a new sense of life:

> There came what seemed a tumultuous rush of new life, other life than his own, pouring like a torrent into his heart, and hurrying through all his veins, as if the mother and the child were communicating their vital warmth to his half-torpid system. The three formed an electric chain. [p. 172]

After Arthur acknowledges Pearl and publicly asks for her kiss, Pearl herself seems reunited with life. The spell that had seemed to separate her from love and feeling "was broken":

> As the tears fell upon her father's cheek, they were the pledge that she would grow up amid human joy and sorrow, nor for ever do battle with the world but be a woman in it. [p. 268]

The implication is, as well, that because of her new warmth, Pearl will no longer be a source of anguish for her mother but rather one of joy and nurturing.

The Nature of Responsibility

Hester believes herself responsible for Chillingworth's moral decline and Dimmesdale's physical and moral torment. Implicitly, by such a stance, Hester raises the question of how much any individual can be responsible for others. Indeed, Hawthorne's point here seems to be the need for individuals to assume responsibility for their actions. Had Dimmesdale publicly acknowledged that he was Pearl's father, he would not have made himself susceptible to Chillingworth's obsession with revenge. Had Chillingworth's acceptance of responsibility for Hester's estrangement included Dimmesdale, he might not have needed revenge at all. That he leaves his fortune to Pearl does suggest a wish on his part to compensate the child and the mother for the pain he has caused them.

An even more interesting question may be that of the individual's responsibility to the community. Dimmesdale, in the end, cannot separate himself from society and so chooses public confession and death rather than exile. Hester, who chose to live neither in the forest nor in the village but at its boundaries, does leave New England after

Dimmesdale's death. Nevertheless, years later, she returns, resumes wearing the Scarlet *A*, and commits herself to a life of service to others in the community.

Although it is tempting to wish for a happier ending to *The Scarlet Letter*, Hawthorne's conclusion is perhaps the most psychologically credible one he might have selected. Regardless of whether Hester and Arthur had earned their right to a life of freedom together, Dimmesdale was so influenced by religious and social values that such freedom may not have been possible for him at all. He had so fully defined himself in terms of Puritan values and so totally embraced the role of minister that he did not believe he could achieve either morality or sanity outside of that framework. That Hester returns to New England, wearing her badge of shame, and devotes herself to others suggests that she, too, ultimately embraces the power of external values. In other words, each had so absorbed society's values, however negatively Hawthorne presents them, that only life which acknowledges society's standards and its values was possible. Moreover, even as Hawthorne throughout the novel rejects society's harshness, he also reaffirms its value.

IV

Adventures of Huckleberry Finn
(Tom Sawyer's Comrade) (1885)

by Mark Twain

IN HIS PREFATORY "NOTICE" TO *Adventures of Huckleberry Finn,* Mark Twain cautions his readers:

> Persons attempting to find a motive in this narrative will be prosecuted; persons attempting to find a moral in it will be banished; persons attempting to find a plot in it will be shot.[1]

The novel's title, with its stress on Huck's adventures and its parenthetical explanation that Huck is Tom Sawyer's comrade, similarly suggests that the novel will be less than serious. But both title and prefatory notice are ironic, for Huck's adventures do indeed have motive and moral, while it is Huck's friendship with Jim, as well as his comradeship with Tom Sawyer, which gives meaning to the book.

Essentially, *Huckleberry Finn* explores the influence of social, political, and religious values on individual choice. In this regard, much of the novel's brilliance lies in Huck's continued innocence. He never comes to recognize the hypocrisy and immorality of the values that dominate his world and that define his attitudes and beliefs. He does not condemn the men who, believing him a carrier of smallpox, do not give him help but rather forty dollars in gold and advice to con others. Nor does Huck understand that what he sees as the aristocratic bearing of the Grangerford family and the "style" of their home disguise their violence toward the Shepherdsons. He does not recognize that beneath the warmth of the Phelps family and the whitewashed facade of their farmhouse lies an unexamined racism.

But most significantly, Huck never realizes that his own instinctive choices are moral and the values of his society are immoral. When he decides to continue to aid Jim's escape from slavery, he is convinced that the action will damn him to hell. And when he decides to "light out for the Territory ahead of the rest" (p. 245), he does so out of personal motives rather than political ones. He is not consciously rebelling against violence, greed, or the institution of slavery. He simply knows from personal experience that he is uncomfortable being "sivilized" (p. 245).

By the same token, Huck's innocence also blinds him to the dangers of the uncivilized life. He disregards what his own experience should have taught him, that individuals are especially vulnerable when they are denied the protections that an ethically based social order normally provides. For example, because there is no one on the river to enforce laws, the steamboat can run down Huck and Jim's raft with impunity. Because there are no laws on the raft itself, the Duke and King can commandeer it and for all practical purposes enslave Huck and Jim. On the shore, too, there is often a breakdown in the social order, characterized by a widespread indifference to law and justice. The results are equally devastating: the Grangerford-Shepherdson bloodbath, Sherburn's murder of Boggs, and mob action.

Twain's much discussed difficulties in concluding the novel further suggest his concern with the interplay between external values and individual choice. As Walter Blair has documented, Twain abandoned the manuscript for several years after taking Huck and Jim past Cairo where Jim might have found freedom.[2] Given the fact that Huck and Jim's journey on the raft was now leading them deeper into the Southern slave states, Twain had created for himself a dilemma. Specifically, how could Huck help Jim achieve freedom and still remain innocent and apolitical? Twain's solution was a *deus ex machina* in the form of Miss Watson's deathbed decision to emancipate Jim. This unexpected twist in the plot allows Huck to aid Jim's escape but without risking social censure or legal punishment. In essence, Twain could now have it both ways. Huck behaves in a manner that Twain's reader can applaud as moral, but he does so without first having to make a conscious decision to repudiate slavery. Moreover, because Jim is already legally "free," Twain does not have to confront within the novel the potential social, legal, or psychological consequences of such a choice.

Because of Huck's failure to come to some sort of moral conscious-ness, the final quarter of the novel is problematic. To begin with, Huck once again acquiesces to Tom Sawyer and his search for adventure but this time at the expense of Jim's humanity. Jim, in his turn, has been reduced to a caricatured figure. But most significantly, Huck and Jim's search for freedom has degenerated from serious drama into slapstick.

On the other hand, it can be argued that the final chapters are successful precisely because they dramatize the power of negative social values to triumph over Huck and Jim's humanity, dignity, and integrity. Only when Huck and Jim are alone on Jackson's Island or on the raft are they able to interact in a genuinely caring way. Once they are within society's boundaries, each readily reassumes those socially assigned roles that deny Jim his humanity and that triumph over moral instincts.

Moral and Values Questions

General Questions: Guide to Reading

1. What is the relationship between individual moral choice and social, political, and religious values?
2. Is it appropriate for an individual to follow the dictates of his or her own conscience if such a choice conflicts with social stan-dards, religious mores, or laws?
3. Is there something about society that is inherently corrupt and that corrupts the individual? Consider Niebuhr's stance that while individuals might be induced to act morally, there are elements inherent "in man's collective behavior which be-long to the order of nature and can never be brought complete-ly under the dominion of reason or conscience"?[3] On the other hand, even given society's limitations, is not some sort of social order necessary to prevent utter anarchy and to protect the weak against the strong? Does Twain reconcile these two points of view?
4. What social and psychological factors allow some people to so dehumanize others that they can enslave them? What factors lead those who are so dehumanized to accept such enslave-ment?
5. What forces typically lead to violence?[4]

Questions for Discussions, Papers, Exams

1. Discuss Huck and Jim's evolving relationship, paying particular attention to the following moments:
   a. Huck's assertion when he and Jim return to Jackson Island that they are "home all safe" (p. 45).
   b. Huck's assertion when he learns that Jim is being sought, "They're after us!" (p. 54).
   c. Huck's apology to Jim after having tricked him (p. 74).
2. In light of Huck and Jim's growing closeness, what is the significance and the effect of Huck's acquiescence to Tom's adventures in the final quarter of the novel?
3. Apart from plot considerations, why does Huck feel relieved and as though he has been "reborn" when the Phelps mistakenly believe him to be Tom Sawyer? In discussing this moment, also take into account the earlier episode when Huck stages his own murder.
4. Discuss Huck's adeptness with disguises.[5]
5. The white characters in the novel celebrate Jim's decision to stay with the wounded Tom Sawyer. Is Jim's choice as simple as those characters believe it to be? Is Jim being unfair to his wife and children by risking his freedom? What values are in conflict here for Jim?
6. Is it credible that Jim agrees to Tom's schemes at the end of the novel? Is Jim's passivity consistent with his earlier ability to chastise Huck for his lack of sensitivity?
7. In various ways throughout the novel, Twain explores the meaning of individual freedom. What is the significance of Huck's several references to Moses (p. 4 and p. 83)? What is the significance of Tom's assertion that Jim is "as free as any cretur that walks this earth!" (p. 241)?
8. What does Huck's description of the Grangerford's house and possessions reveal about the family's values?
9. What sort of values does the Phelps family hold? For instance, what does Aunt Sally reveal about her own values (and what does Huck reveal about his values as well) when the two have the following conversation about Huck's experience on the boat:

"We blowed out a cylinder head."
"Good Gracious! Anybody hurt?"
"No'm. Killed a nigger."
"Well, it's lucky; because sometimes people do get hurt." [p. 185]

10. Huck admires Tom Sawyer's style and dismisses the fact that Tom is blatantly unconcerned about the substance, the consequences, and the morality of his behavior. For example, Tom tells Aunt Sally at the end of the novel that he risked all those lives because he "wanted the *adventure* of it" (p. 242). What is Tom's symbolic role in the novel?

11. Tom's fantasies and his plans generally are violent. Why does Twain juxtapose such youthful, violent fantasies and playacting with the Grangerford-Shepherdson deaths, the Boggs murder, and the mob's abuse of the Duke and the King?

Huck: Instinctively Moral in an Immoral Society

Huck is instinctively moral, Twain suggests, because he has not been fully socialized. His mother is dead, his father is an alcoholic and a social outcast, and Huck apparently went without schooling and religious training until he was in his teens. In other words, Huck was not fully subject to the forces that generally acculturate the individual: family, school, religion, and a valuing of social approval. Indeed, after Widow Douglas has "sivilized" Huck, his father is outraged. Learning that Huck has been taught to read and write in school, Pap hits the boy and warns:

> Now looky here; you stop that putting on frills. I won't have it. I'll lay for you, my smarty; and if I catch you about that school, I'll tan you good. First you know you'll get religion too. I never see such a son. [p. 18]

The irony on which the novel relies of course is that the predominant social, political, and religious values in Huck's world are immoral. Violence, greed, selfishness, mob action, racism, and slavery are tolerated and often justified. Miss Watson, who insists that Huck's behavior be governed by a desire for religious salvation, nevertheless sells Jim even though she knows that her action will separate Jim from his wife and children and take him to the crueler locale of the deep South. In fact, such hypocrisy is rampant in this world. The Grangerfords, who profess to be religious people and who have a library filled with religious books, nevertheless take their guns to church. They also participate, for reasons no one remembers, in a violent feud with the Shepherdsons. Uncle Silas Phelps similarly observes the form of religion as he ignores some of its key moral tenets. He does not find it inconsistent to pray with Jim twice a day at the same time that he imprisons Jim for being a runaway slave.

Huck, for his part, remains essentially innocent. Although at crucial moments he acts in ways that run counter to prevailing societal values, he generally accepts the rightness of those values without question. He believes that slavery is acceptable, that black people are inferior to whites, and that violence and greed are unavoidable if distasteful. Moreover, Huck himself is a skilled liar, able to improvise untruths to cope with uncomfortable situations.

Social Alienation and Individual Choice

Huck's physical and psychological alienation from his society is positive in that it allows him to form a mutually nurturing relationship with Jim. On the other hand, that alienation has left Huck without either a firm sense of himself or a definite moral code by which to live. For this reason, Huck is especially vulnerable to the influence of others, especially to that of Tom Sawyer. For example, when Huck is lonely, he disregards his own instincts and his personal judgments. Even when he believes that Tom's schemes are without profit (p. 12) and foolish (p. 204), he participates in them. He also consistently ignores Tom's lack of morality and wishes to emulate him.

From the opening moments of the novel, Huck is often preoccupied with thoughts of death and a sense of his own loneliness. In the first chapter, his thoughts are permeated with references to death and mourning:

> I set down in a chair by the window and *tried to think of something cheerful, but it warn't no use. I felt so lonesome I most wished I was dead.* The stars were shining, and the leaves rustled in the woods ever so *mournful;* and I heard an owl, away off, who-whooing about *somebody that was dead* and a dog crying about *somebody that was going to die;* and the wind was trying to whisper something to me and I couldn't make out what it was, and so *it made the cold shivers run over* me. Then away out in the woods I heard *that kind of a sound that a ghost makes* when it wants to tell about something that's on its mind and can't make itself understood, and *so can't rest easy in its grave* and has to go about that way every night *grieving. I got so down-hearted and scared, I did wish I had some company.* [p. 5, my emphasis]

Moments later, feeling that the "house was all as still as death now," Huck is comforted by Tom's whistle, deciding simply, "That was good!" (p. 5).

Huck's feelings about life away from society are deeply ambivalent. After Pap has kidnapped him, he first enjoys "being lazy and jolly, off comfortable all day, smoking and fishing, and no books nor study" (p. 22). But weary of his father's beatings and alcoholic violence and finding himself "dreadful lonesome" when his father locks him up (p. 22), Huck stages his own murder and escapes to Jackson's Island. There, too, he alternates between pleasure and loneliness. At first, he is "ruther comfortable and satisfied" and "powerful lazy and comfortable" (p. 32). Soon, however, he admits, "by and by it got sort of lonesome" (p. 34). He even becomes afraid to sleep because "every time I waked up I thought somebody had me by the neck" (p. 35). By the time Jim arrives at the island, himself in flight, Huck is very much in need of human companionship. He is "ever so glad to see Jim" and acknowledges, "I warn't lonesome now" (p. 36).

With Jim present, Huck is no longer frightened by a storm that earlier would have evoked terror. He describes his surroundings now as "all blue-black outside, and lovely" (p. 42). Although the trees "looked dim and spider-webby" and although it seemed to Huck to be as "dark as sin," he tells his new companion, "Jim this is nice . . . I wouldn't want to be nowhere else but here" (pp. 42–43). The camp has become "home" for him now (p. 145).

Huck and Jim: Instinct or Conscience

The degree to which Huck has bonded to Jim is revealed when he learns that Jim is being pursued as a runaway slave and as Huck's possible murderer. Huck tells Jim that they must move quickly to escape because, "They're after us!" (p. 54). As Leo Marx points out, the moment is significant and poignant in that no one is seeking Huck, who is presumed dead.[6]

On the raft, the relationship evolves, and Jim begins to transcend the social strictures which demand that he play a subservient role to whites. He moves into a quasi-parental role in relationship to Huck, standing watch for the boy in order to let him sleep and protecting Huck from the trauma of discovering his father's corpse.[7] He tells Huck, "doan' look at his face—it's too gashly," and then he covers up the body with rags. But most importantly, Jim instructs Huck about his behavior. After Huck has caused the older man worry by pretending to have been thrown overboard in a storm, Jim admonishes him to be more compassionate:

> En when I wake up en fine you back agin', all safe and soun', de tears
> come en I coulda got down on my knees en kiss' you' foot I's so
> thankful. En all you wuz thinkin 'bout wuz how you could make a fool
> uv ole Jim wid a lie. Dat truck dah is *trash;* en trash is what people is
> dat puts dirt on de head er dey fren's en makes em ashamed. [p. 74]

Moved by Jim's lesson, Huck, too, momentarily transcends the
prescribed social roles. Even as he acknowledges his racial biases, he
apologizes to Jim:

> It was fifteen minutes before I could work myself up to go and
> humble myself to a nigger—but I done it and I warn't ever sorry for it
> afterwards neither. I didn't do him no more mean tricks, and I
> wouldn't done that one if I'd a knowed it would make him feel that
> way. [p. 74]

Almost immediately, however, Huck's "conscience" or social
values in regard to slavery resurface. He "blames" himself for not
turning Jim in, believing that his actions in freeing a slave are wrong.
He becomes even more distressed when Jim announces that if he is
unable to buy his wife and children out of slavery, he will "steal" them.
Because Huck views Jim and his family as property and not as human
beings, he thinks:

> It froze me to hear such talk. He wouldn't ever dared to talk such talk
> in his life before. Just see what a difference it made in him the minute
> he judged he was about free. It was according to the old saying, "give
> a nigger an inch and he'll take an ell." Thinks I, this is what comes of
> my not thinking. Here was this nigger which I had as good as helped
> to run away, coming right out flat-footed and saying he would steal
> his children—children that belonged to a man I didn't even know; a
> man that hadn't ever done me no harm. [p. 75]

But however much society's values nag at Huck, he ultimately acts
on his instincts and implicitly acknowledges Jim's humanity. When Jim
reminds him of their friendship, telling him that he is "de on'y white
genlman dat ever kep' his promise to ole Jim," Huck feels "sick" (p. 76).
When he is confronted with the choice of turning Jim in or protecting
him, he lies to preserve Jim's freedom. But he does none of this easily,
convinced as he is that slavery is acceptable and that it is he who is
"wrong." As he attempts to understand his own decisions, he decides
that he simply had been exposed to society's values too late in life:

> I knowed very well I had done wrong, and I see it warn't no use for
> me to try to learn to do right; a body that don't get *started* right when
> he's little, ain't got no show. [p. 78]

46

The Grangerford-Shepherdson bloodbath finally prompts Huck to make a value judgment. After witnessing the battle between the two families, he decides that life on the raft would have prevented him from experiencing such devastation:

> It made me so sick I most fell out of the tree. I ain't agoing to tell *all* that happened—it would make me sick again if I was to do that. I wished I hadn't ever come ashore that night, to see such things. I ain't ever going to get shut of them—lots of times I dream about them. [pp. 97–98]

The raft, Jim, and an Edenic existence again become home for Huck. When he hears Jim's voice, he decides that "nothing ever sounded so good before" (p. 98). When they are on the raft, he judges:

> we was free and safe once more. . . . We said there warn't no home like a raft after all. Other places do seem so cramped up and smothery, but a raft don't. You feel mighty free and easy and comfortable on a raft. [p. 99]

Able to be "always naked, day and night, whenever the mosquitoes would let us" (p. 100) and thus free of social costumes as well as of roles, Huck concludes, "It's lovely to live on a raft" (p. 101).

Huck also is beginning to acknowledge Jim's humanity in other ways. He recognizes, for instance, Jim's depth of caring for his wife and his children, even if nothing in his experience has prepared him for it. With some astonishment, he realizes, "I do believe he cared just as much for his people as white folks does for their'n. It don't seem natural, but I reckon it's so" (p. 131). Later, he becomes actively concerned with Jim's welfare, telling Mary Jane Wilkes that they must use caution in their attempt to thwart the Duke and the King's scheme because if they don't, "there'd be another person that you don't know about who'd be in big trouble. Well, we got to *save* him, hain't we? Of course" (p. 158). Huck is also deeply distressed by the Duke and King's attempt to cheat the Wilkes girls out of their inheritance. Nevertheless, even at this point in his moral development, Huck's language reveals how deeply felt are his racial biases. As he thinks, "Well, if ever I struck anything like it, I'm a nigger. It was enough to make a body ashamed of the human race" (p. 137).

Eventually, those racial biases and Huck's acceptance of social values lead him to consider turning Jim in to the authorities. He reasons, "I was stealing a poor old woman's nigger that hadn't ever done me no harm." (p. 178). But then in a moment rich with irony, he decides that he will risk damnation in order to continue to help Jim to freedom. He rationalizes the behavior he sees as immoral:

> Well, I tried the best I could to kinder soften it up somehow for
> myself, by saying I was brung up wicked and so I warn't so much to
> blame, but something inside of me kept saying, "There was the
> Sunday school, you could a gone to it; and if you'd a done it they'd a
> learnt you, there, that people that acts as I'd been acting about that
> nigger goes to everlasting fire!" [p. 178]

Convinced that he must "decide, forever, betwixt two things," he
embraces what he sees as wickedness. He commits himself to trying to
"steal Jim out of slavery again" and makes his memorable statement,
"All right, then I'll go to hell" (p. 180).

The Cruelty of the Human Race

In these middle chapters of the novel, Huck is repeatedly confronted
with examples of the squalor, the violence, and the greed that characterize small-town life along the Mississippi. In one of the towns he visits,
he realizes, "All the streets and lanes was just mud." Hogs dominate
these roadways. But most significantly, local youths gain their pleasure
by tormenting animals:

> There couldn't anything wake them up all over, and make them
> happy all over, like a dog-fight—unless it might be putting turpen-
> tine on a stray dog and setting fire to him, or tying a tin pan to his tail
> and see him run himself to death. [pp. 118–19]

Huck witnesses violent act after violent act, generally without
comment or apparent judgment. Colonel Sherburn murders the
drunken Boggs simply because Boggs irritates him. The townspeople
initially respond to the murder as though it were good entertainment.
They reward with drinks and attention someone who mimics the
murder. Then, restless and looking for additional excitement, they
form a mob with the intent of lynching Sherburn. Cowed, however, by
Sherburn's speech, which is often assumed to express Twain's own
misanthropic sentiments, they eventually disperse. The crowd at the
circus similarly relishes what they see as danger to someone else, while
later the Duke and King's disgruntled audiences plan to attack the pair
with "sickly eggs and rotton cabbages" and dead cats (p. 128).

Increasingly, Huck makes judgments about what he sees and in
some moments he tries to affect events. For instance, condemning the
Duke and the King, Huck actively foils their plans. Nevertheless, he is
appalled at the behavior of the townspeople when they physically abuse
the King and the Duke. Just as the Shepherdson-Grangerford holo-

caust sickened him, he now feels "sick" to see the Duke and the King tarred, feathered, and ridden out of town on a rail. As Huck puts it, "It was a dreadful thing to see. Human beings *can* be awful cruel to one another" (p. 194). Huck's own compassion, however, confuses him, and he decides that he will simply ignore questions of morality altogether:

> it don't make no difference whether you do right or wrong, a person's conscience ain't got no sense, and just goes for him *anyway*. If I had a yaller dog that didn't know no more than a person's conscience does, I would pison him. It takes up more room than all the rest of a person's insides, and yet ain't no good, nohow. Tom Sawyer he says the same. [p. 194]

Huck's Rebirth as Tom Sawyer

After Huck makes his decision to try to free Jim, he returns to society. His lonesomeness and thoughts of death are reminiscent of the novel's opening chapter:

> it was all still and Sunday-like . . . and there was them kind of faint dronings of bugs and flies in the air that makes it seem so lonesome and like everybody's dead and gone. . . . As a general thing it makes a body wish *he* was dead too and done with it all. [p. 183]

Moments later, hearing a spinning wheel, Huck again has a death wish, thinking, "and then I knowed for certain I wished I was dead—for that *is* the lonesomest sound in the whole world" (p. 184). Given this frame of mind, it is not surprising that Huck welcomes the fact that the Phelpses mistake him for Tom Sawyer. But Huck's language suggests that being able to assume Tom's identity has an appeal far greater than just convenience. Indeed, Huck Finn is relieved to have his identity, his role, and his values defined for him. He recognizes:

> if they was joyful it warn't nothing to what I was; for it was like being born again, I was so glad to find out who I was. . . . Being Tom Sawyer was easy and comfortable. [p. 188]

When Tom Sawyer himself arrives, he abets Huck in maintaining his disguise. He also begins to make most of the decisions, further relieving Huck of responsibility for his actions. The difficulty is that the choices Tom makes and to which Huck acquiesces seem to negate much of what Huck has learned about Jim's humanity. Although Huck does object to many of Tom's ideas, he nevertheless is swayed by Tom's insistence that they must follow "regulations" (p. 201). For this reason, Huck agrees to commit all sorts of unnecessary cruelties in relationship to Jim. For instance, he allows Jim's cell to be filled with rats, snakes, and spiders. He does not interfere with Tom's demand that Jim use his own blood, from rat bites, as ink to write Tom's fictitious messages. He even allows Tom to delay in freeing Jim, even though he knows that the Phelpses are advertising Jim as a runaway slave, an act which might make it impossible for Huck to free Jim after all.

It is important to note that Huck acquiesces to Tom's will while he is publicly assuming Tom's identity. In that role, he seems to ignore his own instincts and accept society's standards. He is thus astonished that Tom would so go against convention and law as to try to free Jim. As Huck understands it:

> Well, one thing was dead sure; and that was, that Tom Sawyer was in earnest and was actuly going to help steal that nigger out of slavery. That was the thing that was too many for me. Here was a boy that was respectable, and well brung up; and had a character to lose; and folks at home that had characters; and he was bright and not leather-headed; and knowing and not ignorant; and not mean, but kind; and yet here he was, without any more pride, or rightness, or feeling, than to stoop to this business, and make himself a shame, and his family a shame, before everybody. I *couldn't* understand it, no way at all. [p. 196]

Nor is Huck able to transcend his own racism. When he is trying to convince Tom to use picks to free Jim, he thinks:

> Picks is the thing, moral or no moral; and as for me, I don't care shucks for the morality of it, nohow. When I start in to steal a nigger, or a watermelon, or a Sunday-school book, I ain't no ways particular how it's done so it's done. What I want is my nigger; or what I want is my watermelon; or what I want is my Sunday-school book . . . and I don't give a dead rat what the authorities thinks about it nuther. [p. 206]

And when Jim risks his own freedom to stay with the injured Tom Sawyer, Huck celebrates Jim's action by thinking, "I knowed he was white inside" (p. 230).

After the adventure is over and Huck has reassumed his own identity, he also once again acts on his more humane instincts. For instance, he insures that Jim is released from the chains that had been binding him. But most significantly, Huck once again decides he is going to leave society. Although he makes no specific condemnation of the values he is leaving behind, he is clear that he prefers alienation from society to participating in it:

> I reckon I got to light out for the Territory ahead of the rest, because Aunt Sally she's going to adopt me and sivilize me and I can't stand it. I been there before. [p. 245]

Jim's Degeneration into a Stereotype

Just as social pressures and the ease of being Tom Sawyer lead Huck to deny Jim's humanity, so does a socially assigned role degrade Jim. After achieving a parental relationship with Huck in any number of instances, Jim becomes totally subservient once he is a captive on the Phelps's farm. He not only agrees to Tom and Huck's dehumanizing schemes, at times he seems to accept their legitimacy. Although he has already proven capable of instructing Huck in matters of behavior and of moving Huck to recognize his human dignity, Jim now allows himself to be subjected to a wide range of abuse. From time to time, he protests feebly, but eventually he fulfills the boys' instructions. When Tom tells him that he must keep a journal on his shirt, using his blood for ink, Jim reluctantly agrees because he defers to their status as whites. As Huck describes it, Jim "couldn't see no sense in the most of it, but he allowed we was white folks and knowed better than him; so he was satisfied and said he would do it all just as Tom said" (p. 208). When Jim later complains about the rats, snakes, spiders, and the other demands Tom makes on him, Tom berates Jim until "Jim he was sorry, and said he wouldn't behave so no more" (p. 221).

Only when the trio are on the water again does Jim assume an adult role. Learning that Tom has been injured, he sends Huck for a doctor and insists on staying with Tom until he is given treatment. He similarly takes on the adult role after he learns he has been free all along. It is at that moment that he very gently tells Huck that his father is dead.

The issue, of course, is complicated.[8] On the one hand, Twain's point may be that only when individuals are freed from prescribed or learned social roles can they behave with dignity, self-respect, and an essential if instinctive morality. If that is the case, then the final chapters of the book are powerful examples of that dynamic. On the other hand, such a reading of the novel seems difficult to accept given Huck and Jim's developing relationship and individual evolutions throughout the novel. Although Huck's youthfulness makes his choices seem slightly more credible, it seems less consistent that Jim would so easily forget his commitment to free his wife and children and so readily play the fool.

The Benefits of a Social Contract

As much as Twain satirizes America's social conventions and attacks its prevailing social and religious mores, the novel also dramatizes ways in which society does offer some measure of protection to individuals. Huck's sense of the cruelty of human beings to one another is apparent in episode after episode. In turn, this sense that individuals may be inherently self-interested suggests that a social contract may be a necessity after all. Certainly, law and social order are forces that counter mob rule, power through force, and anarchy. Thus, even as Twain attacks immoral American values, institutions, and attitudes, he also dramatizes that life for the unprotected and alienated individual may be even more dangerous. At the same time, he also demonstrates the need for that social order to be ethically based. His attack, therefore, is not on society *per se* but on societies whose laws, institutions, and beliefs are hypocritical and without a commitment to morality and the concepts of individual and social responsibility alike.

V

The Death of Ivan Ilych (1886)

by Leo Tolstoy

Leo Tolstoy, in *The Death of Ivan Ilych,* asks his reader to confront perhaps the most difficult question of all; that is, given the inevitability of death, what gives life meaning? His protagonist, Ivan Ilych, has succeeded brilliantly according to society's standards. He has achieved wealth, social status, and professional acclaim. His family shares his values and conforms to his criteria for social presentability. Nevertheless, when confronted with the knowledge that he is dying, Ivan Ilych comes to judge his adult life a sham. He is also desperately afraid of death.

Tolstoy's answer to the question of what gives life meaning is a religious one. Specifically, only two hours before his death, Ivan Ilych triumphs over his physical pain and his fear of dying by rejecting secular values in favor of love, sacrifice, and faith. He decides that he must "act so as not to hurt" his family, is reassured by his new belief "that He whose understanding matters would understand," and gains sight of "the light."[1]

The story also dramatizes the dangers of what Tolstoy presents as the human tendency to deny consciousness, especially consciousness of death. Only Ivan Ilych himself, his youngest child Vasya, and the peasant Gerasim acknowledge death. The others assume, as Ivan Ilych himself once had, that death is something that happens to others but not to oneself (pp. 131–32). This illusion of immortality leads to other illusions. Many of the other characters believe that they can control and shape their lives at will. But, as Ivan Ilych so painfully learns, the individual is totally helpless in the face of illness and impending death. In addition, the illusion of immortality often leads people to ignore what the dying Ivan Ilych comes to define as "the right thing" (p. 155). Instead, they structure their lives around social values and personal comfort and, in so doing, deny their own humanity and that of others.

Ironically, Ivan Ilych becomes the victim of the very value system he had embraced most of his life. He had been governed by his desire for "the pleasures and amenities of life," for "comfort and propriety" (p. 110). In his effort to achieve these goals, he had separated "his real life from the official side of affairs" (p. 118). As a judge, for instance, he learned to "exclude everything fresh and vital . . . and to admit only official relations with people and then on official grounds" (p. 117). But when he is dying, Ivan Ilych is treated as he had treated others. His family, his friends, and his doctors now all deal with him in only formal or official ways. Such moments bring him both torment and the recognition that such detachment on the part of those close to him from the unpleasant and indecorous aspects of life denies him the help he most needs in order to face his impending death.

Tolstoy so relentlessly portrays death's reality and inevitability that he leaves his committed reader no escape from consciousness. Indeed, Tolstoy seems to demand that his readers, like Ivan Ilych, recognize their own desire to escape thoughts of death even as he demands that they acknowledge their own mortality.

Moral and Values Questions

General Questions: Guide to Reading

1. Kierkegaard tells the story "of the absent-minded man so abstracted from his own life that he hardly knows he exists until, one fine morning, he wakes up to find himself dead."[2] How do individuals distance themselves from a sense of mortality? What effect might a sense of personal mortality have on the individual? What are the possible effects of a denial of death?
2. What factors might affect an individual's attitudes toward his or her own death and the deaths of family and friends?
3. Discuss how social values, family relationships, and religious beliefs shape an individual's sense of what gives life its meaning.
4. How do the dictates of an individual's professional role affect

that person's inner life? What are the potential advantages and the potential dangers for the individual who separates the outer from the inner life, the public from the private self?

5. What other illusions—in addition to the illusion of immortality—tend to give meaning and structure to life? What is the potential cost to the individual of being stripped of such illusions? What is the potential cost of continuing to believe in such illusions?[3]

6. Elisabeth Kübler-Ross has outlined a theory of dying in her book, *On Death and Dying.* She describes the typical person as going through the following stages: denial and isolation, anger, bargaining, depression, acceptance, and the letting go of hope.[4] Discuss Ivan Ilych's evolution in terms of the stages Kübler-Ross identifies. In doing so, also note the relationship of psychological anguish to physical pain.

Questions for Discussions, Papers, Exams

1. If the tale is primarily about Ivan Ilych's dying, why does it begin after his death? Why does the first chapter devote itself to his colleagues and his family? What is the effect of Tolstoy's use of a flashback technique, i.e., his tracing Ivan Ilych's life chronologically after he has given the reader the knowledge that Ivan Ilych is already dead?

2. What does Tolstoy mean when he writes, "Ivan Ilych's life had been most simple and most ordinary and therefore most terrible" (p. 104)?

3. Ivan Ilych is preoccupied throughout his life with decorum and comfort, with propriety and pleasure. References to these terms permeate his thoughts. Later, however, Ivan Ilych becomes the victim of this same concern on the part of others for decorum and comfort, for propriety and pleasure. Discuss.

4. Contrast the function of the peasant Gerasim and Ivan Ilych's son, Vasya, to that of his family and friends in relationship to death. In discussing this question, take note of the fact that Ivan Ilych's future son-in-law is an examining magistrate, as Ivan Ilych had been in his youth.

5. Why does Ivan Ilych come to believe that his life had value only when he was a child?

6. Discuss the function of the light imagery in the story. In particular, contrast the light that Ivan Ilych sees when he wins at bridge

(p. 119), the lack of light in his eyes as he approaches death (p. 128), and the light he sees as he dies (pp. 154–56).
7. Tolstoy associates Ivan Ilych's death with that of Christ. Ivan Ilych lay for three days before he finally died and, at his death, "someone near him," echoing Christ's dying words, said, "It is finished!" (p. 156). Ivan Ilych also decides that sacrificing himself for his family will give his life and death meaning. Discuss.

Values: Pleasure and Propriety

Throughout his life, Ivan Ilych had devoted himself to fulfilling "what he considered to be his duty, and he considered his duty to be what was so considered by those in authority" (p. 105). He sought a life that had a combination of "pleasure and propriety" (p. 105), and he judged negatively anything that was not "conducive to the pleasure and amenities of life" (p. 110). Before his illness, his thoughts were dominated by such concerns. For instance, his marriage to Praskovya Fedorovna, a "well connected . . . and sweet, pretty, and thoroughly correct young woman," brought him happiness as long as her presence did not "impair the easy, agreeable, gay and always decorous character of his life, approved by society and regarded by himself as natural" (p. 109). However, when his wife's pregnancy altered her behavior, creating "something new, unpleasant, depressing, and unseemly" (p. 109), Ivan Ilych detached himself from her and their children. The result of this detachment was that "on the whole Ivan Ilych's life continued to flow as he considered it should do—pleasantly and properly" (p. 112).

Ivan Ilych had the same sense of control over his professional life. When a moment of discontent initially brought him to ennui and then to "intolerable depression," he "decided that it was impossible to go on living like that, and that it was necessary to take energetic measures" (p. 113). Yet, Tolstoy makes it clear that Ivan Ilych's success in this instance was more a matter of good luck than an act of will.

In his concern for an orderly, pleasurable life, Ivan Ilych had even been able to distance himself from the deaths of three of his children. In thinking about an episode of unhappiness when his family moved from one city to another, Ivan Ilych seemed to equate the deaths of two of his children with the problems of a higher cost of living. As the narrator explains it: "Though the salary was higher the cost of living was greater, besides which two of their children had died and family life became still more unpleasant for him" (p. 110). Years later, when life had become more comfortable, Ivan Ilych seemed similarly detached from the death of another child. He thought of his life as continuing "to flow as he considered it should do—pleasantly and properly" and "so things continued for another seven years. His eldest daughter was already sixteen, another child had died, and only one son was left" (p. 112).

When his career no longer sustained his interest, Ivan Ilych found a sense of meaning in other external tasks. He changed jobs, bought a new house, and undertook to decorate it himself. As long as his concerns with daily tasks preoccupied him, he was content. His wife and daughter, too, found a sense of purpose in the house, and for a time the family seemed more united than ever before. However, "when nothing was left to arrange it became rather dull and something seemed to be lacking." The family's response to this dissatisfaction was predictable. Once again, they turned to outer tasks, dedicating themselves to making new friends of the appropriate class. The result was that to their minds "life was growing fuller" (p. 117).

Life, Death, and "The Right Thing"

Ivan Ilych's illness and the process of his dying abruptly fling him from his earlier notions. He is confronted with something that he cannot control: his increasing pain and inescapable death. He is also unable to avoid his consciousness of that death, which he calls "*It.*" Eventually, he recognizes the futility of his trying to divert himself with thoughts of work or the other external aspects of his life:

> to save himself from this condition Ivan Ilych looked for consolations—new screens—and new screens were found and for a while seemed to save him, but then they immediately fell to pieces or rather became transparent, as if *It* penetrated them and nothing could veil *It.* [p. 133]

At the same time, Ivan Ilych comes to understand that his dying is unpleasant for others who judge him now by the same criteria he had formerly used. As he thinks:

> the awful, terrible act of his dying was, he could see, reduced by those about him to the level of a casual, unpleasant, and almost indecorous incident (as if someone entered a drawing-room diffusing an unpleasant odour) and this was done by that very decorum which he had served all his life long. [pp. 137–38]

He also recognizes how people detach themselves from the reality of death as long as death is something that is happening to someone other than themselves. Even though death is "bad" for him, he becomes aware that "for the doctor, and perhaps for everybody else, it was a matter of indifference" (p. 122).

Ironically, the devotion to decorum and comfort on the part of others comes to torment Ivan Ilych the most. He despairs that his doctors treat him as though he were an object, much as he had treated legal cases before his illness. They assume "the important air" that Ivan Ilych knew well because it resembled "that which he himself assumed in court" (p. 121–22). Because he recognizes the deception in such public stances, he grows bitter when it is applied to him. His wife, much like the doctors, has "adopted a certain relation" toward him that is false. Instead of acknowledging her husband's suffering or helping him deal with the inevitability of his death, Praskovya Fedorovna acts as though Ivan Ilych "was not doing something he ought to do and was himself to blame" (p. 142). But what gives Ivan Ilych the most anguish is that his wife's response to him does not in any way take into account his sense of the abyss and his fear of facing it alone (p. 127). His friends, too, fail to acknowledge his situation. Schwartz "in particular irritated him by his jocularity, vivacity, and *savoir-faire,* which reminded him of what he himself had been ten years ago" (p. 126). What Ivan Ilych sees as the falsity of those around him eventually comes to "poison his last days" (p. 138).

In time, Ivan Ilych begins silently to rage against those of his circle who are healthy and who are indifferent to death. He thinks:

> Death. Yes, death. And none of them know or wish to know it, and they have no pity for me. . . . It's all the same to them, but they will die too! Fools! I first, and they later, but it will be the same for them. And now they are merry . . . the beasts! [p. 130]

He is especially aware of the contrast between his dying flesh and the younger flesh of his daughter Lisa. Ironically, she now is engaged to a young man who is, as Ivan Ilych once was, an examining magistrate. The message is clear that they, too, will one day have to confront the reality of death. Now, however, "impatient with illness, suffering, and death, because they interfered with . . . happiness" (p. 144), they are distancing themselves from any consciousness of their own mortality.

As death comes nearer, Ivan Ilych anguishes about the injustice of his situation. Once again, he first turns to the external world for some sense of meaning. Because he believes that he has lived with "correctness" (p. 148), he repeatedly questions the justice of his suffering. He is sure that he does not deserve either to suffer so or to die. Initially, he vehemently rejects even the possibility that "Maybe I did not live as I ought to have done" (p. 148). He reminds himself again and again of "the legality, correctitude, and propriety of his life" and insists therefore that there can be no just explanation for the agony of his death (p. 151). Only later, when he views his life from religious rather than secular terms, does he accept his death.

Even though he knows that the denial by others of his dying is a poisonous deception, for a long while he, too, helps preserve the falsity. He does not confront his family with their turning away from him or his death. At the same time, it is only with the peasant Gerasim that Ivan Ilych gains any peace. With Gerasim, who easily accepts death and illness as natural parts of life, Ivan Ilych finds solace and an easing of his physical pain.

Even more significantly, by deciding that perhaps "his life had not been what it should have been," Ivan Ilych begins to come to terms with his death. Dying begins to lose its terror for him. In other words, when he abandons his sense that pleasure and propriety were life's most important values, Ivan Ilych is able to find what he calls "the right thing": the "light" and relief from both pain and fear of death. And when he is able to feel love and sorrow in the face of his son's grief and his wife's rather selfish suffering, he is able to let go of his indifference and antagonism and to gain peace. He achieves the will to release his family and to "free himself from these sufferings." With this decision, he comes as well to an acceptance of what he thinks of as God's grace. Now aware of "the light," Ivan Ilych approaches his death with happiness, "knowing that He whose understanding matters would understand" (p. 155).

Tolstoy surrounds Ivan Ilych's death with none of the ambiguities that readers later will find in Kafka and Camus. The symbolism allying the dying man to Christ is not ironic. Rather, Ivan Ilych's one moment of grace outweighs his earlier empty life and the torment of his death. While it is true that for some readers the emptiness of Ivan Ilych's life and the painfulness of his dying will seem more significant than the peaceful moment of his actual death, Tolstoy's own stance is clear. He is presenting the "light" as positive and desirable and Ivan Ilych's achievement of grace as genuine.

An Ordinary Life

Ivan Ilych led an ordinary life of conformity. He took his values, his goals, and even his tastes from others. His house resembled all others of its kind (p. 116). The parties he and his wife gave were similarly typical. Indeed, "just as his drawing-room resembled all other drawing-rooms so did his enjoyable little parties resemble all other such parties" (p. 118). It is his ordinariness that makes his death so poignant. To begin with, Ivan Ilych had never developed a self. He simply had assumed a persona and, "attracted to people of high station," had become adept at "assimilating their ways and views of life and establishing friendly relations with them" (p. 105). In a sense, neither his life nor his death, until its final moment, had any integrity or genuine meaning for either Ivan Ilych or others.

His ordinariness serves another function as well, tying him to all humanity. He becomes the embodiment of that humanity in the Caius analogy. The link is especially important, for if Ivan Ilych had assumed that "If I had to die like Caius I should have known it was so. An inner voice would have told me so" (p. 132), then so may all people assume that they, unlike the Caiuses and the Ivan Ilyches, are immortal. Tolstoy implicitly asks his readers to recognize, as Ivan Ilych comes to, that no one person is exempt from the conclusion that "all men die"; and once readers recognize their own mortality, they, too, have to ask the question of how they should live their lives.

Ironically, however, Ivan Ilych's own circle does not come to such a recognition. As the opening pages of the story reveal, his friends, his wife, and his daughter have distanced themselves from thoughts of mortality and are preoccupied with the external, daily tasks of their lives. One of his former collegues thinks immediately that Ivan Ilych's death may profit his own career. Another friend, Peter Ivanovich, decides that the death may allow him to secure a job transfer for a relative. At the funeral, Peter Ivanovich concerns himself with observing the proper forms, and he worries neither about mortality nor the loss of a friend but whether he will be able to participate in a card game after the service. Even Ivan Ilych's wife thinks only about the size of her pension and the difficulties her husband's illness caused her. Only Gerasim acknowledges death's inevitability, telling Peter Ivanovich matter-of-factly, "It's God's will. We shall all come to it some day" (p. 103).

VI

The Yellow Wallpaper (1892)

by Charlotte Perkins Gilman

In *The Yellow Wallpaper,* nineteenth-century economist and feminist Charlotte Perkins Gilman dramatizes the ways in which social and sexual expectations can limit an individual's potential for individuality, creativity, and fulfillment. In this rather remarkable piece of short fiction, Gilman also demonstrates just how much such expectations can distort the perceptions of those who resist conformity as well as of those who conform.

The narrator of the tale is a woman whose artistic talent and desire for intellectual and social stimulation is denied by her society, her family, and her friends. Her doctor-husband invalidates her perceptions, insisting that his medical training better qualifies him to make judgments about her condition. In time, he convinces her that her writing and her interesting friends are damaging to her. The husband, John, is, however, as much a victim of social and sexual expectations. His medical training and his sense of propriety have led him to distance himself from his wife emotionally. They also cause him to falsely diagnose her condition. Because he can understand neither her need for intellectual and social interests nor her desire to express herself creatively, he concludes that she suffers from "temporary nervous depression—a slight hysterical tendency."[1] As a result, he prescribes the cure most antithetical to her needs: rest, isolation, and no writing.

The tragedy is that John judges the narrator to be childlike and fails to acknowledge her humanity. Because the narrator has so absorbed his values and society's norms, she begins to distrust her own instincts. Although she has moments of genuine insight, she is not able—as were Hester Prynne or Huck Finn—to defy convention in order to be true to herself. Her only act of self-assertion comes in the form of self-denial: she suffers a mental breakdown and becomes that childlike, dehumanized being to which she had already been symbolically reduced.

Given Gilman's own history, it is somewhat surprising that she presents such a one-dimensional picture of the interplay between social values and individual choice. Although Gilman herself triumphed over a similar experience and eventually conquered her own nervous state by divorcing her husband, giving him and his new wife custody of their child, and writing and lecturing again, she never suggests that her narrator has such options.[2] Rather, the woman is a victim, initially of her husband and society's oppressiveness and later of her own mental instability.

The tale also raises questions about the relationship of values to perception and choice. It is a highly sophisticated example of unreliable narration. Indeed, much of its strength comes from the uncertainty of the narrator's account. Because she is suffering her nervous breakdown as she tells the tale, it is at times difficult for readers to sort out the actual from the fanciful in her narrative. There is the question of whether she is right that her keepers are to be feared (p. 26) or whether her fear is a result of her unbalanced mental state.

The story's symbolic richness emerges with the wallpaper itself. It is the medium onto which the narrator projects her hidden selves. In time, she decides to free herself from the prison her own life has become. She becomes determined to allow these hidden selves to be freed from the wallpaper. But because her perceptions have become distorted, she has also become totally unable to distinguish between the real and the imagined. Thus, when she attempts to destroy the paper, she suffers her own devastating psychotic break.

Much like Kate Chopin's *The Awakening*, which was published several years later, *The Yellow Wallpaper* earned more censure from its reviewers than praise. As Elaine R. Hedges notes, those who admired the tale ignored its concern with sexual politics and focused on its treatment of mental illness and its suspenseful qualities.[3] But, in fact, it is the mixture of the psychological with the political that makes the story both compelling and contemporary. In many ways, Gilman's piece mirrors the point that British psychologist R. D. Laing articulated more than a half-century later in *The Politics of Experience* and elsewhere: in an "insane world" those who are out of step may be the most sane.[4] Unlike Laing, however, Gilman does not present a mental breakdown as a positive experience that leads to deeper understanding. She offers little hope as she presents the narrator creeping around the nursery that has been her prison.

Moral and Values Questions

General Questions: Guide to Reading

1. What pressures encourage individuals to conform to prevailing social norms? What qualities seem to allow some people to resist those pressures without psychological consequences? To what degree are individuals shaped by society's values?
2. What is the effect of expectations related to gender on individual perceptions and choices? What were the prevailing sexual mores in the late 1800s?[5] What was the medical view toward female depression in the nineteenth century?
3. Who decides what is sane and what is insane behavior? What criteria should they use? To what extent does gender affect what is considered sane and insane behavior?[6]
4. What ingredients make life fulfilling for the individual? In particular, how important is self-expression?

Questions for Discussions, Papers, Exams

1. What is the significance of the fact that the narrator's husband so often treats her like a child?
2. What values does John hold? What factors have shaped his values? How do those values affect his response to his wife?
3. How are the narrator's perceptions denied?
4. What is the symbolic function of John's sister?
5. What is the symbolic function of the wallpaper? How and why does the narrator's response to it change throughout the tale?

Social and Sexual Expectations

John's sister epitomizes the role that the narrator's husband would like for his wife. As the narrator explains, "She is a perfect and enthusiastic housekeeper, and hopes for no better profession" (pp. 17–18). The narrator herself fails not only at housekeeping but as a wife and mother as well. Her baby makes her so nervous that she cannot be with him (p. 14). In terms of her husband, she berates herself for failing "to do my duty in any way!" Believing herself unable to provide him help, rest, and comfort, she perceives herself as a burden (p. 14).

Her husband, her brother (who is also a doctor), and, she suspects, her sister-in-law all think that her writing is the major cause of her nervousness. Refusing to acknowledge that she is genuinely ill, her husband nevertheless forbids her to "work" until she is "well again" (p. 10). John also denies her the stimulation of outside companionship. He will not allow her to visit her Cousins Henry and Julia, as she desires. Instead, she is treated with "phosphates or phospites— whichever it is, and tonics, and journeys, and air, and exercise" (p. 10) and then later with "cod liver oil and lots of tonics and things to say nothing of ale and wine and rare meat" (p. 21).

John also gives her a variety of mixed messages. Although he advocates self-control (pp. 11 and 22) and tells her that she should be able to will herself away from what he considers dangerous fancies, he repeatedly treats her as though she were a child. As she explains, "He is very careful and loving, and hardly lets me stir without special direction" (p. 112). He ensconces her in a barred nursery, which she initially detests. He calls her "blessed little goose" (p. 15), carries her to bed (p. 21), addresses her as "little girl," and admonishes her not to walk about their bedroom in the cold (p. 23). At one point, when she confronts him with her own sense that she is sick and that she wants to leave the house they have rented for the summer, he again responds to her in a paternal matter. Hugging her, he tells her, "Bless her little heart! . . . She shall be as sick as she pleases" (p. 24).

John himself is apparently a product of both his medical training and an unqualified belief in rationality. As his wife characterizes him: "John is practical in the extreme. He has no patience with faith, an intense horror of superstition, and he scoffs openly at any talk of things not to be felt and seen and put down in figures" (p. 9). Because he has decided that his wife has "no *reason* to suffer," he is satisfied. That she does suffer is something about which he has little understanding, believing that she should use "will and good sense" instead (p. 16).

Eventually, the narrator becomes imprisoned by her husband's values. Afraid that he will make good on his threat to send her to Weir Mitchell, a famous doctor whom she dreads, if she does not "pick up faster" (p. 19), she begins to hide her true feelings from John, his sister, and the baby's nurse. She cries most of the time but only when she is alone. She also hides from others the fact that she is writing. Eventually, the struggle of that deception wears her down and so she decides that the effort of writing "is getting to be greater than the relief" (p. 21). She thus abandons the one means by which she can express herself.

Values, Expectations, and Perceptions

Perhaps the most devastating effect for the narrator of the conflict between her values and the values of those around her is that she begins to deny the validity of her own perceptions. At the beginning of the story, she understands that she may not be getting well precisely because her husband is a physician. She recognizes that he does not believe that she is sick because he accepts only physical and not mental illness as real (pp. 9–10). She also understands that she would benefit from "congenial work, with excitement and change" (p. 10), and she is convinced that it is not her work but her husband's opposition to it that exhausts her (p. 10). At this point, she is sure enough of herself to disagree privately with the ideas of others even though she is unable to assert those disagreements.

Gradually, the narrator begins to feel guilty that she does not conform to the expected social role. She decides that she is ungrateful because she does not value the fact that her husband has totally scheduled each hour in her day (p. 12). She decides that asserting her own wishes in the face of his preferences would be "silly" and just her own "whim" (p. 15). Because she believes that her husband loves her dearly, she is especially susceptible to his entreaties that she behave as he would like "for his sake" (p. 22). She even goes so far as to believe that it is hard for her to confide in him "because he is so wise and because he loves" her so (p. 23). In other words, despite her initial sense that John's profession may be one of the problems in his response to her, she never counters his insistence that his role as a doctor gives him the right to have authority over her.

It should also be noted that the narrator has no outside source of support. John's sister and the narrator's brother both assume that John's treatment is appropriate. Moreover, as the story progresses, John seems to leave his wife more and more to herself. He sees patients often in town, thus leaving her even more isolated than usual.

As time goes on, denied all outlets of expression, social companionship, and the validity of her own perceptions, the narrator gives up her self. She begins to turn to the wallpaper that she originally detested. At first, she remains alienated from it because it offers her no order and no sense of purpose. Indeed, she is projecting onto it her own sense of the meaninglessness of her life. In time, however, she attempts to gain control and understanding without perceiving the impossibility of her desired task, that she wants to "follow that pointless pattern to some sort of a conclusion" (p. 19).

Eventually, she sees a figure in the design who mirrors her situation, "a strange, provoking, formless sort of figure, that seems to skulk about behind that silly and conspicuous front design" (p. 18). Then, the figure becomes more clear to her and seems "like a woman stooping down and creeping about behind that pattern" (p. 22). Eventually, the wallpaper brings her the sense of excitement that the rest of her life denies her. As she realizes, "I have something more to expect, to look forward to, to watch" (p. 27). Finally, she totally identifies herself with the woman in the paper. Believing that the woman she sees escapes from the paper during the day and creeps along the roads, the narrator locks her door and creeps as well. Then, determined to free the woman and herself, she decides to destroy the paper. Locking herself in the nursery that has become her literal as well symbolic prison, the narrator begins to peel the paper.

As she attempts to assert herself in this way, the narrator also regresses. Similarly, as she attempts to gain control over her situation by means of the wallpaper, she loses total control of herself. For example, frustrated at her inability to move her bed, she "bit off a little piece at one corner," just as she imagined the children who once had inhabited the room had done (p. 34). And although she calls her husband "young man" in an apparent effort to redress the imbalance between them, she is creeping around the room like an infant or an animal when he enters it. Although the narrator is triumphant that she has "pulled off most of the paper" because she now believes that her husband cannot put her back into it, her breakdown is also complete. He faints when he sees her, but her only reaction is to creep over his body as she circles the room again and again.

The Wallpaper as Symbol

In addition to projecting her own image onto the wallpaper, the narrator also projects onto it her own sense of meaninglessness and unhappiness. In an apparently unconscious foreshadowing of her own breakdown, she describes the paper as having "lame uncertain curves for a little distance [that] suddenly commit suicide—plunge off at outrageous angles, destroy themselves in unheard of contradictions" (p. 13). Later, trying to make some order out of the pattern, she decides that the design may be arranged on "laws of radiation" after all with "interminable grotesques [that] seem to form around a common centre and rush off in headlong plunges of equal distraction" (p. 20). She is also aware that because of its "lack of sequence" and "defiance of law," the wallpaper is—as she is—a "constant irritant to a normal mind." Eventually, the paper seems to her to be like a "bad dream," a "fungus," and an "interminable string of toadstools" (p. 25). Then, as her own mental state deteriorates, the paper assumes a bad smell for her and reminds her not of beautiful things "like buttercups but old, foul, bad yellow things" (p. 28).

Throughout the story, the narrator also reveals her sense that her situation is common to all women. For instance, as she contemplates the female figures she sees imprisoned in the paper, she reveals, "Sometimes I think there are a great many women behind" (p. 30). Then, typical of her sense of isolation and her tendency to contradict herself, she immediately reveals that sometimes she sees only one figure.

Nevertheless, even at this point, even when the narrator is on the verge of a breakdown, she understands the dynamics of her situation. She first decides that women are so trapped in their socially assigned roles that "nobody could climb through that pattern—it strangles so" (p. 30). Then, contradicting herself one more time, she decides that even though some women do "get through," the pattern strangles them off and turns them "upside down, and makes their eyes white" (p. 30). In other words, the narrator believes that those women who do defy convention will suffer her fate and either be destroyed or have their own perceptions invalidated, that is, turned "upside down."[7]

The narrator's ultimate perceptions of the wallpaper also indicate just how much she has lost her grip on reality. Although initially she had been aware that she was imagining figures within it, in time she imbues her imagination with a tangible life. The woman in the paper becomes so real to the narrator that she smuggles a rope into her room in order to tie the woman down if she should try to escape. She also tries to pull down the paper because she believes that it imprisons a literal figure.

It may be possible to view the narrator's destruction of the paper as a positive action, as a step toward taking control over her life. Similarly, it may be possible to see her decision to lock herself in and throw away the key as another step toward making her own choices. But in fact, although the narrator may be gaining freedom from the oppression of her husband and society's values, she has done so at the cost of her sanity. Her insanity will no more allow her to write and to live a fully human life than her sanity did. Nor has she gained the independence and maturity of adulthood; rather she continues to "creep" around the nursery that has also been her prison.[8]

VII

The Turn of the Screw (1898)

by Henry James

REGARDLESS OF THE READER'S CONVICTIONS about the governess's re-liability and the ghosts' reality, Henry James's *The Turn of the Screw* draws special attention to the relationship between values and percep-tions and to the ways in which each affects moral choice. In particular, the novella suggests that values derived from class and, in the gov-erness's case, from religious training shape perceptions that in turn influence behavior. *The Turn of the Screw* also demands that readers attend to their own values and perceptions. Those readers who accept the governess's version of events, who share her professed abhorrence of evil, and who celebrate the destruction of that evil, whatever the cost, are likely to see her efforts to save the children as understandable and perhaps even admirable. In contrast, readers who view the governess as unreliable and the ghosts as nothing more than a product of an unstable mind are apt to view her story either as a study in madness or to judge her behavior toward the children as both "cruel"[1] and an "act of violence" (p. 396).

Critical controversy over the tale has raged since Edmund Wilson's 1934 essay, "The Ambiguity of Henry James."[2] In that essay, Wilson attributed the ambiguities about the governess's reliability to James's conscious artistry. After acknowledging Edna Kenton's observation a decade earlier that the governess is the only person to see the ghosts,[3] Wilson concluded that the governess "is a neurotic case of sex repres-sion and the ghosts are not real ghosts at all but merely the governess's hallucinations."[4] Vehement criticism of this reading led Wilson to modify it and then to modify it again. Eventually, he decided that the tale's ambiguities were not deliberate on the author's part. Rather, he explained, "not merely is the governess self-deceived but . . . James is self-deceived about her."[5]

The debate has continued with most subsequent readers tending either to affirm Wilson's initial Freudian perspective or to insist that the governess is sane and reliable and that the novella is a ghost story after all. Eric Solomon has offered yet a third—albeit whimsical—interpretation, making the case that Mrs. Grose is the villain of the piece. Noting the several references in the text to moments or actions of "grossness," Solomon argues that the housekeeper manipulates the naïve governess in order to maintain her authority over Flora.[6]

In a sense, the final twist of the tale's screw lies in its defiance of definitive critical resolution. Because its ambiguities are so unrelentingly preserved, the tale ultimately demands that the readers ask, as the governess does, whether their perceptions float "into clearness" or "into a darker obscure" (p. 401). Even the introductory section, which ostensibly validates the governess's character, raises as many questions about the validity of individual perception and the relationship of perception to judgment and choice as does the tale itself.

Moral and Values Questions

General Questions: Guide to Reading

1. If Mrs. Grose believes the governess to be insane, then she is confronted with the need to choose between the dictates of her position as housekeeper under the authority of the governess and the dictates of her own conscience. How do individuals make judgments about appropriate action when their roles come into conflict with their personal morality? What are the possible consequences to those who choose to defy authority? What are the consequences to their sense of self and to the larger society if they acquiesce?
2. How do individuals know whether or not they are "seeing" their worlds objectively, particularly if their perceptions are not in accord with prevailing social norms? How do values affect perceptions?
3. The governess asks herself about Miles, "if he *were* innocent, what then on earth was I?" (p. 401). What steps might indi-

viduals take to protect themselves from unpleasant truths a-
bout themselves?

4. What is the obligation of the individual in regard to others?
   Assuming the governess to be right that Miles was "possessed"
   by the evil Quint, were her actions in attempting to "save" him
   justified, particularly in light of the consequences of that
   attempt?

Questions for Discussions, Papers, Exams

1. How does the governess's religious training figure in her self-
   definition and in her perception of the situation? How do matters of
   class affect both the governess and Mrs. Grose?
2. Many of the critical arguments that assert the governess to be sane
   depend upon Mrs. Grose's identification of the ghosts as Quint
   (pp. 318–21) and Jessel (pp. 328–32). The governess herself insists
   that the validity of her tale is proven by her ability "to give, of each of
   the persons appearing to me, a picture disclosing to the last detail,
   their special marks—a portrait on the exhibition of which [Mrs.
   Grose] had instantly recognized and named them" (p. 333). Is the
   governess's characterization of these scenes accurate? Might she
   have manipulated Mrs. Grose's responses or, in turn, might Mrs.
   Grose have manipulated hers? Once again, consider how values
   affect both perception and choice.
3. What is the function of the introductory narrator and of Douglas?
   Is there any evidence that the introductory narrator is reliable? Is
   Douglas a reliable judge of the governess's character? In discussing
   the reliability of narrative perceptions and expression, also consider
   the relationship in the tale of fantasy or imagination to reality,
   specifically noting the repeated references in the tale to imagination
   and to art.
4. Discuss the governess and Mrs. Grose's interaction in general. What
   is the significance of the governess's tendency to define Mrs. Grose's
   responses for her and to assume the nature of her thoughts when
   the housekeeper is silent?
5. What is the function of the repeated use of the word "gross" or
   variations on it throughout the narrative (p. 313, p. 340, p. 397, and
   p. 398)?
6. Discuss the governess's relationship with each of the children. How
   do her expectations for the position and her background affect her
   relationships with them? In particular, consider the circumstances

surrounding her rejection of Flora and her subsequent sense that she and Miles are like "some young couple who, on their wedding journey, at the inn, feel shy in the presence of the waiter" (p. 394).

Values and Perceptions: The Governess

Whether the governess is combating genuine ghosts for the souls of Flora and Miles or whether she is in the grip of a "spell" (p. 315), a "fancy" (p. 305), or an "impulse" (p. 338), the governess is a product of her background. The daughter of a parson, she wishes to be a moral savior (p. 323). She is determined that the children be "enclosed and protected" (p. 309) and elevates her role from that of governess to heroine. When she believes that the figure she encounters is that of the evil and deceased Quint, she is moved not to fear, as might be expected, but to a feeling of "joy in the extraordinary flight of heroism the occasion demanded" (p. 325). She is also pleased that the situation provides her with an opportunity to prove her worth to the children's uncle, thinking:

> I now saw that I had been asked for a service admirable and difficult; and there would be a greatness in letting it be seen—oh, in the right quarter!—that I could succeed where many another girl might have failed. It was an immense help to me—I confess I rather applaud myself as I look back! that I saw my service so strongly and so simply. I was there to protect and defend the little creatures in the world the most bereaved and the most lovable. [pp. 325–26]

It seems likely that the governess's impoverished and sheltered childhood made her particularly susceptible to the uncle's charms. Her infatuation with him, coupled with her self-definition as defender of the good, led her to believe that protecting Miles and Flora would earn her employer's approbation:

> I was giving pleasure—if he ever thought of it!—to the person to whose pressure I had responded. What I was doing was what he had earnestly hoped and directly asked of me, and that I *could,* after all, do it proved even a greater joy than I had expected. I daresay I fancied myself, in short, a remarkable young woman and took comfort in the faith that this would more publicly appear. [p. 309]

Ultimately, recognizing the uncle's indifference to her, the governess turns her devotion to the children. She repeatedly thinks of them as "my girl" and "my boy." When she comes to believe that Miles and Flora are possessed by evil in the form of Quint and Jessel, she asserts,

"I would have given . . . all I possessed on earth really to be the nurse or the sister of charity who might have helped to cure Miles" (p. 370).

The influence of her childhood is manifest in other ways as well. Certainly, the governess's response to Bly and the children stems in part from the relief they gave her from her eccentric father (p. 355) and from the disturbing letters she is receiving from home (p. 315). In fact, she sees the children as "an antidote to any pain." Emphasizing her new proprietary role in relationship to the youngsters, she decides, "with my children, what things in the world mattered?" (p. 315). Bly also gives the governess peace, time alone, and a sense of her importance, all things she had previously been denied. As she characterizes her initial responses:

> [I] learned to be amused, and even amusing, and not to think for the morrow. It was the first time, in a manner, that I had known space and air and freedom, all the music of summer and all the mystery of nature. And then there was consideration—and consideration was sweet. [pp. 308–309]

It is likely that the poverty of the governess's childhood further prompts her to romanticize her new surroundings and her charges. For example, she takes great pleasure in the fact that Flora and Mrs. Grose receive her as if she "had been the mistress or a distinguished visitor" (p. 299). Flora seems to her "the most beautiful child" she had ever seen (p. 299). To Miles, she attributes "something divine that I have never found to the same degree in any child—his indescribable little air of knowing nothing in the world but love" (p. 307). Bly itself becomes in her mind "a castle of romance inhabited by a rosy sprite, such a place as would somehow . . . take all color out of storybooks and fairytales" (p. 302).

But in the same way that the governess initially sees beauty and love wherever she looks, she sees only evil shortly after. When Flora rejects her, she turns against the child. She no longer sees her as "one of Raphael's holy infants" (p. 300) but as repulsive. She decides that Flora's beauty "had suddenly failed, had quite vanished . . . she was literally, she was hideously hard; she had turned common and almost ugly" (p. 382). As importantly, now believing the child both lost to evil and unattractive, she relinquishes her to the questionably named Mrs. Grose's care and turns her thoughts and energies to Miles.

The governess's feelings for Miles are especially charged, suggesting that her desire is not to save him (p. 390) but to possess him herself. She holds him with "hands of such tenderness," believing that he "had" her (p. 349). Upset by his wish to return to boarding school, she feels betrayed and considers leaving Bly because she "wanted to get away from him" (p. 364). She increasingly treats him as her equal (p. 371), and, during their dinner the night after Flora and Mrs. Grose have left Bly for London, she feels as though they are like a young couple on their wedding night (p. 394).

There are other suggestions that the governess has subconsciously defined the situation so that she can play out her chosen role of remarkable young woman and moral savior. For example, when she first encounters Quint, she is walking in the garden fantasizing about meeting the children's uncle. What "arrests" her with a shock when she first sees the figure "was the sense that my imagination had, in a flash, turned real" (p. 310). She may have imagined Quint in order to create a situation that would require moral action on her part.

There are also suggestions that she is mentally unstable. Even as she rejoices in her role of serving the children, she herself acknowledges that her state of mind may have been approaching insanity. As she explains it, she was now watching the children "in a stifled suspense, a disguised excitement that might well, had it continued too long, have turned to something like madness" (p. 326). She also begins, by her own admission, to move overtly into the world of invention with the children, encouraging them to create fictive worlds in which she seems always to play the role of "some remarkable person or thing" (p. 326).

But what may be most telling about the governess's state of mind is her responses to the children as the tale evolves. Despite her professed wish to protect them, she often seems to put her own interests before theirs. For example, wishing that events might have been different, she thinks, "I might have spared myself" (p. 344), a thought that shows an astonishing insensitivity to Miles's fate. Similarly, when she learns that Flora is speaking "horrors," she feels not the grief that Mrs. Grose evidences but rather relief. She exclaims, "Oh, thank God!" When the housekeeper expresses puzzlement at her response, the governess explains, "It so justifies me" (p. 388). Then, when she leads Miles to "confess," she is triumphant that she has been vindicated. In her own words, she is "infatuated . . . blind with victory" (p. 40), a reaction that is oblivious to Miles's obvious pain.[7]

There are moments when the governess does question both her perceptions and her actions. She recognizes that she initially romanticized Bly, noting that her "older and more informed eyes" tell her that Bly was not the fairy castle of her earlier vision but rather "a big, ugly, antique, but convenient house" (p. 302). More significantly, she expresses some concern about the morality of her actions. Before she confronts Miles with her knowledge of his expulsion from school, she has doubts, noting specifically that she felt:

a perverse horror of what I was doing. To do it in *any* way was an act of violence, for what did it consist of but the obtrusion of the idea of grossness and guilt on a small helpless creature who had been for me a revelation of the possibilities of beautiful intercourse. [pp. 396–97][8]

As she pressures Miles to confess, she thinks with similar alarm that he might not have been possessed by evil at all: "It was for that instant confounding and bottomless, for if he *were* innocent, then what on earth was I?" (p. 401).

Such questions raise the possibility that the governess is either evil or insane or both. Because such possibilities are apparently too dreadful for her to contemplate, she retreats from them. Instead, she devotes her energy to self-justification, insisting particularly upon the validity of her perceptions. Thus, she asserts early in the tale that she "saw with a stronger sharpness" (p. 311) and decides that her shock in seeing Quint "must have sharpened my senses" (p. 313). When she tells Mrs. Grose about her meeting with Quint, she notes with pleasure and relief that the housekeeper "accepted without directly impugning my sanity the truth as I gave it to her" (p. 332). Later, she addresses the issue directly, explaining that her belief then "was not, I am as sure today as I was sure then, my mere infernal imagination" (p. 354). Yet, much like every other statement of the governess's, these assertions, too, are ambiguous. That she sees her imagination as being "merely infernal," given the consequences of her actions, itself suggests that Mrs. Grose might have been wise to question her sanity.

There is, then, the possibility that the governess has presented her account of events in order to justify her actions in relationship to Miles and Flora. There is also the even more distressing possibility that she frightened Miles to death and terrified Flora into illness in order to convince herself that she was acting morally.

Values and Perceptions: Mrs. Grose

Mrs. Grose's actions, too, seem products of her background, particularly her social status. Whatever her private reservations about the governess's sanity (or, if Eric Solomon is right, whatever her villainy), Mrs. Grose never waivers publicly from her role as housekeeper. She acquiesces to the governess's authority just as she had apparently deferred to Peter Quint because the children's uncle had put him in charge of Bly. She indicates that she acts out of a sense of duty (p. 320) and at times out of fear (p. 324). If Mrs. Grose is in fact innocent of any villainy and if she believes the governess to be mentally unbalanced, her dilemma becomes especially acute. She must choose between the dictates of her conscience and the requirements of her job and her social status. If that is the case, much of her behavior can be attributed to a desire to keep the governess calm and the children from suffering (p. 368). For example, she often discusses the situation with the governess, counseling her at one point, "we must keep our heads" (p. 330).

Only at the end of the tale, when Flora seems terrified of the governess and seriously ill, does Mrs. Grose make independent decisions. She tells Flora that the governess is wrong and that Miss Jessel does not exist (p. 382). She also keeps the governess away from the distraught Flora. Even so, she secures the governess's approval for her choices. Despite her apparent preference that the governess leave Bly, Mrs. Grose agrees instead to take Flora to her uncle and to leave Miles at Bly with the governess. The latter decision, which the governess perceives her to be reluctant to make, is a fatal one for the boy. By giving the governess one final chance to make Miles "confess" so that she can "save him," Mrs. Grose has contributed to the child's death.

Of course if Solomon is right that Mrs. Grose is the villain, that the governess is the victim of someone's taking "a liberty rather gross" with her (p. 313), all of the housekeeper's actions assume a new meaning. Under such circumstances, Mrs. Grose becomes a skilled actress who adeptly plays the role expected of someone in charge "below stairs only" (p. 296) for her own evil purposes. Her apparent respectability and deference to the governess would then be seen as part of her efforts to manipulate her naïve supervisor, a woman deeply susceptible to the power of suggestion.

Values and Perceptions: Douglas

Douglas's assessment of the governess is unhesitatingly positive. He describes her as "a most charming person" and as "the most agreeable woman I've ever known in her position; she would have been worthy of any whatever" (p. 293). He found their conversations to be "awfully clever and nice" (p. 29). But Douglas apparently was in love with the governess, much as she had been infatuated with her employer. His judgments of her then might well be biased. Moreover, Douglas bases his confidence in her on the same sort of intuition upon which the governess relied. He insists that she had not shared the tale with anyone other than himself. As he put it, "It wasn't simply that she said so, but that I knew she hadn't. I was sure: I could see" (p. 293).

Although it is perfectly possible that Douglas's assessment of the governess, approximately fifty years after the event, was accurate—either because she had always been sane or because she had gained her sanity—it is equally possible that he is deceived about her. In any event, the introductory section invites the reader in yet another way to question the validity of what people see and what they believe they see.

Imagination or Reality

James calls attention in other ways as well to the question of whether or not the governess's manuscript is an artful and imaginative recreation of events or a historical account. He infuses the tale with references to artfulness and to imagination. Douglas draws his audience into the ghost story of the two children "with quiet art" (p. 292). In her turn, the governess wants to give Flora "the sense of knowing me" and contrives to use "the gentlest arts" to do so (p. 302). Soon after arriving at Bly, she decides that her work there would not be "gray prose" but rather "the romance of the nursery and the poetry of the schoolroom" (p. 314). She later notes, "We lived in a cloud of music and love and success and private theatricals" (p. 340). It is not unexpected that she eventually so confuses fantasy and reality that she decides of her relationship with Miles, "nothing in the whole world of reality was perhaps at that moment so fabulous as our actual reality" (p. 370).

James also suggests, although rather obliquely, that the manuscript itself may be more artful than authentic. The governess has written it after the events and given it to Douglas years later. He in turn has given it to the narrator to copy, and that transcription, which the narrator promises is exact (p. 295), becomes the body of the tale itself. This narrator is himself explicit that his enthusiastic response to the story is influenced by Douglas's oral presentation in that Douglas read it with "a fine clearness that was like a rendering to the ear of the beauty of his author's hand" (p. 298). The ambiguities about the text's reliability are one more way in which James draws attention to the complexities of perception and expression.

Finally, as several critics have noted, those moments in the text which suggest the ghosts are real are themselves suspect. As Harold C. Goddard points out, Mrs. Grose does not react to the specific details of the governess's description of Quint but rather to the more generalized thought that he looked like an "actor" and seemed to be dressed in clothes not his own (p. 302).[9] In other words, Mrs. Grose may be easily influenced by her superior. Even so, Mrs. Grose is openly doubtful that the governess has seen Jessel. For example, when the governess describes her vision of Jessel, the housekeeper first asks her, "How can you be sure?" (p. 329) and then twice questions, "Tell me how you know?" (p. 330). She is convinced ultimately not by the detail that the woman was "extraordinarily beautiful" or "wonderfully handsome" (details that Grose herself had earlier supplied), but she is moved by the governess's assertion that Jessel was "infamous" (p. 331). The latter detail might well appeal to Mrs. Grose's ostensible concern with respectability.

Miles's "confession" that he sees Quint is equally problematic. When the governess insists that there is a figure at the window, Miles first asks her, "It's he?" When she pushes him to reveal whom he means, only then does the boy reply, "Peter Quint—you devil!" (p. 402). But that phrase, too, is ambiguous. It might simply express Miles's fearful acquiescence to what he believes the governess wishes to hear or it might be a defiant accusation on his part that it is the governess and not Quint who is the devil after all.

The governess herself, except in the moments noted earlier, generally overlooks both ambiguity and nuance. Her concern may not then be to protect the children or, in terms of her account, to present the truth. Rather, it is possible that she turns each episode—both as it occurred and as she later describes it—into "evidence" for her perspective and her actions. If so, her narrative may be deliberately artful, just as many of her encounters with the children reinforced her imaginative sense of her world. On the other hand, both her choices and her presentation may be unconscious and even self-deceiving. James's refusal to resolve this issue and others has the effect of immersing his readers in these issues, demanding that they make the final judgments about the governess, Mrs. Grose, Douglas, and the ghosts and in so doing question the motives behind, and the validity of, their own perceptions and choices.

VIII

Heart of Darkness (1899)
by Joseph Conrad

MARLOW, THE NARRATOR OF JOSEPH CONRAD'S *Heart of Darkness,* comes to reject the dehumanizing and materialistic values of the white colonialists he encounters on his journey down the Congo. As he does so, he mentally allies himself with Kurtz, despite his ambivalence about the man. For instance, he recognizes that Kurtz, whom he had judged to be "hollow at the core,"[1] has succumbed to "the fascination of the abomination" (p. 6). He is also aware that in the wilderness Kurtz "lacked restraint in the gratification of his various lusts" (p. 59), including that of murder. In a larger sense, Marlow is turning "to the wilderness really" (p. 63) rather than to the dying Kurtz even though he believes that the wilderness corrupts. In other words, given the choice between Kurtz and the wilderness on the one hand and a corrupt society on the other, Marlow judges Kurtz a "remarkable man" and makes him his "choice of nightmares," a choice to which he vows to remain loyal (p. 66).

This is not the only moment when Marlow is confronted with the need to choose between nightmares. He must decide whether to take Kurtz away from the wilderness against his will or to leave him to die in the village where his lusts were gratified and where he was worshiped as a deity. Marlow must himself choose between giving in to the evil offered by the wilderness or returning to the civilized world for which he feels contempt. And when he does return to society, Marlow must choose whether to preserve the illusions of those who worshiped Kurtz or to tell the truth about Kurtz's evil. In particular, Marlow must decide whether to adhere to his own code of truthfulness or whether to protect Kurtz's Intended from a truth he judges "too dark—too dark altogether" (p. 79).

Conrad complicates both Marlow's choices and the readers' responses to those choices by infusing the tale with ambiguities. Marlow himself is aware that he may not always correctly be interpreting that which he sees. He is initially unsure whether the wilderness, great and invincible, is "like evil or truth" (p. 23). He questions whether Kurtz's ability to talk, his "gift of expression" was "bewildering" or "illuminating," was "the most exalted" or "the most contemptible," was "the pulsating stream of light, or the deceitful flow from the heart of an impenetrable darkness" (p. 48). Marlow's uncertainty about such matters suggests that his interpretation of other events may be unreliable. For example, Marlow rests much of his allegiance to Kurtz on his belief that Kurtz has recanted his earlier evil. Marlow's evidence for his belief is Kurtz's dying words, "The horror! The horror!" (p. 71). It is equally possible that Kurtz was not recanting evil at all but embracing it and that his dying words were his despairing judgment about the death that was denying him his lusts.

The response of Marlow's listeners to his tale creates additional questions about his validity as a narrator. On the one hand, all but the unidentified narrator appear to have fallen asleep during his account. On the other hand, that narrator is compelled enough by Marlow's tale to perceive the Thames in the same terms Marlow does, as a river leading into darkness and evil. In any event, such questions about Marlow's reliability raise their own questions about the complexities of perception, judgment, and moral choice and the difficulties inherent in discovering and expressing truth.

Moral and Values Questions

General Questions: Guide to Reading

1. To what degree are social restraints necessary to protect individuals from being exploited by others? Are human beings innately corrupt and therefore in need of societal restraints? On the other hand, do societies tend to assume powers that go beyond that of preserving the general good, becoming themselves forces that are dangerous for the weak?
2. What forces lead one group of people to exploit others? What

social, political, and economic factors conventionally have led one society to perceive another as its colony and its property? What psychological factors enable one group to so perceive another?

3. What crimes against humanity have been committed in the name of the social good, religious beliefs, and morality? What crimes against humanity have been committed when social good, religious belief, and morality have been ignored?

4. To what degree and under what circumstances should any individual assume responsibility for another?

5. What is the cost to an individual of being stripped of those illusions which give meaning and structure to that person's life? On the other hand, what is the cost to the individual of continuing to believe in such illusions?[2] By what criteria should one person decide whether another should be allowed to maintain certain illusions which might sustain but which might also be destructive?

6. Are lies ever moral?[3]

Questions for Discussions, Papers, Exams

1. Is *Heart of Darkness* primarily about Kurtz or about Marlow? In what ways are they confronted with the same moral dilemmas?

2. Is *Heart of Darkness* primarily an attack on colonialism or a dramatization of the dangers of the wilderness? If it is both, is there anything affirmative about the tale? In answering this question, take into account the following aspects of the tale:

a. The French gunboat.

b. The chain gang.

c. The grove of the dying.

d. The attack that Marlow's companions made on the village as they took Kurtz away.

e. The accountant who always wore white.

f. The snake imagery associated with the map of the Congo.

g. Marlow's perception of Brussels as a "sepulchral city" (p. 72).

h. Marlow's description of the Intended's home with its many death images.

i. The shrunken heads on Kurtz's gate.

j. Kurtz's stance as a deity.

k. Kurtz's attitude toward the villagers, the ivory, and his Intended.

3. What did Kurtz mean when he said, as he died, "The horror! The horror!" (p. 71)?
4. Is Marlow's lie to the Intended an act of morality and maturity or does the lie suggest that Marlow, because of his encounter with Kurtz, has betrayed his own ideals?
5. What is the function of the unidentified narrator? of Marlow's listeners?

Civilization versus the Wilderness

Heart of Darkness begins and ends with negative images of society. The story's setting, the Thames near London, is characterized by death and darkness. The narrator explains that "the air was *dark* above *Gravesend*" and "seemed condensed into a *mournful gloom, brooding* motionless" over London behind it (p. 3, my emphasis). Marlow similarly characterizes Brussels, the location of his company's offices. He describes the city as "a white sepulchre" (p. 9). The offices, moreover, are located in a "narrow and deserted street in deep shadow," a place of "dead silence." The entrance is an "ungarnished staircase, as arid as a desert" (p. 10). The secretary, although compassionate, seemed "full of desolation" as well as "sympathy" (p. 10). The two women "knitting black wool" later would seem to Marlow to have been "guarding the door of Darkness, knitting black wool as for a warm pall" (p. 11). The doctor's office, too, seems "as still as a house in a city of the dead" (p. 11).

Marlow's experiences with Kurtz and the wilderness do not cause him to alter his perceptions of Brussels. On his return from the Congo, he still thinks of Brussels as the "sepulchral city" (p. 72). He similarly defines the Intended and her home in deathlike terms. He notes that the Intended is dressed in black. He describes her house as cold and dark. He likens the top of her piano to "a sombre and polished sarcophagus" (p. 75).

Conrad presents an equally bleak view of civilization. The unidentified narrator and Marlow both think about the crimes committed in the name of society and progress. In the opening pages of the story, the narrator recalls that Britain's heroes, the "great knights-errant of the sea," had plundered other cultures for money, fame, and the expansion of the British Empire. This thought prompts Marlow to remark that England itself "has been one of the dark places of the earth" (p. 5). Marlow extends the attack on imperialism to the early Roman conquerors of England, characterizing them as criminal, greedy, immoral, and racist:

They grabbed what they could get for the sake of what was to be got. It was just robbery with violence, aggravated murder on a great scale, and men going at it blind—as is very proper for those who tackle a darkness. The conquest of the earth, which mostly means the taking it away from those who have a different complexion or slightly flatter noses is not a pretty thing when you look into it too much. [pp. 7–8]

Marlow professes to believe, however, that such exploitation can be "redeemed" if there is behind it "an idea, and an unselfish belief in the idea—something you can set up, and bow down before and offer a sacrifice to" (p. 8). But significantly, he argues that contemporary European efforts in Africa were not redeemed by such an idea. Rejecting his aunt's view that the Company for which he works is motivated by idealistic reasons, Marlow instead "ventured to hint that the Company was run for profit" (p. 12). In addition, he contrasts the noble idea with the reality that Kurtz created. Indulging his appetite and his greed, Kurtz set himself up as a figure before whom others bowed and to whom they made material and apparently human sacrifices.

Marlow's account is filled with images of the human devastation that the European colonial adventures brought to the African population. A French gunboat fires into the bush, attacking the "camp of natives" whom they deem "enemies" (p. 14). Marlow sees a chain gang of blacks which an inner "ominous voice" tells him "could by no stretch of the imagination be called enemies" (p. 16). He is sickened by the grove of death. He is appalled by the shrunken heads on Kurtz's gate.

Marlow is especially disdainful of the ways in which the whites use language to justify their violence and their greed. When he is told that the shrunken heads "were the heads of rebels," he laughs and thinks: "Rebels! What would be the next definition I was to hear? There had been enemies, criminals, workers—and these were rebels. Those rebellious heads looked very subdued to me on their sticks" (p. 59). Marlow himself refuses to allow political language to elevate immoral acts to some ideal. He is adamant that the destruction he sees stems from "a flabby, pretending, weak-eyed devil of a rapacious and pitiless folly" (p. 17).[4]

Despite his negative feelings about civilization, Marlow is keenly aware of its protections. He recognizes that society prevents the "pure, uncomplicated savagery" of a Kurtz (p. 59) for whom "there was nothing on earth to prevent him killing whom he jolly well pleased" (p. 57). Marlow also believes that the wilderness, where all is permitted, has the power to change the individual who previously had acted morally. Kurtz was originally a member of the "new gang of virtue"

(p. 26), was considered "a prodigy . . . an emissary of piety, and science, and progress" (p. 25). He had apparently come to Africa determined to "exert a power for good practically unbounded" (p. 50). Despite such ideals, Kurtz became totally corrupt within the wilderness. Almost immediately, his principles gave way to his "appetite for more ivory" (p. 58). He came to believe that he was entitled to possess everything he desired. As Marlow tells his listeners: "You should have heard him say, My ivory. Oh yes, I heard him. My Intended, my ivory, my station, my river, my—everything belonged to him." (p. 49).

Kurtz also gave way to the savagery within him. Instead of working for the "Suppression of Savage Customs," he began to "preside at certain midnight dances ending with unspeakable rites" (p. 51). Eventually, he set himself up as a god (p. 51). The natives worshiped him. He placed the shrunken heads of those he killed as symbols of his power on the gates to his house. Indeed, his initial desire to promote the good was transformed into a wish to "exterminate all the brutes" (p. 51).

Kurtz is not the only character who lacks the innate strength and the capacity for faithfulness which, according to Marlow, prompt individuals to act morally even when they are away from social restraints. Fresleven, Marlow's Danish predecessor, had been "the gentlest, quietest creature that ever walked on two legs" (p. 9). Yet, two years in the wilderness made him lose control. After a quarrel over two black hens, Fresleven attacked the chief of the village, an act that brought about his own death. Another white whom Marlow meets becomes similarly violent, demanding for no reason that Marlow "kill somebody" (p. 21).

Marlow himself eventually is in danger of changing in the wilderness. He symbolically suggests that evil tempts him when he notes that it was the serpentine quality of the image of the Congo on the map that had enticed him to take the journey. As he puts it, "The snake had charmed me" (p. 8). Later, on a more literal level, he finds the "pure, uncomplicated savagery" of the wilderness a relief. The lack of restraints leads him momentarily to devalue human life, much as Kurtz had. For example, when Kurtz resists being taken away from the wilderness, Marlow considers killing him but then almost casually rejects that action for practical reasons. He thinks that the idea "wasn't so good, on account of unavoidable noise" (p. 68). Ultimately, Marlow identifies himself with Kurtz, catching his sickness and taking it upon himself to preserve Kurtz's reputation. There is no question that, sometimes at least, like Kurtz he was tempted by the abomination.

The Elusiveness of Truth

Although Marlow seeks to understand and to express the meaning of his experiences, he essentially believes that truth is elusive and genuine communication between people impossible. As he tells his companions:

> It is impossible; it is impossible to convey the life-sensation of any given epoch of one's existence—that which makes its truth, its meaning—its subtle and penetrating essence. It is impossible. We live, as we dream—alone. [p. 28]

Marlow's language, filled as it is with double entendres in regard to his simultaneous physical and psychological journey, further points to the uncertainty of his perceptions and judgments. For example, he admits of his journey down the Congo:

> It was the farthest point of navigation and the culminating point of my experience. It seemed somehow to throw a kind of light on everything about me—and into my thoughts. It was sombre enough too—and pitiful—not extraordinary in any way—*not very clear either. No, not very clear. And yet it seemed to throw a kind of light.* [p. 7, my emphasis]

The tale's unidentified narrator, like Marlow, acknowledges the difficulty in discovering and communicating meaning. He contrasts Marlow to the typical seaman for whom the "whole of meaning . . . lies within the shell as a cracked nut." For Marlow, he recognizes, the truth is less tangible:

> the meaning of an episode was not inside like a kernel but outside, enveloping the tale which brought it out only as a glow brings out a haze, in the likeness of one of those misty halos that sometimes are made visible by the spectral illuminations of moonshine. [p. 3]

When Marlow has moments of assuming that he is capable of communicating meaning, the narrator undercuts him. He notes that Marlow is prone to recounting "inconclusive experiences" (p. 7). And when Marlow tells his listeners that they can "see more" of Kurtz because "You see me, whom you know . . ." the narrator immediately notes, "It had become so pitch dark that we listeners could hardly see one another" (p. 28). The irony is sharp. In this moment, Marlow has become for his companions what Kurtz had been for him, a voice that he may or may not "see" or interpret correctly. On the other hand,

Marlow's companions do not appear to be as compelled by Marlow and his tale as Marlow was compelled by Kurtz and his voice. In fact, all but the unidentified narrator may be asleep.

The question of Marlow's reliability and of the elusiveness of truth in general makes suspect some of Marlow's most important judgments and choices. For instance, when Marlow interprets Kurtz's "The horror! The horror!," he may well be projecting his own needs onto the dying man. Disappointed that his illness, which he caught from Kurtz, brings him no moral vision, Marlow values Kurtz for what he perceives to be Kurtz's dying "affirmation, a moral victory paid for by innumerable defeats, by abominable terrors, by abominable satisfactions. But it was a victory" (p. 72). It is this interpretation of Kurtz's dying words that leads Marlow to champion Kurtz. But Kurtz's words, in fact, may not have signified a moral recantation. Instead, they may have been in response to a vision of the horror of death itself. They may have been a negative judgment on Kurtz's part of the death that was taking him away from the people who worshiped him and indulged his appetites. Or they may have simply been an exclamation of physical pain.

Marlow's loyalty to Kurtz in turn leads Marlow to lie to the Intended, despite his own abhorrence of dishonesty. Early in the tale, he explains:

> You know I hate, detest, can't bear a lie, not because I am straighter than the rest of us, but simply because it appalls me. There is a taint of death, a flavour of mortality in lies—which is exactly what I hate and detest in the world—what I want to forget. It makes me miserable and sick, like biting something rotten would do. [p. 27]

Marlow's lie to the Intended itself points to the difficulty of discovering meaning, for it is an act filled with ambivalent implications. On the one hand, the lie is based on loyalty and a conviction that the truth might damage. Seen in this way, the lie becomes an act of morality, maturity, and compassion. It leaves the Intended with an illusion that sustains her, justifies her grief, and allows her to avoid that darkness which Kurtz, Marlow, and the narrator confront. On the other hand, by his lie, Marlow betrays his own moral code. Certainly he is aware as well of the devastation wrought by illusions. Seen in this light, the lie becomes negative in that it will, in all likelihood, perpetuate the Intended's imprisonment in her mourning and in her tomblike house. It may encourage her to spend her life devoted to the memory of a man whom she did not genuinely know, a man who had embraced evil, a man who had found another woman to worship him while he was in the wilderness.

The complexities of truth actually lead Marlow to the conviction at some moments that some individuals should avoid knowledge, particularly if that knowledge is evil. He values trivial tasks for this reason; such tasks, he believes, can hide "the inner truth . . . luckily, luckily" (p. 34). In his mind, attending "to the mere incidents of the surface" will distract people so that they do not have to face a "reality" which is so dark that it may destroy their sanity. At other moments, however, Marlow takes an opposing view. Here, he advocates genuine work precisely because it does lead to an understanding of the self, which he concludes is the only knowledge possible: "I don't like work— no man does—but I like what is in the work—the chance to find yourself. Your own reality—for yourself, not for others—what no other man can ever know. They can only see the mere show and never can tell what it really means" (p. 28). Such a discovery of self can be sustaining and itself a triumph, Marlow believes, but only if the individual in question has an "innate strength," a "capacity for faithfulness" (p. 50), and a "deliberate belief" (p. 37) in an idea that redeems (p. 7).

Ultimately, Marlow is confronted repeatedly with a "choice of nightmares," whether it be the choice of society or the wilderness, taking Kurtz or leaving him, championing his cause or judging him harshly, telling the lie or presenting the truth. Again and again, he demonstrates the difficulties inherent in perceiving reality, interpreting it, and communicating it. Again and again, he demonstrates that most people struggle with such questions and that in the end most people are neither totally committed to evil nor totally committed to good. Indeed, he can only conclude that all of life is a balance, explaining that most people are not solely devils nor "exalted." Rather, he decides: "Most of us are neither one nor the other. The earth for us is a place to live in, where we must put up with sights, with sounds, with smells, too, by Jove!—breathe dead hippo, so to speak, and not be contaminated" (p. 50).

IX

The Awakening (1899)

by Kate Chopin

ALTHOUGH KATE CHOPIN's *The Awakening* directly explores the ways in which prescribed social roles limit individual freedom, the novel's focus is ultimately as much on the psychological as it is on the social or the political. Even after Edna Pontellier, Chopin's protagonist, has asserted a relatively large measure of social and sexual independence, she remains tormented by her failure to achieve self-realization. Even after she has evolved to the point where she can defy those conventions that she believes deny the self, she fails to complete the inner journey that, Chopin suggests, is necessary for personal fulfillment.

Chopin asks the reader to consider how much Edna is a victim of conditioning and circumstances and how much her choices are a product of her own personal failure of will and spirit. Throughout the novel, Chopin maintains a tension between the social and psychological forces that influence Edna. On the one hand, she points to the external values that constrain women and mold their attitudes. On the other hand, she emphasizes Edna's personal inadequacies, particularly her failure to be reflective about her choices, to assume responsibility for others, and to accept the aloneness that accompanies the independence she seeks. Although it could be argued that Edna's conditioning as a woman has taught her to be unreflective, irresponsible, and dependent, Chopin offers woman characters who achieve more self-knowledge, maturity, and autonomy than Edna does.

Chopin draws attention to the complexities of individual choice and responsibility by raising the question of just how much freedom any one person has. She infuses the narrative with references to fate, suggesting that Edna's actions were preordained. Chopin also emphasizes the power of social convention by demonstrating that even though Edna herself is able to disregard social strictures with "neither shame nor remorse,"[1] she is still affected by their power over others. Robert leaves Edna because he is unable to understand her perception of herself as a free agent. He continues to see her as "one of Mr. Pontellier's possessions to dispose of or not" (p. 178). He also believes that his love for her demands that he protect her from social censure. Robert's decision to end their relationship leaves Edna despondent. She recognizes that Robert "did not understand" and "would never understand" her sense of individuality. She also realizes that she no longer will be able to gain "possession of the beloved one" (p. 185). But most of all, Edna believes that she is and will always be alone.

In the end, then, it is a combination of the social and the psychological that prompts Edna to swim to her death. She is unable to reconcile her need for social independence with her despondency over her growing conviction that she is alone in the universe. Although she is determined to allow no one to "possess her body and soul" (p. 190), she lacks the inner strength necessary to sustain her in the aloneness such independence brings.

As the narrator explains after Robert leaves Edna:

> Despondency had come upon her there in the wakeful night and had never lifted. There was no one thing in the world that she desired. There was no human being whom she wanted near her except Robert; and she even realized that the day would come when he, too, and the thought of him would melt out of her existence, leaving her alone. [p. 189]

Edna's relationship with her children typifies her ambivalence about her own needs and desires. On occasion, she is capable of "giving them all of herself, and gathering and filling herself with their young existence" (p. 157). She is equally capable of forgetting about them (p. 33 and p. 158). Only a day before her death, believing that she will have a life with Robert, she tells Dr. Mandelet:

> I don't want anything but my own way. That is wanting a good deal, of course, when you have to trample upon the lives, the hearts, and the prejudices of others—but no matter—still, I shouldn't want to trample upon the little lives. [p. 184]

Nevertheless after her "wakeful night," Edna reaffirms what she had insisted earlier to Adèle Ratignolle, "that she would give up the unessential, but she would never sacrifice herself for her children" (p. 181). Instead, she now decides that her children are her greatest burden:

> The children appeared before her like antagonists who had overcome her, who had overpowered and sought to drag her into the soul's slavery for the rest of her days. [p. 189]

Believing that suicide is "a way to elude" her children and feeling herself absolutely alone, Edna succumbs to the seductive voice of the sea, which invites "the soul to wander into abysses of solitude," and drowns herself (p. 189).

It is fitting that reader response to *The Awakening* at various points in its history dramatizes, much as the novel does, the power of social values to influence individual perceptions. Following its publication in 1899, *The Awakening* aroused a vehemently negative reaction. Offended by Edna's awakened sexuality and her lack of guilt, most reviewers damned the book, and some libraries refused to shelve it. In her native St. Louis, Chopin was ostracized by both social and literary circles.[2] According to her biographer, Per Seyersted, Chopin "became 'stunned and bewildered,' and even broken-hearted at the reaction to *The Awakening*."[3] Edmund Wilson similarly reports that the novel brought Chopin "into such ill-repute that she is said to have been reluctant to publish anything more."[4] In contrast, the women's movement in the sixties and seventies occasioned a Chopin revival, rediscovering *The Awakening*, which had been out of print for more than half a century. Readers now typically laud Edna's struggle for independence and celebrate her suicide as a heroic act of liberation.[5] But as instructive about readers' biases as these reactions are, neither those who damned Edna nor those who sanctify her do justice to the novel's complexities. In the first instance, they ignore the courage of Edna's struggle, and in the latter, her personal inadequacies. In addition, Chopin's readers have too readily equated the author with her character. But the novel's language and its imagery suggest that Chopin may well have viewed Edna with a more critical eye.

Moral and Values Questions

General Questions: Guide to Reading

1. To what degree are individuals responsible for their own actions and to what degree are they shaped by childhood and social conventions?

2. If individuals are fated to live their lives in certain ways, can they be held responsible for their actions?

3. Edna tells Dr. Mandelet: "perhaps it is better to wake up after all, even to suffer rather than to remain a dupe to illusions all one's life" (p. 184). What is the cost to the individual of being stripped of those illusions that give meaning and structure to life? On the other hand, what is the cost to the individual of continuing to believe in such illusions?

4. Dr. Mandelet suggests that nature creates illusions about the parental bond in order to perpetuate the race. What is the legitimate obligation of parent to child? Does the parental bond demand that parents (historically, mothers) "idolize" and devote their lives to their children as the "mother-women" do? Or is it possible and acceptable for them to choose themselves first, as Edna does?

5. What is the nature of human responsibility? What would be the implications of large groups of individuals asserting as Edna did that they would be willing "to trample upon the lives, the hearts, the prejudices of others?"

6. What ingredients go into making a fulfilled person? What is the importance of work, of relationships, and of artistic self-expression to an individual's fulfillment?

7. Is suicide ever an affirmative act?[6]

Questions for Discussions, Papers, Exams

1. What are the symbolic roles of the other women in Edna's life: Adèle, Mademoiselle Reisz, Mrs. Highcamp, Edna's mother-in-law, Mariequita, Mrs. Lebrun, the woman who fingers her rosary beads, and the woman who, with her lover, so often appears in the opening chapters of the book? Why does Edna reject them as models?

2. What values does Léonce Pontellier hold? In particular, what are his attitudes toward his wife and his children?

3. What is the novel's stance toward Edna's suicide? Take into account the thematic significance of the following aspects of the novel:
   a. The validity of Edna's perceptions about her children and her husband as enslavers.
   b. The bird imagery that permeates the novel.
   c. The changes in the language in the narrative refrain about the sea (p. 25, p. 189).
   d. The snake imagery associated with the water.

e. Edna's failure to make deliberate choices.
f. Edna's choice of Arobin as a lover even though she believes it is Robert whom she loves.
g. Edna's earlier infatuations.
h. Edna's artistic abilities and the degree of her commitment to her painting.
i. Edna's vision that Mademoiselle Reisz would sneer at her if she knew that Edna was going to kill herself.
j. Edna's failure to seek Dr. Mandelet's help.
4. What is the function of the fact that Edna often falls asleep or is without energy?[7] What is the thematic significance of the title?
5. What is the significance of Edna's reading Emerson and falling asleep as she does so?[8]
6. What is the function of the following passage:

> Edna was what she herself called very fond of music. Musical strains, well rendered, had a way of evoking pictures in her mind. She sometimes liked to sit in the room of mornings when Madame Ratignolle played or practiced. One piece which that lady played Edna had entitled "Solitude." It was a short, plaintive, minor strain. The name of the piece was something else, but she called it "Solitude." When she heard it there came before her imagination the figure of a man standing beside a desolate rock on the seashore. He was naked. His attitude was one of hopeless resignation as he looked toward a distant bird winging its flight away from him. [p. 44]

7. What is the significance of Edna's sense that life is a "monster made up of beauty and brutality" (p. 140)?

Social Barriers to Self-Realization

Léonce Pontellier assumes that Edna belongs to him. When she is sunburned, he chides her for being "burnt beyond recognition," appraising her "as one looks at a valuable piece of personal property which has suffered some damage" (p. 7). Because Pontellier is a man who "valued his possessions, chiefly because they were his" (p. 83), he is unable to acknowledge Edna's individuality or her humanity. He wakes her from a deep sleep to tell her of his evening's gambling adventures and then demands that she get out of bed to tend to one of their children whose sleep he has also disturbed. Moments later, he easily falls asleep, leaving Edna awake and distraught. Eventually, he compensates her materially for his lack of consideration, giving her half of his gambling winnings and sending her a box of delicacies.

At this point in the novel, Edna does not understand her unhappiness nor the terms of her relationship with her husband. She accepts his gift of his winnings "with no little satisfaction" because "she liked money as well as most women." Nor does she quarrel with the judgment of the other women at Grand Isle that the box of delicacies qualifies Pontellier as "the best husband in the world" (p. 15).

At other times, Léonce adopts a parental stance toward his wife. He "instructs" her to send Robert away if she finds him boring (p. 8), and he commands her to come into the house when she prefers to stay outside. When she balks at the latter direction, Léonce insists, "I can't permit you to stay out there all night. You must come in the house instantly" (p. 53). On the other hand, Léonce is dismayed when Edna does not conform to his expectations for her as a wife and a mother. He reproaches her "with her inattention, her habitual neglect of the children" (p. 13) and becomes enraged when, in his estimation, she fails to supervise properly the preparation of their dinner.

When Edna begins actively to defy her husband by ignoring his commands, by failing to receive guests on Tuesdays as usual, and by disregarding "her duties as a wife" (p. 95), Léonce begins "to wonder if his wife were not growing a little unbalanced mentally" (p. 96).[9] Unable to accept her "peculiar" behavior, he turns to Dr. Mandelet for advice (p. 110). Only then, after he has been advised by this male whose authority he respects, does Léonce relax about Edna's behavior. But even though he chooses to tolerate what Mandelet assures him is "some passing whim" (p. 110), he makes no attempt either to understand Edna or to see her as an individual in her own right. For instance, when she moves out of his house into the "pigeon house" in order to be free of his "bounty" as she is "casting off her allegiance to him" (p. 133), Léonce's concern is not their relationship or Edna's psychological state. Rather, "simply thinking of his financial integrity," he concocts a face-saving scheme that will not be harmful to his "business prospects" (p. 155).

Léonce Pontellier's perceptions of the husband-wife relationship were not unique to his society. In fact, they reflect existing laws that designated women as the property of their husbands. As Margaret Culley points out in her discussion of "The Context of *The Awakening*," the Napoleonic Code was still in effect in New Orleans at the turn of the century:

> All of a wife's "accumulations" after marriage were the property of her husband, including money she might earn and the clothes she wore. The husband was the legal guardian of the children, and until 1888 was granted custody of the children in the event of a divorce. The wife was "bound to live with her husband and follow him

wherever he [chose] to reside." A wife could not sign any legal contract (with the exception of her will) without the consent of her husband, nor could she institute a lawsuit, appear in court, hold public office, or make a donation to a living person . . . and divorce was a scandalous and rather rare occurrence.[10]

It should not be surprising, given the current mores, that Robert Lebrun shares Léonce's assumptions about the marital rights of men. Nor should it be surprising that Edna's experience offers her few alternative role models. Most of the women she knows fall into the category of "mother-women," the role that Léonce desires for her. These are women who seem always to be

> fluttering about with extended, protecting wings, when any harm, real or imaginary, threatened their precious brood. They were women who idolized their children, worshipped their husbands, and esteemed it a holy privilege to efface themselves as individuals and grow wings as ministering angels. [p. 16]

The embodiment of the "mother-woman" is "the sensuous Madonna," Adèle Ratignolle (p. 22). Adèle resembles "the bygone heroine of romance and the fair lady of our dreams" (p. 17). She so caters to her husband that she refuses Edna's request for company one evening because "Monsieur Ratignolle was alone, and he detested above all things to be left alone" (p. 67). When Adèle is pregnant, she confines herself to their home, only leaving "to take a languid walk around the block with her husband after nightfall" (p. 126). Adèle even seems to feel the necessity to justify her accomplishments as a musician in terms of her family, telling a social gathering at Grand Isle:

> she was keeping up her music on account of the children, she said, because she and her husband both considered it a means of brightening the home and making it attractive. [p. 42]

Madame Lebrun and Mrs. Highcamp appear similarly dedicated to their familes. Aline Lebrun, widowed in the early years of her marriage, has for over twenty years held the "fixed belief . . . that the conduct of the universe and all things pertaining thereto would have been manifestly of a more intelligent and higher order" had her husband lived (p. 39). After her husband's death, she turned her attention to her sons, especially the youngest. As Mademoiselle Reisz tells Edna:

> Aline Lebrun lives for Victor, and for Victor alone. She has spoiled him into the worthless creature he is. She worships him and the ground he walks on. [p. 81]

Mrs. Highcamp is more complicated in that she embraces the role of "mother-woman" with almost blatant hypocrisy. She uses her daughter's social needs "as a pretext for cultivating the society of young men of fashion" (p. 123). Nevertheless, she publicly plays the role of the devoted wife. Ignoring her husband's unresponsiveness to her at dinner, she treats him with "delicate courtesy and consideration. . . . She addresses most of her conversation to him" (p. 25).

Mademoiselle Reisz embodies an antithetical alternative, that of the artist. In contrast to Adèle, whose art exists for her family's pleasure, and to Edna, who can only paint when in the mood, Mademoiselle Reisz has given her life over to her art. She is a "courageous soul" who dares and defies" (p. 106). The cost, however, has been high. She possesses no femininity, and her refusal to observe social amenities has made her an outcast. As with Edna, Mademoiselle Reisz's defiance of convention leads others to see her as mentally unbalanced. Alcée Arobin sees her as "partially demented." Edna, for the moment sure of her own antisocial impulses, rejects Arobin's view, telling him that she finds Reisz "wonderfully sane" (p. 138). Nevertheless, Chopin symbolically suggests that Mademoiselle Reisz has failed to achieve her maturity. At Edna's dinner party, because of her diminutive size, the artist is seated upon cushions "as small children are sometimes hoisted at table upon bulky volumes" (p. 145).

Unhappily, Edna is unable to emulate the best aspects of the lives that Mademoiselle Reisz and Adèle offer. She is unable to accept for herself the solitude that characterizes the artist's life. She also cannot achieve her friend's self-discipline. Nor can she embrace the sort of responsibility that marks Adèle's life. On the other hand, neither these two women nor the others have accomplished Edna's ultimate goal, the integration of their outer and inner lives, or what the narrator describes as "the outward existence which conforms, the inward life which questions" (p. 26). The woman who fingers the rosary beads, for instance, has so immersed herself in religion that she appears to have no life other than the spiritual one. Nameless, without an individual identity, she is always referred to as "the lady in black." Mariequita, a flirtatious young girl, is dismissed as "a sly one, and a bad one" (p. 81). The young lovers, like the lady in black, have no individuality. Finally, Miss Mayblunt, apparently herself an artist and an intellectual, publicly denies her accomplishments and her talents for "it was suspected of her that she wrote under a *nom de guerre*" (pp. 144–45).

Edna is comfortable in none of these roles. She is not a woman-mother nor does she find value in the Ratignolle's apparently perfect understanding and harmony. She characterizes their peaceful union as "a colorless existence," and she can see in it only "an appalling and hopeless ennui" (p. 93). She is equally unable to contemplate a life of aloneness. And despite the pleasure that her painting brings her and despite the fact that she is able to earn an independent income by selling her work, she cannot make the commitment to art that Mademoiselle Reisz has made. Edna is also alienated from the religious life. As a child, she tried to escape from what she perceived as the gloom of her father's reading of the Presbyterian service (p. 30) and as an adult, she finds the atmosphere in a church oppressive (p. 60). She also rejects an unmarried, promiscuous life. Although she feels no regret or guilt about her loveless but passionate affair with Arobin, she eventually decides that such relationships are meaningless to her. She also sees them as potentially harmful to her children. As she walks on the beach just before her suicide, she said "over and over to herself: 'Today it is Arobin; tomorrow it will be someone else. It makes no difference to me, it doesn't matter about Léonce Pontellier—but Raoul and Etienne!' " (p. 188).

Edna's Social Freedoms

Despite the prevailing social attitudes and limited options available to women in general, Chopin makes it clear that Edna has advantages, opportunities, and freedoms not usually available to women of her generation. An inheritance from her mother gives her enough financial independence so that she can set up her own residence with servants. Her mother-in-law is happiest when she can care for Edna's children. Even when Raoul and Etienne are with Edna, servants take care of her children, leaving Edna the leisure and the opportunity to begin her summer flirtation with Robert, to visit friends, to paint, and to form her liaison with Arobin. Finally, although Adèle attempts to influence Edna to give up her affair with Arobin and to "think of the children" (p. 185), neither she nor any of Edna's other friends ever withdraw their friendship from Edna. Mademoiselle Reisz offers Edna support in her relationship with Robert. Dr. Mandelet directly offers her help. A group of friends and acquaintances even attend Edna's party to celebrate her moving into her own home. In other words, Edna Pontellier is not as enslaved by her children as she seems to think, nor is she the victim of extreme social pressure.

Edna's Incomplete Mystical Journey

Chopin universalizes Edna's awakening to her "position in the universe as a human being, and to ... her relations as an individual to the world within and about her" by infusing it with some of the ingredients of the mystical journey. Edna, for instance, goes through three of the stages that Evelyn Underhill identifies as characteristic of the mystical journey: awakening, illumination, and the dark night of the soul. On the other hand, Edna experiences neither the third stage of the journey, contemplation or purgation of the senses, nor the final stage of union.[11]

Edna has her first "awakening of the self" when she learns to swim. As Underhill describes it, this moment is "usually abrupt and well-marked" and "accompanied by intense feelings of joy and exaltation."[12] In this moment, Edna is "like the little tottering, stumbling, clutching child, who of a sudden realizes its powers, and walks for the first time alone, boldly and with overconfidence." She is overcome by a "feeling of exultation" and "wanted to swim far out, where no woman had swum before" (p. 47). Swimming out into the sea alone, Edna is "intoxicated with her newly found power" and "seemed to be reaching out for the unlimited in which to lose herself" (p. 48).

For Edna, this initial awakening is almost immediately followed by "self-knowledge." In Underhill's terms, the soul here realizes its "own finiteness and imperfection, the manifold illusion in which it is immersed, the immense distance which separates it from the One."[13] Edna's moment of such self-knowledge comes just as she learns to swim. Then, "a quick vision of death smote her soul" (p. 48). Able to muster the strength to swim back to shore, Edna is deeply affected by the experience. She tells Robert:

> I never was so exhausted in my life. But it isn't unpleasant. A thousand emotions have swept through me tonight. I don't comprehend half of them ... I wonder if any night on earth will ever again be like this one. It is like a night in a dream. [p. 49]

Robert, sharing her mood, tells her that perhaps a spirit has possessed her which might never release her again (p. 50).

The experience still has power for Edna the following day. As she sails across the bay with Robert:

> Edna felt as if she were being borne away from some anchorage which had held her fast, whose chains had been loosening—had

snapped the night before when the *mystic spirit* was aboard, leaving her free to drift whithersoever she chose to set her sails. [p. 58, my emphasis]

Edna fails to enter the next stage in the mystical journey, that of contemplation. She does not achieve "illumination," the state in which "the Self has become detached from the 'things of the sense.' "[14] In fact, she denies contemplation and indulges in her sensuous responses. She behaves unreflectively and impulsively, planning to think only later. As she tells Arobin:

> One of these days . . . I'm going to pull myself together for a while and think—try to determine what character of woman I am, for, candidly, I don't know. [p. 137]

But instead, as time goes on, "a feverish anxiety attended her every action. There was no moment of deliberation, no interval of repose between the thought and its fulfillment" (p. 141). Overwhelmed by a feeling of irresponsibility (p. 140), she gives herself over to Arobin and "her latent sensuality, which unfolded under his delicate sense of her nature's requirements like a torpid, torrid, sensitive blossom" (p. 173).

Chopin repeatedly refers to Edna's unreflectiveness. For example, after her awakening while swimming, Edna spends a night "disturbed with dreams that were intangible, that eluded her" (p. 55). When she awakens, although she felt somewhat renewed, she again avoided conscious thought. As the narrator explains:

> she was not seeking refreshment or help from any source, either external or from within. She blindly followed whatever impulse moved her, as if she had placed herself in alien hands for direction, and freed her soul of responsibility. [p. 55]

Later, it becomes clear that Edna neither learns from her past nor thinks of her future (p. 76). She also does not attempt to understand her oscillating moods of happiness and unhappiness:

> There were days when she was very happy without knowing why. She was happy to be alive and breathing, when her whole being seemed to be one with the sunlight, the color, the odors, the lux-uriant warmth of some perfect Southern days. . . . There were days when she was unhappy, she did not know why—when it did not seem worth while to be glad or sorry, to be alive or dead, when life appeared to her like a grotesque pandemonium and humanity like worms strugging blindly towards inevitable annihilation. [p. 97]

Edna's tendency to fall asleep further signals her unreflectiveness. As George Arms notes, Edna is often tired. She sleeps much of her day with Robert on the Cheniere. She is overwhelmed by feelings of ennui at her own dinner party. She falls asleep while reading Emerson, the advocate of self-reliance.[15] But most significantly, Edna commits suicide without apparent reflection. Although she has spent a "wakeful" night in contemplation, she nevertheless decides to kill herself without prior thought. She has sent Victor and Mariequita off in search of fish for her dinner and asked that they make a room ready for her, gestures that suggest she had not intended to drown herself. Moreover, as she walks on the beach, she does so "rather mechanically, not noticing anything special except that the sun was hot" (p. 188). As the narrator explains, because "she had done all the thinking which was necessary after Robert went away," she now acts without thinking about her situation at all (p. 188).

Having skipped the important step of purgation of the senses and having failed to achieve illumination, Edna nevertheless goes through a "Dark Night of the Soul," the aspect of the mystical journey in which the individual suffers a deep sense of loss and believes itself "abandoned by the Divine." As Underhill describes it, "the Self now surrenders itself, its individuality, and its will completely. It desires nothing, asks nothing, is utterly passive."[16] Edna, at this point in her development, is often overcome by feelings of ennui, defines herself as having "a little more comprehension than a machine, and still feels like a lost soul" (p. 166). She then enters a state in which she has neither hope nor despondency (p. 173). She now sees life as a "monster made up of beauty and brutality" (p. 140).

In short, Edna does not achieve Union or oneness with the universe. She does not complete the journey. Instead, she is overwhelmed by her aloneness and her hopelessness. Although Edna has told Dr. Mandelet, "Perhaps it is better to suffer than to have one's illusions" (p. 184), she makes this statement when she believes that Robert is waiting for her. After she loses him, she becomes totally despondent.

Edna's tragedy is that she is one of those souls whom the narrator described earlier, whose consciousness leads to bewilderment, "to dreams, to thoughtfulness, to . . . shadowy anguish" (p. 25), but not to a sense of meaning or to the "peaceful joy," the sense of "enhanced powers" or the "intense certitude" that Underhill describes as accompanying her final, desired state of the journey, that of Union.

In the end, then, Edna's journey is not a successful one. Although she is awakened to a new sense of her own potential, to a new understanding of her social role, and to her sexuality, Edna's consciousness does not lead to self-realization or to fulfillment. The narrator was right that such growing awareness "may seem like a ponderous weight of wisdom to descend upon the soul of a young woman of twenty-eight—perhaps more wisdom than the Holy Ghost is usually pleased to vouchsafe to any woman" (p. 25). On the other hand, the narrator suggests that Edna's failure is not unusual because "the beginning of things, of a world especially, is necessarily vague, tangled, chaotic, and exceedingly disturbing. How few of us ever emerge from such beginning! How many souls perish in its tumult!" (p. 25).

Edna's Suicide: A Jungian Reading

Edna's evolution can be further illuminated by a Jungian perspective. Specifically, Edna's tendency to project her needs onto a love object denies her self-realization and maturity or what Jung calls individuation.

Before her marriage, Edna was infatuated with a series of men with whom no genuine relationship was possible. She first became obsessed with "a dignified and sad-eyed cavalry officer who visited her father in Kentucky" (p. 31). She was so drawn to him that "she could not leave his presence when he was there nor remove her eyes from his face" (p. 31). After the officer "melted imperceptibly out of her existence," Edna became enamored of a young man engaged to one of her neighbors. Although her emotions were "deeply engaged," the young man did not notice her, and "he, too, went the way of dreams" (p. 32). Next, Edna began to be haunted by "the face and figure of a great tragedian. The persistence of the infatuation lent it an aspect of genuineness. The hopelessness of it colored it with the lofty tones of a great passion" (p. 32). In other words, in her first three romances, Edna projected onto the object of her love her own needs.

Determined to escape this last infatuation and "inwardly disturbed" by her propensity for falling in love with men who did not return her love (p. 31), Edna married Léonce Pontellier. She did not love him but hoped that by marrying him "she could take her place with a certain dignity in the world of reality, closing the portals forever behind her upon the realm of romance and dreams" (p. 33). But once again she was projecting onto a man her desires, perceiving "a sympathy of thought and taste between them, in which fancy she was mistaken" (p. 32).

The marriage brought her neither happiness nor, initially, self-awareness. Rather, when faced with the inadequacies of her marriage, Edna gave herself over unreflectively to dark moods: "An indescribable oppression, which seemed to generate in some unfamiliar part of her consciousness, filled her whole being with a vague anguish. It was like a shadow, like a mist passing across her soul's summer day. It was strange and unfamiliar; it was a mood" (p. 41).

It is in this state of mind that Edna becomes infatuated with Robert. Similar in appearance to her (p. 9), he seems to be her alter ego. As the narrator points out, the two are also similar in that they talk about themselves because they are "very young, and did not know any better" (p. 10). Under the spell of her feelings for Robert, Edna believes that "she was seeing with different eyes" and that her present self was somehow different from what it had been in the past (p. 67). She ignores her recognition that her feelings for Robert have the "symptoms of infatuation" that she had experienced in the past. She also tries to hide from herself the emotion she feels when Robert leaves for Mexico.

After Robert's departure, Edna decides that her life lacks meaning. Even as she attempts to assert her independence from her husband, she is growing dependent on her love for Robert. She now sees his love as the means for her fulfillment: "Robert's going had some way taken the brightness, the color, the meaning out of everything. The conditions of her life were in no way changed, but her whole existence was dulled, like a faded garment which seems to be no longer worth wearing. She sought him everywhere—in others whom she induced to talk about him" (p. 77). Edna believes that when Robert went to Mexico, he left "a void and wilderness behind him" (p. 78).

Edna does try to find meaning elsewhere but without success. One evening she seeks to find herself in nature, "but the voices were not soothing that came to her from the darkness and the sky above and the stars." Instead of nurturing her, the voices "jeered and sounded mournful notes without promise, devoid even of hope" (p. 87). When she tries consciously to forget Robert, she is equally unsuccessful: "Still under the spell of her infatuation," she is continually obsessed with him, and her thoughts of him "filled her with an incomprehensible longing" (p. 90). Nor does Emerson offer her guidance. Edna first grows sleepy and then restless reading him.

Even her art does not fulfill her. Although her painting offers her increasing satisfaction, Edna is still defeated by fluctuating moods:

> On rainy or melancholy days Edna went out and sought the society of the friends she had made at Grand Isle. Or else she stayed indoors and nursed a mood with which she was becoming too familiar for her own comfort and peace of mind. It was not despair, but it seemed to her as if life were passing by, leaving its promise broken and unfulfilled. Yet there were other days when she listened, was led on and deceived by fresh promises which her youth held out to her. [p. 123]

There are nevertheless moments of growth. With Mademoiselle Reisz, Edna's spirit seemed free. By moving out of her house, Edna changes:

> There was with her a feeling of having descended in the social scale, with a corresponding sense of having risen in the spiritual. Every step which she took toward relieving herself from obligations added to her strength and expansion as an individual. She began to look with her own eyes; to see and to apprehend the deeper undercurrents of life. [p. 156]

Perhaps most significantly, Edna gains confidence in her own ideas and instincts: "No longer was she content to 'feed upon opinion' when her own soul had invited her" (p. 156).

But such progress does not sustain Edna nor subdue her restlessness. At times, she seems to lose her sense of reality. After she has left her husband, "She had abandoned herself to Fate, and awaited the consequences with indifference" (p. 172). Adèle chides her during this period for her lack of maturity and deliberateness, telling her, "In some ways you seem to me like a child, Edna. You seem to act without a certain amount of reflection which is necessary in this life" (p. 160). Edna also ignores the signs that Robert may be nothing more than a projection of her own needs. After he has returned from Mexico, she realizes that she felt closer to him when he was in Mexico (p. 170). Nevertheless, she tells him that she is willing to give up everything to be with him, and she believes that there would be "no greater bliss on earth than possession of the beloved one" (p. 185).

Because Robert is still governed by social norms, he cannot accept or understand Edna's independence. His decision to end their relationship negates Edna's fantasy that she and Robert could be "everything to each other" (p. 179). Without that belief and with her growing awareness of her essential solitude and her new sense of obligation to her children, she chooses death.

Chopin's imagery underscores just how much Edna has failed to achieve maturity. First, just before she enters the water, she sees that "a bird with a broken wing was beating the air above, reeling, fluttering, circling, disabled down, down to the water" (p. 189). Unlike the bird who had flown away from the naked, solitary man of Edna's earlier vision (in Jungian terms, perhaps Edna's "animus"), Edna is identified with this crippled bird. She does not have wings that are strong enough, to use Mademoiselle Reisz's analogy, to "soar above the level plain of tradition and prejudice" (p. 138).

Second, Edna now succumbs to the seductive voice of the sea as she had on the night of her awakening but with a difference. Although the sea once again has a voice that is "never ceasing, whispering, clamoring, murmuring, inviting the soul to wander in abysses of solitude" (p. 25 and p. 189), Edna's choice now is a permanent one. No longer is she being invited to wander only "for a spell" (p. 25). Even more significantly, the sea does not offer her the promise of "inward contemplation" as it once had. Rather, it now promises the "abysses of solitude."

Although Edna's stripping herself of her "unpleasant, pricking garments" is positive, the other images surrounding this moment are ambivalent. Even as they suggest rebirth, they also hint that Edna may be regressing rather than maturing. For instance, she stands naked, "like some new-born creature, opening its eyes in a familiar world that it had never known" (p. 189). She has failed to understand her world, much as she has failed to learn about herself. The moment for her, then, is "strange and awful." It is also "delicious." In the end, it is the sea's sensuousness that draws Edna into its "soft, close embrace."

As Edna swims out to sea, she recognizes that she might have sought help from Dr. Mandelet, who appeared to understand the importance of the inner life. Thus she realizes that there were avenues open to her that she had not explored. Experiencing momentary terror, Edna responds by retreating into her memories much as earlier she had retreated into fantasy. She gives herself over to thoughts of her childhood, of her father's and sister's voices, of the sound of "the spurs of the cavalry officer" who had been her first infatuation, and of her childhood walks across the fields. Although these memories now seem positive to Edna, she is ignoring the fact that her relationships with her father and her sister were troubled, that the cavalry officer had not acknowledged her existence, much less returned her love, and that her youthful walks had been unthinking and impulsive attempts to escape from her father. Then, as at her death, Edna was unsure whether her experiences "frightened or pleased her" (p. 30). Then, as now, her inability to reconcile her inner and her outer life led her to attempt to escape, "aimlessly, unthinking and unguided" (p. 30).

Edna and Whitman

Whitman's influence can be felt throughout *The Awakening*. As James E. Miller points out, "Song of Myself" is itself an inverted mystical journey in which the poet achieves union not by the purgation of the senses but by giving himself over to them.[17] Moreover, Whitman imbues the sea with the combination of sensuous invitation and death in "Out of the Cradle Endlessly Rocking." The differences, however, are as telling. Whitman eventually merges himself with the universe, with nature, and with other people, whereas Edna's journey leads her to solitude and alienation. Whitman's journey also reconciles the inner and the outer life and the sensual and the contemplative sides of himself. Edna, in contrast, rejects the outer life but without having first developed the contemplative side of herself.[18]

The Metamorphosis (1915)

by Franz Kafka

FRANZ KAFKA'S *The Metamorphosis,* a tale about the transformation of the traveling salesman Gregor Samsa into a "monstrous vermin,"[1] immediately and insistently demands that its readers suspend disbelief. Human beings do not wake up in the morning to discover that they have become huge beetles. Nevertheless, once the improbability of this event is accepted as reality within the fiction, the remainder of the action is logical and credible. Indeed, the story operates as more than an allegory in that Gregor and his family become characters in a very compelling human drama.

Gregor's metamorphosis has a variety of implications. It demands that both he and the reader examine their preconceptions about life, question their expectations for their futures, and consider the nature of individual responsibility. It occasions questions about identity, the degree to which humans have free will, and the validity of reason. But perhaps most brilliantly—and also paradoxically—Gregor's transformation into a giant bug raises the question of what it means to be human as it dramatizes how families and institutions dehumanize the individual.

In *The Metamorphosis,* Kafka demonstrates a mastery of point of view. Specifically, in the early part of the story, he presents Gregor as a sympathetic character. In light of Gregor's pain and disbelief at his condition, his family's revulsion for him seems distasteful. So does their habit of exploiting Gregor's penchant for self-sacrifice. As the story progresses, however, Kafka subtly shifts the point of view and the sympathy from Gregor to his family. Their distress over the beetle, whom they can no longer perceive to be their son and brother, becomes understandable. It is their pain and disbelief that now comes to the fore.

Moral and Values Questions

General Questions: Guide to Reading

1. What does it mean to be human? What differentiates humans from animals?
2. What aspects of life generally nurture the individual? What is the potential impact on an individual for whom the world offers no such nurturing?
3. What expectations do most people hold about their futures? about the certainty of their own identities? about their relationship to their family and those with whom they work? What might be the effect on an individual who suddenly finds all such expectations voided?
4. To what degree and under what circumstances are individuals responsible for others? In particular, what is the nature of familial responsibility?
5. To what degree do individuals assume that the world is governed by rationality? What happens to the individual who is confronted with a very different reality, i.e., that reason has little usefulness?
6. Is suicide ever a positive act?[2]

Questions for Discussions, Papers, Exams

1. What are the possible implications of the title? Discuss the title in terms not only of Gregor but also in terms of his family.
2. What does Gregor's metamorphosis symbolize? What is the symbolic significance of his having been changed into a beetle?
3. The tale is permeated with Christian symbolism. When Gregor is caught at the door to his room, his father's shove is described as "truly his salvation" (p. 20). The apple that his father later throws at him made him feel "nailed to the spot" (p. 39). When he dies, the

clock strikes three (p. 54). His death itself is his sacrifice for his father, his mother, and his sister. What is the significance of such symbolism?

4. The story ends with the family, freed of Gregor, spending a day in the country. The senior Samsas are suddenly aware that Grete "had blossomed into a good-looking, shapely girl" and that it "would soon be time, too, to find her a good husband." When Grete stretches her young body, it "was like confirmation of their new dreams and good intentions" (p. 58). What is the function of this paragraph? Have the Samsas changed because of Gregor's metamorphosis and his death? Why or why not?

Kafka and the Absurd

Camus, in *The Myth of Sisyphus* written decades after *The Metamorphosis*, defines the absurd in ways that illuminate the Kafka story. As Camus puts it:

> A world that can be explained by reasoning, however faulty, is a familiar world. But in a universe that is suddenly deprived of illusions and of light, man feels a stranger. His is an irremediable exile, because he is deprived of memories of a lost homeland as much as he lacks the hope of a promised land to come. This divorce between man and his life, the actor and his setting, truly constitutes the feeling of Absurdity.[3]

When Gregor awakens to find himself transformed, he is experiencing absurdity as Camus was to define it. He first attempts to reassure himself that all is well by using reason. He notes that his room was "a regular human room" (p. 3). He assumes that he needs to sleep a little more so that he would wake up "forgetting all this nonsense." He attributes his new sense of himself to his work schedule (p. 4). He also continues to try to reassure himself of his own humanity by thinking, "this getting up so early . . . makes anyone a complete idiot. Human beings have to have their sleep" (p. 4).

But reason does not work, and Gregor's body communicates to him that new truth. As the story goes on, Gregor will eventually lose a great many other prior conceptions about the world and himself. He will become disillusioned about his family, will lose all hope of the future and all nurturing memories of the past, and will recognize that he has limited free will.

The irony in all of this is that Gregor was, in many ways, living in an absurd world even before he became a beetle. Although he was exceedingly generous to his parents and his sister, they gave him neither the affection nor the acknowledgment that he comes to believe his self-sacrifice warranted. He was alienated from the other salesmen and had no intimate friends of his own. He spent his free evenings at home, generally reading train timetables. His prized possession was a magazine photograph of a "lady done up in a fur hat and a fur boa . . . [wearing] a heavy fur muff in which her whole forearm had disappeared" (p. 3). Gregor's separateness was so complete that he locked his bedroom door at night, even when he was in his family's apartment.

Gregor's family, especially his father, had exploited him. Mr. Samsa's failure to tell his son of his savings chained Gregor unnecessarily to a job he detested. Gregor's parents and his sister had also assumed helpless roles. Mr. Samsa walked with a shuffle. His mother "spent every other day lying on the sofa, gasping for breath" (p. 29). For his sister Grete, life "had consisted of wearing pretty clothes, sleeping late, helping in the house, enjoying a few modest amusements, and above all playing the violin" (p. 29). But after Gregor's metamorphosis, all three become capable of working again, and Gregor's father for a time becomes vigorous and assertive.

Gregor's work also dehumanized him. His life as a traveling salesman did not allow him to form friendships or romantic attachments. His superiors at work, moreover, failed to acknowledge his worth or his individuality. His employer, who sat on his desk, "talks down from the heights to the employees" (p. 4). The assistant manager is quick to suspect Gregor of irresponsibility, even theft. Although "during his five years with the firm Gregor had not been sick even once" (p. 5), the assistant manager suggests sinister motives for Gregor's absence now. He suspects Gregor of stealing company funds and warns him that his "job is not the most secure" (p. 11).

Although Gregor does not understand until much later just how much his family had exploited him, he is aware that the assistant manager has dehumanized him. He asks himself bitterly, "Were all employees louts without exception, wasn't there a single loyal, dedicated worker among them who, when he had not fully utilized a few hours of the morning for the firm, was driven half-mad by pangs of conscience and was actually unable to get out of bed?" (p. 9). In short, before his metamorphosis, Gregor was already metaphorically a "monstrous vermin." His reasoning powers had not served him well for he had ignored his family's parasitical behavior. His situation and his personality both circumscribed his freedom. Although it is true that Gregor's illusions about family and work had given him a sense of meaning and purpose, it is also true that he was living not for himself but for Grete and his parents. Ironically, only after Gregor becomes a beetle does he begin to discover his own humanity.

The Meaning of Being Human

When Gregor comes to realize the emptiness of his earlier life, he begins to recognize his own feelings and needs. He suffers a wide range of emotions about his family. At moments he continues to feel "shame and grief" over his inability to support them (p. 29); in other moments he is "filled with rage at his miserable treatment (p. 43). He recognizes that his family had been capable of supporting themselves all along. He learns of his father's savings, watches his parents go through physical metamorphoses that allow them to work, and sees Grete assume responsibility. At the same time, Gregor begins to see his sister more clearly. He is no longer totally devoted to her, recognizing that her apparent kindnesses are often self-serving. Just as he comes to see the hospital across the street from his window as bleak rather than healing, so he realizes that his family had exploited rather than nurtured him. Then, in an especially painful moment, Gregor understands that his family is starving him. He grieves that he is dying of hunger even as the family's new boarders are "gorging themselves" (p. 47).

Kafka complicates the ambiguities surrounding the question of Gregor's humanity in several ways. Gregor's resistance to his new insect state stems, for instance, from his desire to hold onto the trappings of being human. He fears that when his mother and sister strip his room of his material possessions, he will begin to forget "his human past" (p. 33). He is aware that to a great extent it is his meager possessions that have given him a sense of his identity: his tools, the desk at which he had done his schoolwork, and his cherished picture of the woman in the fur. The irony, however, is that by such a limited self-definition, Gregor has lived less than a fully human life.

Even more significant is his response to his sister's music. Although Gregor had not himself cared about music before his metamorphosis, Grete's music now moves him profoundly. In another irony, Gregor sees this response to music not as a sign of humanity but of his new bestiality. As he thinks, "Was he an animal, that music could move him so. He felt as if the way to the unknown nourishment he longed for was coming to light" (p. 49).

Despite his new consciousness of his situation, Gregor chooses to die in acquiescence to his family's wishes. He is moved to this decision in part because he has heard Grete assert that if he were human he would kill himself. Grete rejects the beetle, denying that he is her brother. As she tells their parents:

> But how can it be Gregor? If it were Gregor, he would have realized long ago that it is not possible for human beings to live with such a creature, and he would have gone away of his own free will. Then we wouldn't have a brother, but we'd be able to go on living and honor his memory. But as things are, this animal persecutes us, drives the roomers away, obviously wants to occupy the whole apartment and for us to sleep in the gutter. [p. 52]

When Gregor overhears his sister's words, he decides "to disappear" and thinks of his family with "deep emotion and love." Such love brings him to a "state of empty and peaceful reflection" (p. 54). When the clock outside strikes three, a moment reminiscent of the cock that crowed three times as Peter betrayed Christ, Gregor dies. This allusion to Peter's betrayal of Christ and the sense that Gregor is sacrificing himself out of love suggest the possibility that Gregor's death should be celebrated. This question, however, like so much else in *The Metamorphosis,* has its ambiguities.

On the one hand, Gregor's suicide may be a fulfillment of his deepest human instincts. Certainly, by his death, he has responded with genuine love to the suffering he has caused his family. The decision brings him a new peacefulness as well. Moreover, given Gregor's inability to change his current situation, itself a death-in-life, his choice of suicide may be a heroic response to the absurdity and meaninglessness of a life which holds no hope for the future and which lacks freedom, love, and nurturing from work, friends, or family.

On the other hand, Gregor's suicide may itself be a meaningless act. His death serves little purpose in that his parents and his sister seem to learn nothing from either Gregor's life, his metamorphosis, or his death. The senior Samsas now turn to Grete as their hope for the future. Their thoughts of her marriagability indicate that they hope she will find a husband who will take Gregor's place as their support. Their pleasure in her attractive young body is even more painful in light of the fact that Gregor's body had become so desiccated by his starvation. In addition, Gregor's resumption of the sacrificial role is problematic. Although it is a role with which he is obviously happy, it may also be a sign that he is reverting to old, self-destructive behavior rather than maturing.

XI

The Great Gatsby (1926)

by F. Scott Fitzgerald

IN ESSENCE, F. Scott Fitzgerald's *The Great Gatsby* is an indictment of an American culture that was built not on morality or on what Nick Carraway, the novel's narrator, in another context refers to as "the hard rock."[1] Rather, Fitzgerald suggests, America is flawed because it based itself on a "fairy's wing" that was as unsubstantial and amoral as Daisy *Fay* Buchanan herself (my emphasis). In particular, the novel dramatizes how those social values and cultural myths associated with the American dream shape individual choice. Gatsby, Daisy, and Tom seek material possessions, status, and security without regard for morality or individual responsibility. Nick, too, comes to abandon his professed moral code in the midst of his own culturally defined quest for self-realization.

The novel simultaneously operates on a more universal level. On the one hand, it demonstrates the destruction wrought by false and amoral dreams. On the other hand, it emphasizes the way certain illusions appeal to people in a world which offers little that sustains them. Repeatedly, Fitzgerald points to just how much individuals need to create order and find meaning. The irony in *The Great Gatsby*, however, is that the dreamers seem eventually to mirror their culture. Thus, in their search for fulfillment in what Fitzgerald presents as a modern *Waste Land*,[2] the major characters often perpetuate the amorality and sense of meaninglessness they wish to escape. In a world that tends to dehumanize the individual and to devalue responsibility and genuine caring, they often act in dehumanizing, irresponsible, and uncaring ways.

The Great Gatsby is rich in other ways as well. It explores the complexities inherent in any point of view, focusing particularly on the relationship between values and perceptions, judgments, and choices. Certainly, Nick's own values and his need for order and meaning prompt his various responses to the other characters and to the events he narrates. The novel also reveals how patterns of language and imagery can reinforce theme. The flower, the birth, and the nursing imagery that permeate the novel, for instance, ally Gatsby's dream of success with his larger desire for Daisy and then link both with the larger American dream.

Moral and Values Questions

General Questions: Guide to Reading

1. What is the American dream as it is conventionally understood? What are the differing versions for men and women? What place does morality have in the dream?[3]
2. What forces generally shape an individual's values? Nick describes Gatsby as having "invented just the sort of Jay Gatsby that a seventeen-year-old boy would be likely to invent, and to this conception he was faithful to the end" (p. 99). What values would a teenage boy have been likely to embrace in the second decade of this century in America?
3. Gatsby builds his life on a series of myths, specifically the American dream and his vision of Daisy as the embodiment of that dream. What in general are the costs to individuals of basing their lives on myths or illusion? What are the costs to individuals of being stripped of such myths or illusions?
4. When Nick realizes that it is Daisy whom Gatsby seeks, he rejoices: "Then it had not been merely the stars to which he had aspired on that June night. He came alive to me, delivered suddenly from the womb of his purposeless splendor" (p. 79). What is the cost to individuals whose need for purpose or order overrides other considerations?

Questions for Discussions, Papers, Exams

1. What is the significance of Gatsby's dream being allied symbolically to Daniel Boone and Buffalo Bill Cody, to Benjamin Franklin, to Hopalong Cassidy, and to James J. Hill?

2. What is the significance of Nick's allying himself with Christopher Columbus when he thinks of East and West Egg as being like eggs "in the Columbus story" (p. 5)? What is the significance of his implicitly likening himself to James Fenimore Cooper's hero, Leatherstocking, when he describes himself as "a guide, a pathfinder, an original settler" (p. 4)?

3. The language describing Gatsby and Daisy's first kiss is akin to the language of Nick's final reverie about the American dream. Gatsby's desire to "suck on the paper of life, gulp down the incomparable milk of wonder" (p. 112) calls to the mind the image of the "fresh green breast of the new world" and the Dutch sailors' capacity for wonder (p. 182). Compare the function of the two passages.

4. Why is it significant that Daisy's voice is characterized as having promise (p. 9), much like Gatsby's smile (p. 48)? Why also is it significant that her voice seems to Nick to be a "deathless song" (p. 97) and to Gatsby as being "full of money" (p. 120)?

5. What was Daisy's dream? Why did she twice abandon Gatsby, whom she loved, for Tom? Also, what is the significance of her treatment of her daughter, her failure to assume responsibility for killing Myrtle Wilson, her failure to attend Gatsby's funeral, and her apparent ability to detach herself from his death?

6. What does Dr. T. J. Eckleburg stand for?

7. Fitzgerald reportedly had memorized almost all of T. S. Eliot's *The Waste Land*. How does *Waste Land* imagery function in the novel?[4]

8. It is Nick who presents and judges the events and the other characters in the novel. Do his values change, and if so, do those changes affect his perceptions and his choices? For example, what is the significance of his moving from a tolerance of others to a conviction that he wishes no more "riotous excursions with privileged glimpses into the human heart" (p. 2)? In other words, what is Nick's function as both narrator and character?

9. What is the significance of Nick's acceptance of Jordan's "incurable" dishonesty (pp. 58–59) and his tolerance of Daisy's lack of integrity in light of his own insistence that he is "one of the few honest people" he has ever known (p. 60)?

10. What is the significance of Gatsby's desire to stop time?

11. What does Nick's description of the guests at Gatsby's party reveal about the world of West Egg?
12. Religious imagery permeates the novel, often in unexpected ways. Dr. Eckleburg is allied with God. Wolfsheim plays with the "faith" of fifty million people (p. 74) and gives Gatsby "a sort of benediction" (p. 73). Gatsby is described as going about "His Father's business" (p. 99) and later as holding a sacred "vigil" over nothing (p. 146). His quest for Daisy is likened to the search for the grail (p. 149). What is the function of this imagery, particularly in light of the abundance of *Waste Land* imagery?

Gatsby and the American Dream

Jay Gatsby has embraced the version of the American dream for men: financial success, status, security, and eventually marriage to the woman he loves. Although Nick asserts that Gatsby "invented" the identity he chooses for himself, he qualifies this judgment with another, explaining that "the truth was that Jay Gatsby of West Egg, Long Island, sprang from his Platonic conception of himself" (p. 99). That conception, as the novel makes clear, came primarily from American culture.

As a child, Gatsby admired James J. Hill, attempted to emulate Ben Franklin, and apparently read *Hopalong Cassidy*. His first mentor was Dan Cody, whose name suggests an amalgam between Daniel Boone, a genuine American folk hero, and his carnival descendent, Buffalo Bill Cody. Gatsby's Cody was "the pioneer debauchee, who during one phase of American life brought back to the Eastern seaboard the savage violence of the frontier brothel and saloon" (p. 101). Seeking the success of these models but ignoring whatever moral or aesthetic values Franklin and Boone embodied, Gatsby devoted himself to making his fortune. Meyer Wolfsheim, the gambler who fixed the world series, "made him" a success (p. 172). Other incidents in the novel further suggest the illegality of Gatsby's activities.

In many ways, Gatsby's vision is as unseeing as Dr. Eckleburg's eyes. He does not understand the need to base his conduct on a moral premise. He falsely believes that material possessions will make him "safe and proud above the hot struggles of the poor" (p. 150). He fails to understand that the future cannot recreate the past, believing that he can "repeat the past" (p. 111) and negate the last five years of Daisy's life. Nor does he understand the importance of appearances to the American dream.

Because of their vulgarity, Gatsby's possessions are not worthy of the aesthetic contemplation that America once inspired in the Dutch sailors. Rather, "a universe of ineffable gaudiness spun itself out" in Gatsby's imagination, and it is the gaudiness of that universe which the Buchanans and Nick scorn. Tom, for example, is contemptuous of Gatsby's pink suit, while Daisy is offended by the "raw vigor" of West Egg (p. 108) and by people who "conducted themselves according to the rules of behavior associated with amusement parks" (p. 41). Nick is as explicit, acknowledging that Gatsby "represented everything for which I have unaffected scorn" (p. 7).

Gatsby's story is essentially a morality tale in that his dream brings him nothing. Daisy, who embodies the dream in both its elusive promise and its tainted substance, ultimately betrays him. By refusing to accept responsibility for driving the "death car" that kills Myrtle Wilson, Daisy indirectly causes Gatsby's death. Her failure to call him the day after the accident or to acknowledge his death in any way, coupled with the fact that almost no one attended his funeral, suggests the bleakness of Gatsby's life. Gatsby did choose the wrong "grail" (p. 149), and that choice led him to a sacred "vigil . . . watching over nothing" (p. 146).

The religious imagery associated with Gatsby's quest is almost always ironic and further reinforces the notion that Gatsby's dream was a corrupt one. Specifically, Gatsby, whom Nick describes as "the son of God," defines his "Father's business" as "vast, vulgar and meretricious" (p. 99). His goals, then, are material, not moral or spiritual. In addition, Fitzgerald tends to join the religious imagery with references to *The Waste Land*, further suggesting the death of morality and spirituality in the modern world. The only godlike figure in the novel is the billboard of the unseeing Dr. Eckleburg, who faces the waste land of the valley of ashes (pp. 23–24), while Wolfsheim, the gangster who betrayed the "faith" of the American people and fixed the world series, strikes a priestly pose, giving Gatsby his benediction (p. 73).

Daisy: Symbol and Seeker of the Dream

Daisy Fay Buchanan is an appropriate embodiment of Gatsby's dream. Her voice, which promises so much (pp. 9–10), seems to Nick to be "a deathless song" (p. 97). But it is Gatsby who understands the promise in Daisy's voice, that it is a voice "full of money" (p. 120). Gatsby's tragedy is that he learns too late that money does not bring immortality or security and that wealth "imprisons" as much as it "preserves" (p. 150).

Daisy herself repeatedly chooses material possessions, status, and security at the expense of love, responsibility, and even human life. She first marries Tom Buchanan rather than Gatsby because Tom promises her the version of the American dream that applies to women: marriage to a successful man. Then, five years later, despite her unhappiness and her knowledge that her marriage is a sham, Daisy again chooses to stay with Tom.

Although *Waste Land* imagery permeates the novel, it especially applies to Daisy and her friend Jordan. Both women have "cool" and "impersonal eyes" that are "absent of all desire" (p. 12). At their first meeting, Daisy greets Nick by telling him: "I'm p-paralyzed with happiness" (p. 9), and at least two of their later conversations are reminiscent of those of the upper-class people in the "A Game of Chess" section of *The Waste Land*. For instance, early in the novel Daisy and Jordan decide with indifference and even with ennui that they ought to plan something. Daisy asks, "What'll we plan? . . . What do people plan?" (p. 12). Later, before Tom, Daisy, Jordan, Gatsby, and Nick decide to go to the Plaza, Daisy similarly asks, "What'll we do with ourselves this afternoon . . . and the day after that, and the next thirty years?" (p. 118). In both instances, she echoes the woman in *The Waste Land* who asks, "What shall I do now? What shall I do? . . . What shall we do tomorrow? What shall we ever do?"[5]

It is not surprising that Daisy most admires the movie star at Gatsby's party who is a "gorgeous, scarcely human orchid of a woman" (p. 106), who is all gesture and no emotion (p. 108). In fact, it is at the Plaza, when Gatsby moves beyond the realm of successful gestures, that Daisy once again distances herself from him.

Like Gatsby, Daisy is very much a product of her culture. She believes that her choices are only among suitors. But whereas Gatsby believes marriage is a symbol of success, Daisy sees marriage not as a symbol of success but success itself. Thus, after Gatsby had gone into the army, Daisy had turned to Tom because, as Nick explains, she was "young," because her world was "artificial," and most of all because "something within her was crying for a decision. She wanted her life shaped now, immediately—and the decision must be made by some force—of love, of money, of unquestionable practicality—that was close at hand" (p. 151). She married Tom Buchanan because his wealth, and his wedding gift of a $350,000 string of pearls promised her the security and meaning she assumed she could not create alone.

Tom's frequent infidelities and Daisy's general unhappiness in her marriage do not alter her convictions that women need men to take care of them. She insists that the very independent Jordan will benefit from Nick's care, declaring, "Nick's going to look after her" (p. 19). Both Tom and Gatsby were aware as well of Daisy's need. Gatsby originally "had certainly taken her under false pretenses. . . . He had deliberately given Daisy a sense of security; he let her believe that he was a person from much the same stratum as herself—that he was fully able to take care of her" (p. 149). Tom, in his turn, threatened that Daisy might leave him for Gatsby, assures her, "I'm going to take better care of you from now on" (p. 134).

It is apparently out of her sense of the limitations imposed on women in American society that Daisy weeps when she learns that her newborn child is a girl. Almost immediately, however, Daisy begins to perpetuate for her daughter the same values that had already constrained her. For instance, she announces: "All right. . . . I'm glad it's a girl. And I hope she'll be a fool—that's the best thing a girl can be in this world, a beautiful little fool" (p. 17).

As time goes on, Daisy does treat her daughter as though she were a beautiful decoration. She does not acknowledge her individuality, speaks of her "irrelevantly" (p. 10), and seems to bring the child out only for show. It is telling that Daisy never addresses the child by name (only the governess does). Instead, in language that reverberates with irony in this novel about the material side of the American dream, Daisy refers to her daughter twice as "bles-sed pre-cious" and once as "You dream, you. You absolute little dream" (p. 117).

At the end of the novel, Daisy once again plays "the beautiful little fool," abdicates responsibility, and chooses money and security. This time, however, the consequences of Daisy's choices are, in literal terms, deadly. Her failure to tell Tom or the police that it was she and not Gatsby who was driving the car that killed Myrtle Wilson leads George Wilson to murder Gatsby and then to commit suicide. As Nick notes at the end of the novel, Daisy and Tom are "careless people . . . they smashed up things and creatures and then retreated back into their money or their vast carelessness, or whatever it was that kept them together, and let other people clean up the mess they had made" (pp. 180–81).

The American Dream and Individual Responsibility

Nick seems to make contradictory judgments about both Gatsby and Daisy. On the one hand, he points out his "unaffected scorn" for all that Gatsby represents. Then, moments later, he praises Gatsby for his "extraordinary gift for hope, a romantic readiness such as I have never found in any other person and—which it is not likely I shall ever find again" (p. 2). He also judges Daisy somewhat negatively, describing her conversation as having a "basic insincerity" to it (p. 18). He concludes, in fact, that Daisy's revelations to him the evening they met "had been a trick of some sort to enact a contributory emotion from me" (p. 18). Nevertheless, as with Gatsby, Nick almost immediately offers a very different judgment. He indicates that he is enchanted by Daisy and describes her as "opening up again in a flower-like way" (p. 20).

Nick reconciles these differing responses by deciding that social values and cultural myths, not Gatsby and Daisy themselves, are responsible for that of which he disapproves. Of Gatsby, Nick explains, "No, Gatsby turned out all right at the end; it is what preyed on Gatsby, what foul dust floated in the wake of his dreams" that arouses Nick's scorn. Nick similarly absolves Daisy of responsibility by relegating her to the role of child and of the culturally accepted "beautiful little fool." Having done so, he can think of her detachment from Gatsby's death "without resentment" (p. 176). He is also able to consider the knowledge that she had been driving the car an "unutterable fact" (p. 180).

Nick does see himself as "responsible" (p. 165). It is he who handles Gatsby's funeral arrangements out of the belief that everyone, at death, is entitled to some "intense personal interest" (p. 165). It is also Nick who erases the obscenity scrawled on the steps of Gatsby's house (p. 181) and who sees himself as the person who cleans up the mess that people like Tom and Daisy make.

Nevertheless, Nick ultimately embraces his own dream at the expense of his personal moral code. He also disregards his new knowledge about the importance of individual responsibility. Despite his characterization of himself as one of the few honest people he knows, Nick does not reveal the truths he has learned about the various deaths, either to Tom or at the inquest. He even inverts his usual value system by praising Catherine's lying under oath at the inquest as showing "a surprising amount of character" (p. 164).[6] Although he leaves the East because it is haunted for him with images of indifference, he chooses to return to a Midwest that he knows is not a place of morality. Moreover, he does so in spite of his conviction that the Midwest is a series of "bored, sprawling, swollen towns . . . with their interminable inquisitions which spared only the children and the very old" (p. 177). But most significantly, Nick no longer concerns himself with whether the basis for individual action is moral or not. Desiring instead that the world be "in uniform and at a sort of moral attention forever," he asserts, "Conduct may be founded on the hard rock or the wet marshes, but after a certain point, I don't care what it's founded on" (p. 2).

The Need for Dreams

Nick in part is able to justify his praise for Gatsby and his acceptance of Daisy because he makes a distinction between the dreamer—or at least the ability to dream—and the dream itself. He is thus able to affirm Gatsby's quest for material success despite his recognition that Gatsby's material desires are "vast, vulgar and meretricious." He similarly is able to affirm Gatsby's quest for Daisy despite the fact that Daisy herself eventually betrays Gatsby. Indeed, even as Nick refers to Gatsby's "corruption" and acknowledges that he "disapproved of him from beginning to end" (p. 154), he characterizes Gatsby's dream as "incorruptible" (p. 155).

Nick also distinguishes between dreamer and dream in terms of the larger, American dream. He values the Dutch sailors for their sense of wonder when they first envisioned America as a New Eden but describes their dream as having been prostituted from its inception. As Nick explains it, the American dream, much like Daisy, had "flowered" only momentarily in an irrecoverable past:

> I became aware of the old island here that flowered once for Dutch sailors' eyes—a fresh, green breast of the new world. Its vanished trees, the trees that had made way for Gatsby's house, had once pandered in whispers to the last and greatest of all human dreams; for a transitory enchanted moment man must have held his breath in the presence of this continent, compelled into an aesthetic contemplation he neither understood nor desired, face to face for the last time in history with something commensurate to his capacity for wonder. [p. 182]

Nick is also sympathetic to what he sees as Gatsby and Daisy's need for order. He presents Daisy as turning to Gatsby, as she earlier had turned to Tom, because she feels everything is "so confused" (p. 118) and because she wishes to mold "senselessness into forms" (p. 119). He similarly perceives Gatsby's life as having been "confused and disordered" since Daisy left him the first time for Tom (p. 111). In other words, Nick recognizes the importance that dreams have for those who seek meaning and who need order in a world that seems to offer neither.

Even more specifically, Nick himself is drawn to dreams. When Gatsby and Daisy have their first reunion and the green light on Daisy's dock becomes merely a green light again, Nick seems to note regretfully that Gatsby's "count of enchanted objects had diminished by one" (p. 94). Nick further recognizes that Daisy in reality could not match "the colossal vitality of [Gatsby's] illusion" (p. 97). Conjecturing that Gatsby has been denied his dream altogether, Nick imagines Gatsby's pain in language that reveals Nick's need as much as it does Gatsby's state of mind. Referring to the phone call from Daisy, which never came, Nick explains:

> I have an idea that Gatsby himself didn't believe it would come, and perhaps he no longer cared. If that was true he must have felt that he had lost the old warm world, paid a high price for living too long with a single dream. He must have looked up at an unfamiliar sky through frightening leaves and shivered as he found what a grotesque thing a rose is and how raw the sunlight was upon the scarcely created grass.[7] [p. 162]

On the other hand, Nick has come to recognize that dreams without a moral foundation bring destruction. He believes that Americans denied the country's Edenic promise because they were willing from the beginning to sacrifice America's natural beauty to make the material part of their dream real. When they cut down "the vanished trees" to build gaudy and artificial structures, like Gatsby's house would be, the "fresh green breast of the new world" became a waste land, with literal valleys of ashes. Nick explicitly connects this dream to Gatsby's when he imagines Gatsby having a vision just before he was murdered of "a new world, material without being real, where poor ghosts, breathing dreams like air, drifted fortuitiously about" (p. 162).

In addition to being a dreamer of sorts, Nick is like Gatsby in other ways as well. After his disillusioning experience in World War I, which he dismisses sarcastically as "that delayed Teutonic migration known as the Great War," Nick himself went East to make his fortune. Like Gatsby who tried to emulate Hill and Franklin, Nick spends his evenings studying Midas, Morgan, and Maecenas. Aware of his own restlessness, he goes East in hopes of finding a permanent way to live. There, too, he becomes aware of his own need for order. For example, when he learns that Tom is having an affair, he considers calling the police (p. 16). He also wishes that Daisy would take her child and leave Tom (p. 21). When he becomes enamoured of Jordan, Nick delays an involvement because, as he puts it, "I am slow-thinking and full of interior rules that act as brakes on my desires" (p. 59). At the end of the novel, believing himself "half in love" with Jordan (p. 179), Nick leaves her because he is "five years too old to lie to myself and call it honor" (p. 179). He confronts Jordan with his decision because he wanted "to leave things in order and not just trust that obliging and indifferent sea to sweep my refuse away" (p. 178).

In the end, it is to preserve that sense of order, however illusory it may be, that Nick returns to "the thrilling, returning trains of my youth, and the street lamps and sleigh bells in the frosty dark and the shadows of holly wreaths thrown by lighted windows on the snow" (p. 177). Even though Nick knows that the Middle West is buried in his youth, he seeks the past because he believes it will give him protection. Much as Gatsby thought his dream would serve him and much as Daisy thought her marriage would protect her, Nick believes that returning home will make him less vulnerable to "grotesque reality" (p. 147) and to the "abortive sorrows and short-winded elations" that characterize life itself (p. 2).

Nick and Point of View

When Nick was young, he followed his father's advice and was tolerant of others. After his experiences with Gatsby, he no longer wishes to be so open to others. He also gives the impression of preferring to see things from only one point of view, deciding, "life is much more successfully looked at from a single window after all" (p. 4). He also thinks about how distressing multiple perspectives can be. He first sees West Egg through Daisy's eyes, accepting it as "a world complete in itself, with its own standards and its own great figures." Eventually, he looks at it more critically but observes of this new perspective, "It is invariably saddening to look through new eyes at things upon which you have expended your own powers of adjustment" (p. 105). Such remarks serve to draw attention to the question of point of view in general and to the fact that it is Nick who is shaping the tale and who is making a wide range of judgments.

When Nick characterizes himself as being "within and without, simultaneously enchanted and repelled by the inexhaustible variety of life" (p. 36), he is calling even further attention to his dual role as narrator and character. At the same time, he is echoing Walt Whitman's initial stance in *Song of Myself* that he, Whitman, was "both in and out of the game and watching and wondering at it."[8] Significantly, Nick never fully enters the game. He never takes Whitman's step of truly merging with those figures whom he observes. Nor does Nick ever fully embrace democracy and America's diversity as Whitman does. Even though Nick momentarily, in his imagination, enters into the lives of those whom he observes, in the end he is more like the clerks in "The Fire Sermon" section of *The Waste Land*. As he puts it, he "felt a haunting loneliness sometimes" that he identified in others but particularly in those "young clerks in the dusk, wasting the most poignant moments of night and life" (p. 57).

Nick Carraway eventually succumbs to his own need for order, his own inability to involve himself in the risk that life is. By choosing to distance himself from others, by returning to the Midwest of his childhood memories, and by valuing uniformity over morality, Nick disregards all that he has learned from watching Gatsby, Tom, and Daisy about the need for engagement in the world, for an acceptance of the changes that time brings, and for responsible, moral choice.

XII

"Dry September" (1931)

by William Faulkner

IN "DRY SEPTEMBER," William Faulkner focuses on an individual caught between what he knows is right and the power of those forces that demand a terrible price for his being true to a higher sense of morality. Although Hawkshaw, the barber, is clear in his own mind about matters of truth and justice, he is almost totally powerless to act on his convictions. In his case, the barrier to moral action is the racism that impels a group of white men to murder a black man unjustly accused of raping a white woman. Hawkshaw tries to prevent the killing by appealing to reason, but his efforts are futile. In the middle of a September drought, where emotions are enflamed by heat and boredom, rationality holds no sway, and truth and justice become irrelevant. Moreover, had Hawkshaw attempted physically to prevent the murder, he would have risked his own well-being and perhaps his life. Instead of taking that course, in a moment devastating in its implications, the barber momentarily succumbs to mob psychology. Despite his certainty that Will is innocent, Hawkshaw joins the others in striking Will.

"Dry September" also dramatizes the extent to which some individuals will go to achieve a sense of personal importance and even power. For example, both McLendon and Minnie Cooper suffer from a sense of class inferiority. Both seek to regain the attention they had attracted in their youth. In addition, Minnie wants her sexuality to be publicly reaffirmed while McLendon seeks to prove his masculinity.

Because their racism and that of the community dehumanizes Will, he becomes their victim. Minnie accuses him of raping her, and McLendon directs the lynching.

The white population of Jefferson, Mississippi, share some of the same motives that prompt McLendon and Minnie. Oppressed by sixty-two rainless days and desirous of reasserting their control over the black community, Jefferson's whites conspire in Will's murder. Minnie's friends, in fact, are titillated both by Minnie's story, which they don't believe, and by the expression of white control. After the murder, as they walk on the square, "their voices sounded like long, hovering sighs of hissing exultation. 'There's not a Negro on the square. Not one.'"[1]

Moral and Values Questions

General Questions: Guide to Reading

1. What is the responsibility of one individual for another? To what degree should one person risk his or her well-being to protect the rights of the innocent or be true to a moral principle?
2. What is the relationship between repressed sexuality and violence? What is the impact of racism on violence?[2]
3. What are the factors that allowed the whites of Jefferson, Mississippi, to so dehumanize the blacks that they would be able, with apparently no regret and certainly with impunity, to lynch a man they believed innocent?
4. What are the dynamics of mob psychology?[3]

Questions for Discussions, Papers, Exams

1. Did Will Mayes rape Minnie Cooper? What evidence is there to support the possibility that he did? What in the text indicates that he did not? Even more significantly, does it matter to McLendon and his companions whether Minnie's accusation is true? Why or why not?
2. What factors in Minnie's background motivate her to accuse Will of rape?

3. What factors in McLendon's background lead to his decision to direct the murder?
4. What does Hawkshaw's defense of Will reveal about the town's value system and his own? What in particular is the significance of his insistence that Will is "a good nigger" (p. 62) and his repeated references to the fact that Minnie is unmarried.
5. Discuss Will's early acquiescence to his captors, his attempts to identify them, his naming their names, and his brief impulse to fight back.

Racism's Indifference to Truth and Justice

Faulkner makes it clear in the opening pages of the story that matters of truth and justice are irrelevant to the barber's white clientele. Having heard "the rumor, the story, whatever it was. Something about Miss Minnie Cooper and a Negro" (p. 62), the men immediately seek "a Negro" to be their scapegoat. They reject the barber's defense of Will and ignore his plea that they "find out the truth first" (p. 64). McLendon, in fact, is explicit that the truth is irrelevant. As he puts it, "Happen? What the hell difference does it make? Are you going to let the black sons get away with it until one really does it" (p. 65)?

For McLendon and his companions, Minnie's accusation provides an occasion to assert power over the black people of Jefferson. Thus, they ignore the substance of Hawkshaw's defense of Will, labeling the barber an outsider because of his stance. They accuse him of being a "damn nigger lover" and sarcastically label him "a hell of a white man" and "a fine white man" (p. 63). A client who cautions patience is similarly attacked as an alien. Even though he "was born and raised in Jefferson" (p. 64), he is charged with being a Northerner. Ultimately, McLendon demands that the men choose between being part of the group and being alienated from it. When one of the customers advises, "Let's figure this thing out. Who knows anything about what really happened?" McLendon bursts out, "Figure out hell! . . . All that're with me get up from there. The ones that aint—" (p. 66).

In addition to setting up this us-them dichotomy, McLendon and one of the others inject the powerfully emotional ingredient of the Southern code of honor, which demands that white males protect and preserve the honor of white women.[4] When Hawkshaw first defends Will, one of the clients challenges him, "Do you accuse a white woman of lying?" (p. 63). McLendon invokes the code immediately. His first words in the story are, "Well. . . . are you going to sit there and let a black son rape a white woman on the streets of Jefferson?" (p. 64). Moments later, he, too, confronts Hawkshaw about his skepticism of Minnie's accusation: " 'You mean to tell me,' McLendon said, 'that you'd take a nigger's word before a white woman's? Why, you damn niggerloving—' " (p. 65).

Minnie's friends are equally skeptical of her story. Moreover, despite their obvious pleasure in the events, they condescend to her. For example, they ask one another, " 'Do you suppose anything really happened?' their eyes darkly aglitter, secret and passionate. "Shhhhhhhhhh! Poor girl! Poor Minnie!' " (p. 76).

Social Status and Behavior

Minnie's accusation of Will seems to be the product of at least three factors: her failure to maintain her youthful popularity because of her social class, her status as an unmarried woman nearly forty years old, and the monotony of her life. Minnie had once been popular but at a time when her companions were "still children enough to be unclass-conscious" (p. 67). Although "she was of comfortable people—not the best in Jefferson, but good people enough," both men and women eventually abandon her. The men reject her out of snobbery, and the women retaliate against her because of her earlier popularity.

Minnie's only romantic relationship had ended six years earlier. It has been a relationship that had "relegated [her] into adultery by public opinion" (p. 68) and had made her conscious of growing older. In fact, at the beginning of this affair, Minnie "began to ask her old schoolmates that their children call her 'cousin' instead of 'aunty' " (p. 68). After four years, Minnie's lover moved to Memphis. When he returned each year for a Christmas bachelors' party, Minnie's neighbors seemed to delight in tormenting her, telling her "how well he looked, and how they heard that he was prospering in the city" (p. 68).

Minnie's life, filled with "idle and empty days," offers her little. Her mother is an invalid; her aunt, who manages the household, is described as "gaunt" (p. 67). Minnie spends her days wearing bright dresses, strolling downtown, shopping for merchandise she has no intention of buying, and going to the movies with her female neighbors. During such excursions, she is keenly aware of the budding sexuality of her friends' children. She is also drawn to the romances she sees on the screen but is distressed that the men lounging in the square "did not even follow her with their eyes any more" (p. 69).

Minnie's desire for male attention has led her to earlier "man scares" (p. 65). A year earlier, she had told others "something about a man on the kitchen roof, watching her undress" (p. 65). When that episode did not bring her the desired attention, Minnie apparently decided to up the ante. She accuses a black man of raping her, an accusation that she certainly knew would bring her attention and that would endanger the accused. Her plan is successful. Her women friends minister to her and, as she passes the drugstore after Will has been murdered, "even the young men lounging in the doorway tipped their hats and followed with their eyes the motion of her hips and legs when she passed" (p. 75). On the other hand, her friends doubt her story, and the men in the square will soon direct their gaze elsewhere. The reality is that Minnie herself will never again be as "divinely young" and as sexual as the "scented and sibilant. . . . delicate and sleek" young girls in the movie theater (p. 75). The horrifying tragedy is that Minnie Cooper has caused the death of another human being in order to attract to herself momentary attention.

McLendon's motives are in many ways similar. A former soldier "who had commanded troops at the front in France and had been decorated for valor" (p. 64), McLendon apparently has no social or professional status in Jefferson. He also leads an unsatisfying life. His marriage is an unhappy one, and although his is a "neat new house," it is "almost as small" as a birdcage (p. 76). By arousing the other men to murder Will, McLendon, like Minnie, gains the desired attention. Once again, he is in command of troops. Once again, he can tell himself that he is acting nobly.

McLendon's actions, however, contain only dreadful ironies. His justification for murdering Will, that he is protecting white Southern women, proves empty in that McLendon emotionally and physically abuses his own wife. When he returns home after the murder, he first verbally assaults her, then holds her shoulder until it hurts her, and finally "half struck, half flung her across the chair" (p. 77). His wife's response makes it clear that McLendon has previously tyrannized her.

Like Minnie, McLendon also gains only a temporary sense of importance and pleasure from Will's murder. His reality is that his home has become no larger and his marriage no happier. He still has to deal with the oppressive heat. Even his use of his pistol has not brought him the satisfaction he seeks. In a passage replete with sexual innuendos, the narrator describes McLendon's frustration:

> He took the pistol from his hip and laid it on the table beside the bed, and sat on the bed and removed his shoes, and rose and slipped his trousers off. He was sweating again already, and he stopped and

hunted furiously for the shirt. At last he found it and wiped his body again, and with his body pressed against the dusty screen, he stood panting. [p. 77]

The Barber: Moral Man in an Immoral Society

Hawkshaw, the barber, may be the most complicated character in the story. Although he wishes to protect Will, he too has inculcated the negative social values of racism and sexism that allow both the murder and McLendon's abuse of his wife. Although at moments he personalizes his association with Will ("I know Will Mayes"), he bases his defense of Will on the fact that Will knows his place as a black man in a Southern town. He insists that Will could not have raped Minnie because "he's a good nigger" (p. 62). Hawkshaw similarly stereotypes Minnie. Although he knows her (p. 62), he attributes her criminal irresponsibility solely to her unmarried state. As he explains it, "She's about forty, I reckon. She aint married. That's why I dont believe—." Later, he elaborates: "I dont believe anybody did anything. I dont believe anything happened. I leave it to you fellows if them ladies that get old without getting married dont have notions that a man cant—" (p. 63).

There are two moments of crisis for the barber, and he is impotent in both. The first crisis occurs when Will resists being tied up and lashes out at the group of white men around him. Then, as Will "slashes the barber upon the mouth . . . the barber struck him also" (p. 72). Although the barber's response is probably reflexive, it also denies his commitment to justice. Specifically, even as Hawkshaw is struggling to help Will, he cannot tolerate Will's striking him. He loses his own individuality and becomes victim to the group's psychology. Hawkshaw's second crisis occurs when the group is driving Will to his death. Will appeals to the barber for help by speaking his name twice. But despite Will's need, Hawkshaw literally flings himself out of the car and the situation. The decision is a troubling one. Although it is likely that the barber would have been unable to prevent the murder, he nevertheless chooses to dissociate himself from it. He chooses self-protection rather than his principles. His subsequent nausea may be as much a response to that particular failure as it is to the impending murder.

Will Mayes: Victim of Racism

The opening lines of the story make it clear that McLendon and his friends are looking for a scapegoat who is black. The rumor that circulates is about "Miss Minnie Cooper and a Negro" (p. 62). Minnie is personalized. Apparently any black man will do, even one who historically has pleased whites by his behavior. Will's own actions indicate that the role of "good nigger" (p. 62) is one he plays consciously and reluctantly. When he is initially assaulted by the whites, he acquiesces. His first remarks are, "What is it, captains? . . . I aint done nothing. "Fore God, Mr. John" (p. 71). His subsequent actions reveal his political intelligence. Although he submits to being handcuffed by men who treat him "as though he were a post" (p. 71), Will attempts to humanize the situation. He looks from face to face, asking, "Who's here, captains?" and he identifies those whom he knows (pp. 71–72).

Eventually, Will also reveals his own humanity. When McLendon and the others strike him, he finally loses control and abandons the mask he normally dons: "he whirled and cursed them, and swept his manacled hands across their faces" (p. 74). When he is put in the car, he calms down, sitting carefully "so as not to touch" his white captors. Nevertheless, he looks at them, moving from face to face, and he appeals to the barber directly.

Faulkner reinforces the sense of Will's innocence by several symbolic motifs. To begin with, both his white murderers and Minnie's friends are associated with evil. Like snakes, they hiss. The men give out a "hissing explusion of breath" as they capture Will (p. 71). The women, in their triumph that the square is empty of blacks, give out their own sighs of "hissing exultation" (p. 75). In contrast, Will is likened to Christ. Manacled, put upon by the mob, he is ultimately crucified for sins that were not his own. The terrible horror of his death is intensified by the fact that Will's death redeems no one. His suffering brought no salvation or redemption; rather, it simply left "the dark world . . . stricken beneath the cold moon and the lidless stars" (p. 77).[5]

That Will works in an ice factory is also significant. It distinguishes him from those in the town who are described repeatedly as being feverish and bright. Faulkner adds to the ironies here. On the one hand, Will is murdered in an abandoned brick kiln. On the other, the women use ice, apparently from Will's workplace, to minister to Minnie after her breakdown.

Faulkner uses both the snake symbolism and that of heat in other ways throughout the story. He extends the snake symbolism to include sexual connotations. He suggests the sexuality of the young people in the movie theater by his use of "s" sounds, describing them as being "scented and sibilant" with bodies that are "in silhouette, delicate and sleek." There are ironies here, too. The young people, like Minnie, still seem to find their sense of life, "beautiful and passionate and sad" in the illusions of the movies rather than in the realities of their own lives.

The oppressive heat reinforces the suggestion that Jefferson is a moral waste land. As in T. S. Eliot's poem, the lack of rain is devastating.[6] Unlike Will, who perspires freely, the whites in "Dry September" "sweat dryly" (p. 71). The world is also one in which stems are "sapless" (p. 73) and the the air is "lifeless" (p. 69) and "flat and dead" (p. 66). The death imagery which permeates the narrator's descriptions of the environment further emphasizes the stagnation of the town and foreshadows Will's death. As the narrator explains: "The day had died in a pall of dust; above the darkened square, shrouded by the spent dust, the sky was as clear as the inside of a brass bell. Below the east was a rumor of the twice-waxed moon" (p. 69). The image of the moon also has its significance and its ironies. Minnie's rumor seems to be her attempt to have, like the moon, a second "waxing," but she cannot recover her youth. Eventually, the imagery associated with the moon itself becomes deathlike in that "Below the east, the wan hemorrhage of the moon increased" (p. 71).

The weather—with its heat, its dryness, and the metallic taste of the air—seems almost a character in the story. As one of the clients in the barbershop suggests, the weather may be responsible for the events, "It's this durn weather—it's enough to make a man do anything" (p. 63). In any event, the weather provides the context for the rumor and for Will's murder as the story's opening line makes clear: "Through the bloody September twilight, aftermath of sixty-two rainless days, it had gone like fire in dry grass, the rumor, the story, whatever it was" (p. 62). In this world of "furious unreality" (p. 69), oppressive heat, and metallic-tasting air, even violence, tragically, seems a welcome outlet.[7]

XIII

"Barn Burning" (1939)

by William Faulkner

SARTY, the ten-year-old protagonist of Faulkner's "Barn Burning," is repeatedly faced with the conflict between "the old fierce pull of blood"[1] and what he later comes to understand is "truth, justice" (p. 9). Tormented because his father, Abner Snopes, burns the barns of those with whom he comes in conflict, the boy nevertheless feels an intense loyalty to the man. He sees those who oppose his father as "*our enemy . . . ourn! mine and hisn both!*" (p. 3). It is a loyalty that Sarty's father has deliberately cultivated. For example, when he believes that Sarty might have testified against him, Snopes strikes the child and then instructs him, "You're getting to be a man. You got to learn. You got to learn to stick to your own blood or you ain't going to have any blood to stick to you" (p. 9).

But even as the story focuses on Sarty's need to choose between morality and family, it also raises the question of just how much free will any individual has. Although Sarty's mother and aunt do experience a conflict between their almost reflexive loyalty to Snopes and their more conscious rejection of his arson, ultimately they are trapped by their poverty, their lack of alternatives, and their apparent fear of Abner. Sarty's brother has so totally inculcated Abner's values that he had become a carbon copy of his father. Even Sarty, with his consciousness, has begun to mimic some of his father's behavior. Like Abner, Sarty treats his mother with disdain. The boy also suggests that the family not acquiesce to the legal judgment against them in the case involving Major de Spain's rug.

Sarty, in fact, struggles throughout the story with the question of free will in regard to both his father and himself. When he first sees de Spain's house, he hopes that its peace, its dignity, and its courthouse size will dissuade his father from further arson. He thinks, *"Maybe he will feel it too. Maybe it will even change him now from what maybe he couldn't help but be"* (p. 12). But despite his awareness, Sarty fears that his age makes him powerless. He believes that he is a victim of his still being a child, that he is too old to escape from the world "as it seemed to be ordered" and too young "to resist it and try to change the course of events" (p. 10). The moral of the story is bleak. On the one hand, Sarty comes to understand that he can affect the course of events after all. On the other hand, he learns that the cost to himself and to his family of such tampering with events is extreme.

Faulkner complicates the story in one final way. Although he neither condones nor justifies Snopes' illegal actions, he does suggest that Abner is in part motivated by outrage at social injustices. Snopes' poverty is set against de Spain's wealth. More significantly, Abner is embittered by the system of tenant farming and by the fact that the affluence of white Southern landowners like de Spain was based on the exploitation of blacks and poor whites. Thus, although Snopes's actions are contemptible, Snopes himself acts out of commitment to his own version of justice and personal integrity (pp. 7–8).

"Barn Burning" also dramatizes, in poignant ways, how individuals must live with the consequences of their actions. Twenty years later, Sarty is still attempting to make sense out of his choice to stop his father from burning de Spain's barn. Twenty years later, he is still attempting to reconcile his conflict between morality and love. The last line of the story, "He did not look back" (p. 27), is painfully ironic for it is clear that Sarty will always do so.

Moral and Values Questions

General Question: Guide to Reading

1. Faced with a conflict between morality and/or social law, on the one hand, and love and loyalty, on the other, what should the individual choose? What criteria should determine the choice?
2. Does the victim or protester of social injustices have the right to

act illegally in an effort to right inequities? Are acts of violence ever justified?[2]

3. How much free will do people really have? What personal and social forces limit individual choice?

4. Sarty's mother and aunt are women who appear to have no good options. Abner is their source of livelihood, yet they fear him and condemn his arson. What social, psychological, and economic factors lead people to be loyal even to those who abuse them? Even more specifically, what other choices might Sarty's mother and aunt, in the 1930s, have been able to make?

Questions for Discussions, Papers, Exams

1. Abner Snopes was a horse thief, a mercenary in the Civil War, and a tenant farmer who burned barns when he held grudges. Yet, he was also a man who believed that fire preserves his integrity and who feels outrage at class and racial inequities. Discuss the significance of these apparent inconsistencies in Snopes's character. How might these details about his attitudes affect the reader's response to him?

2. Why does Sarty believe that the size, peace, and dignity of de Spain's home will make it immune to his father's arson? Why is he wrong?

3. The story is filled with references to time. Sarty feels in certain moments that time has stopped. His mother's dowry is a clock that would no longer run. Snopes himself moves with "clocklike finality" (p. 12) and "wooden and clocklike deliberation" (p. 16). What is the significance of these references to time in terms of the story's larger meaning?

4. What is the thematic significance of Sarty's "bovine" sisters?

5. Abner is defined at one point as seeming to Sarty to be "without face or depth—a shape black, flat, and bloodless, as though cut from tin" (p. 8). He is subsequently allied to tin in several other instances. Discuss.

Justice Versus the Old Fierce Pull of Blood

Sarty's name, Colonel Sartoris Snopes, signifies his conflict. On the one hand, he is a Snopes and thus the product of "the old blood which he had not been permitted to choose for himself, which had been bequeathed him willy nilly and which had run for so long (and who knew where, battening on what of outrage and savagery and lust) before it came to him" (p. 23). On the other hand, he is named after Colonel Sartoris, by now a larger than life embodiment of the same values of honor and tradition and courage and gentility that de Spain purports to represent. As the Justice tells Sarty during the story's first trial, "I reckon anybody named for Colonel Sartoris in this country can't help but tell the truth, can they?" (p. 5).

Initially, Sarty is more Snopes than Sartoris. He sees the Justice as "*Enemy! Enemy!*" (p. 5). He physically attacks a much larger boy who hisses "Barn burner" at his father (p. 6). Although he is in terror that his father might burn another barn, he believes himself unable to affect his father's actions. He only secretly wishes that new events will lead Snopes "*to stop forever and always from being what he used to be*" (p. 18). When he realizes that Abner wants to burn de Spain's barn, Sarty considers running away but decides that he cannot: "*I could keep on. I would run on and on and never look back, never need to see his face again. Only I can't. I can't*" (p. 23).

When Sarty ultimately acts, he makes a choice that would be dreadful for any human being but that is almost intolerable for a child. He warns de Spain that his barn is in danger and then, still overwhelmed with his own ambivalence, he tries to warn his father of his betrayal of him. He runs toward the barn, even after he hears the shots that make him think, "It was too late" (p. 26). Although the story does not reveal the meaning of the shots, what is important is that Sarty believes that de Spain has killed his father. He thinks immediately about Abner in the past tense and mourns him, feeling "grief and despair," thinking, "*Father. My father* . . . He was brave!" (p. 26).

Twenty years later, Sarty is still reliving in his mind the moment his father warned him to stick to his own blood. Twenty years later, he is still torn between his love for Abner and his sense of despair that his father would never have changed. Twenty years later, he is still trying to reconcile his own commitment to truth and justice with his sense that his father was brave. Sarty's fear that he was too young to affect events has been replaced by an adult awareness. He now recognizes that he did after all have the freedom to act but that, in his case at least, his action had terrible consequences.

Sarty's mother and aunt are faced as well with the choice between justice and family. When Snopes is on his way to burn de Spain's barn, he recognizes that Sarty might try to warn the plantation owner. He orders his wife, Lennie, to hold the boy, an act that reveals some of Snopes's essential cruelty. Just as he had earlier required Sarty to participate in the rug incident and in the barn burnings, he now forces his wife to be an accomplice in his actions. Although the aunt offers to restrain Sarty, Abner insists that his wife do so, telling her, "Take hold of him. I want to see you do it." He then instructs her, "You'll hold him better than that. If he gets loose don't you know what he's going to do" (p. 24). When Abner threatens to tie Sarty to the bed, Lennie whispers her promise that she will hold the boy.

More significantly, both the mother and the aunt almost instinctively abet Abner. After he leaves, Sarty struggles to free himself. The aunt, speaking her only lines in the story, reveals her distress at Abner's actions. She pleads with Lennie, "Let him go! . . . If he don't go, before God, I am going up there myself" (p. 24). But neither woman can escape her loyalty to Abner and her fear of him. When Sarty breaks free, both women attempt to grab him again, to prevent him from warning de Spain about Abner's intentions.

Personal Integrity and Social Injustice

During the Civil War, Abner Snopes was a horse thief who hid from both sides (p. 8). He went to war not for patriotic or moral reasons but for material ones. He was a mercenary who fought "for booty—it meant nothing and less than nothing to him if it were enemy booty or his own" (p. 27). He strikes his son and physically abuses his wife. He destroys the property of those who cross him. Indeed, the language of the story suggests Abner's dehumanization. Not only does he seem to Sarty to be "without face or depth—a shape black, flat, and bloodless as though cut from tin" (p. 8), his voice, too, is without human qualities, "harsh like tin and without heat like tin" (p. 9). But for all Abner's faults, Faulkner gives to the reader a sense of the human factors that brought Snopes to his criminality. For example, Sarty realizes: "the element of fire spoke to some deep mainspring of his father's being, as the element of steel or of powder spoke to other men, as the one weapon for the preservation of integrity, else breath were not worth the breathing, and hence to be regarded with respect and used with discretion" (p. 8).

Abner deeply resents the social system of tenant farming that allows others, as he puts it, to own "me body and soul for the next eight months" (p. 10). But his ultimate outrage seems to be that de Spain's wealth is the result of exploitation of others. When he takes Sarty to de Spain's house, he tells his son, "Pretty and white, ain't it . . . That's sweat. Nigger sweat. Maybe it ain't white enough to suit him. Maybe he wants to mix some white sweat with it" (p. 13).

In his own life, Snopes seems committed to some notion of equity. With care and deliberation, for instance, he cuts lunch into three equal parts—for himself, for Sarty, and for Sarty's brother. In his own mind, the barn burnings and his damaging de Spain's rugs seem to be deliberate acts of retaliation meant to right the inequities that characterize his life. Thus, he soils de Spain's rug with "machinelike deliberation" (p. 12), and he throws the rug back on his employer's porch with "wooden and clocklike deliberation" (p. 16). Essentially, Abner Snopes is an outlaw. He acknowledges neither the authority of the courts nor of his employer. He refused to pay allegiance during the Civil War to region, serving neither the South nor the North but rather his own interests. For that reason, the size, dignity, and courtlike appearance of de Spain's house do not dissuade or intimidate Abner. Rather, those qualities are more likely to lead him to destructive acts.

Tragically, the legal system has been unable to contain Snopes's destructiveness. Only Sarty's commitment to truth and justice stop the barn burning. The irony is that Sarty turns to de Spain, whom he thinks embodies a higher morality and the values of the legal system, only to discover that de Spain, like Abner Snopes, takes the law into his own hands. de Spain's use of his gun, much like Abner's use of fire, lies outside the judicial system, dehumanizes others, and values the material over all other considerations.

Time

The references to time which pervade the story serve a variety of functions. Perhaps most significantly, they draw attention to time's movement. Even though Lennie's clock has stopped, time does not. Sarty grows older, and events demand that he act. By the same token, time carries with it memories. Although the narrator may be right that the universe is indifferent to human events as its "slow constellations wheeled on" (p. 27), for Sarty, the movement of time brings with it a continued grief and a continued struggle over the legitimacy of his choices.

XIV

The Stranger (1942)

by Albert Camus

MEURSAULT, protagonist of Albert Camus's novel *The Stranger,* (*L'Etranger* in its original French), is, as the title suggests, an outsider, the alienated one, the other. Specifically, Meursault is estranged from social conventions and social law. As Camus explained it in his preface to the novel's first English version: "the hero of the book is condemned because he doesn't play the game. In this sense he is a stranger to the society in which he lives; he drifts in the margin, in the suburb of private, solitary, sensual life."[1]

Meursault is equally estranged from what the prosecutor calls a "moral sense."[2] Alienated from religion, indifferent to love, and unconcerned with questions of responsibility, Meursault comes to decide that even the act of murder is of no consequence. As he confronts the Arabs on the beach, he acknowledges, "And just then it crossed my mind that one might fire, or not fire—and it would come to absolutely the same thing" (p. 72).

As the novel evolves, Meursault's attitude toward human life becomes more complex. His imprisonment and later the sentence of death bring him to celebrate life in itself. Now conscious that all are "condemned to die," Meursault defines the living as "the privileged class" (p. 152). In particular, he values his own life, reaffirming the validity of his having lived it as he did. But even as he cherishes life, Meursault paradoxically never once regrets that "because of the sun" (p. 130), he had unnecessarily taken another's life. Instead, his recognition of death's inevitability leads him to justify both his alienation and the murder:

> What difference could they make to me, the deaths of others, or a mother's love, or his God; or the way a man decides to live, the fate he thinks he chooses, since one and the same fate was found to "choose" not only me but thousands of millions of privileged people who . . . called themselves my brothers. [p. 152]

Meursault's relationship to social convention is similarly problematic. In his preface, Camus praised Meursault's insistence on truth.

> He refused to lie. Lying is not only saying what is not true. It is also and especially saying more than is true, and, as far as the human heart is concerned, saying more than one feels. This is what we all do every day to simplify life. Meursault, despite appearances, does not wish to simplify life. He says what is true. He refuses to disguise his feelings, and immediately society feels threatened.[3]

Camus's appraisal notwithstanding, Meursault does not always commit himself so fully to truth. Although he does put his life at risk by refusing to pretend to mourn his mother's death and to regret the murder, there are other moments, both before and after the killing, when he easily engages in dishonesties.

The Stranger ultimately raises questions about the nature of social and individual responsibility. On the one hand, it dramatizes the dangers to human freedom and to human life of a legal system that is not committed to justice. On the other hand, the novel suggests that the prosecutor may be right after all, that a man who is estranged from social customs, who is indifferent to the deaths of others, and who has no "moral sense" may always be a potential threat to the lives of others and to the social fabric.[4] Given the fact that Meursault has once murdered gratuitously and without regret, the prosecutor may also be right that Meursault has "no place in a community whose basic principles he flouts without compunction" (p. 129).

Moral and Values Questions

General Questions: Guide to Reading

1. What are the usual sources of an individual's moral sense?
2. What are the possible dangers to human life and to society from an individual who has not developed a moral code and who is indifferent to social customs and to law?

3. Meursault indicates that he lost all "ambition" and sense of life's meaning when he had been forced to give up his studies. What are the implications for individual choice of such hopelessness?
4. Meursault lives primarily in the present, and he is motivated more often by feeling and physical sensation than by thought. What are the implications for both the individual and society of such an orientation?
5. To what degree and under what circumstances should one individual assume responsibility for another? In particular, what is the responsibility of child for parent? of friend for friend? of lover for lover?
6. What are the dangers of a judicial system that makes judgments based on whether an individual conforms to social values rather than on issues of justice?
7. In what ways has organized religion historically been a force for the good? In contrast, in what ways has organized religion been a negative force, used to justify dehumanizing actions?

Questions for Discussions, Papers, Exams

1. Is the prosecutor right when he charges that Meursault is a threat to society?
2. Is Meursault's refusal to fulfill the social expectations that he grieve for his mother and feel remorse for the murder a sign of his inhumanity or is it a courageous act?
3. Why does the prosecutor argue that Meursault's murdering the Arab is related to his indifference to his mother during her lifetime and after her death? Is this argument logically valid?
4. What does the prosecutor mean when he argues that Meursault's act of murder "authorized" the parricide that was to be tried later (p. 28)? Is he right?
5. Meursault blames the sun for the murder. Is that a justifiable defense in this case? Why or why not?
6. What is the significance of Meursault's writing the letter for Raymond? of his refusing to interfere or to send for the police when Raymond is beating up his girlfriend? What is the significance of Meursault's testifying in Raymond's favor at the police station?
7. How does Meursault evolve during the course of the novel? What is the significance of his outburst to the priest and of his final acceptance of death? Why does he welcome "the howls of execration" of those who will attend his execution (p. 154)? Why does he feel kinship to "the benign indifference of the universe" (p. 154)?

Meursault: Hero, Victim, or Threat to Society?

Meursault's crime is not premeditated. Indeed, Celeste and Raymond are technically right when they argue that it happened by chance. An argument might also be made that Meursault shot in self-defense. The man he killed had earlier attacked Raymond with a knife and had again pulled his knife out when Meursault approached him. In addition, Meursault earlier had tried to prevent violence. He had taken the gun away from Raymond, arguing, "it would be a low-down trick to shoot . . . in cold blood." He also tells Raymond that if the Arab "doesn't get out his knife you've no business to fire" (p. 71).

The judicial process is a travesty. The examining magistrate, the press, and the jury all seem more intent on Meursault's lack of remorse than on justice. The suggestion is that if Meursault had pretended regret and, more significantly, had assumed a religious stance, his life would have been spared. He might even have been acquitted. The trial seems, in fact, to ignore the murder, focusing instead on Meursault's unconventional behavior at his mother's death. When his lawyer exclaims, "Is my client on trial for having buried his mother, or for killing a man" (p. 121), he is pointing to the process's greatest inequity. Abhorrent as Meursault's indifference may be, it is not sufficient grounds for his conviction and his execution.

In light of this context, it is possible to judge Meursault's refusal to acquiesce to the system and to convention as heroic. Despite the magistrate's entreaties, for instance, Meursault refuses to pretend to embrace religion. Acquiescence might have brought freedom; defiance, in contrast, earns the prosecutor's epithet, "Mr. Antichrist" (p. 88) and his determination that Meursault is beyond redemption. During the trial, Meursault also refuses to act in a self-serving manner. He gives the doorkeeper support even though the doorkeeper's testimony is harmful to his case. He refuses to deny his friendship with Raymond even though he recognizes the negative implications that friendship carries for the jury (p. 121). Even when he despairs that the spectators at the trial loathe him, Meursault refuses to compromise himself. His final revolt, his anger at the priest, is in keeping with these decisions to be true to himself and does bring him some happiness. First, he feels "a sort of ecstasy of joy and rage" (p. 151) and then later a feeling of "calm" (p. 153).

On the other hand, Meursault is not always and actively committed to truth. He writes the letter for Raymond under Raymond's name. He gives evidence to the police in Raymond's favor without knowing the full truth of the matter. He initially pretends to agree with the magistrate's enthusiasm about Christ, thinking, "As I usually do when I want to get rid of someone whose conversation bores me, I pretended to agree" (p. 86). Moreover, Meursault is often unable to express his thoughts or feelings to others. He cannot bring himself to tell Marie that she looks pretty when she comes to visit him in prison. When he feels affection for Celeste, he "wanted to kiss" her but "didn't say anything, or make any movement" (p. 116). Nor does he interrupt the court proceedings when he wishes to "put in a word" himself (p. 124). Many of Meursault's choices grow out of his passivity.

When he does act, it generally is in response to the immediate and the sensuous rather than out of deliberate choice. Nor does he consider either the moral implications of his actions or their future consequences. Although initially his behavior is harmless, eventually he makes choices that are harmful to others and that ultimately lead him to commit murder. Later, in prison, he does gain consciousness but then uses this consciousness to justify his earlier nonthinking actions. Thus, Meursault moves from a state where he acts simply out of impulse to a philosophical stance that affirms impulses as valid criteria for action.

It is his justification of his own actions and his inability to value the lives of others that give credence to the prosecutor's charges that Meursault had "no soul," "nothing human" about him, no "moral sense," and that he lacked "every decent instinct" (p. 127). It is his inability to value other lives that makes Meursault "a menace to society," however despicable and dehumanizing in its own right the society happens to be.

Meursault's Commitment to the Present

Meursault's indifference to all but the immediate is apparent in the opening line of the novel. He is unconcerned with the date of his mother's death because that detail has no effect on his own life. In contrast, he worries that his request for a work-leave will annoy his employer. Throughout the novel, especially in the first section, Meursault repeats this pattern. He seldom visited his mother in the home because it "would have meant losing my Sunday—not to mention the trouble of going to the bus, getting my ticket, and spending two hours on the journey each way" (p. 4). He is also aware that her funeral interferes with the pleasure the day might otherwise have brought him, thinking: "A morning breeze was blowing and it had a pleasant salty tang. There was the promise of a very fine day. I hadn't been in the country for ages, and I caught myself thinking what an agreeable walk I could have had, if it hadn't been for Mother" (p. 14).

His mother's death does not, however, dissuade Meursault from, in the prosecutor's words, "on the next day after his mother's funeral . . . visiting the swimming pool, starting a liaison with a girl, and going to see a comic film" (p. 118). Nor does it alter Meursault's pattern of life in other ways. He spends the Sunday following the funeral sitting on his balcony observing the crowds walk by. As he himself recognizes: "It occurred to me that somehow I'd got through another Sunday, that Mother now was buried, and tomorrow I'd be going back to work as usual. Really, nothing in my life had changed" (p. 31).

Meursault's indifference extends to romance and to friendship, but here indifference is mingled with passivity. When Marie asks him if he loves her, he responds, "that sort of question had no meaning, really" and then adds that he supposes he did not (p. 44). Later, he reiterates to Marie that the question of love "meant nothing or next to nothing—but I supposed I didn't" (p. 52). Nevertheless, he accepts Marie's marriage proposal because "she was keen on it." Although he explains to her that "it had no importance really," he agrees to an early wedding "if it would give her pleasure" (pp. 52–53). He even goes so far as to tell Marie that if another woman whom he had liked had proposed, he would have accepted that proposal.

With Raymond, he is similarly compliant. He accepts his neighbor's overtures of friendship despite Raymond's disreputable life. As he thinks, "I've no reason for freezing him off" (p. 34). He agrees to have dinner with Raymond because it "would save my having to cook my dinner" (p. 35). He accepts Raymond's suggestion that they become "pals" because he "had no objection" (p. 36). His only response to Raymond's story about beating up his girlfriend was that it was "interesting" (p. 38). He even writes the letter Raymond uses to entice the girlfriend back so that he can punish her because "I wanted to satisfy Raymond, as I'd no reason not to satisfy him" (p. 41).

Meursault's indifference allows him to be passive in the face of human suffering. He had already placed his mother in the home despite her objections and her unhappiness. He does not stop Raymond from beating his girlfriend. He refuses to call the police to put a stop to the beating because he "didn't like policemen" (p. 45). Eventually, his indifference extends to murder. Moments before he pulls the trigger and kills the Arab, Meursault is aware that he would not have to shoot: "It struck me that all I had to do was to turn, walk away, and think no more about it" (p. 74). But his earlier thought that "one might fire, or not fire—and it would come to absolutely the same thing" enables him to stay, to fire, and to kill another human being.

But even though Meursault seems to feel no emotion in most instances, he is deeply influenced by his physical sensations. During his mother's wake, the "glare off the white walls" made his "eyes smart" (p. 9) while the warm coffee, the scent of flowers, and a cool breeze made him feel comfortable enough to sleep. Thus, when Meursault argues that it was the sun that impelled him to shoot, he is telling the truth. Even though he knew that approaching the Arab "was a fool thing to do," he took a step closer to the man in response to the oppressive heat, which "was just the same sort of heat as at my mother's funeral" (p. 75). Significantly, Meursault presents the act of pulling the trigger as being caused by something outside of himself. Unable to stand the heat and the sunlight flashing off the Arab's knife, Meursault describes himself as being out of control: "Then everything began to reel before my eyes, a fiery gust came from the sea, while the sky cracked in two, from end to end, and a great sheet of flame poured down through the rift. Every nerve in my body was a steel spring, and my grip closed on the revolver. The trigger gave" (p. 76).

Meursault's immediate response to the murder is in keeping with his self-concern. His thought is not for the life he has just taken unnecessarily but rather for himself. "I knew," he thinks, "I'd shattered the balance of the day, the spacious calm of this beach on which I had been happy" (p. 76). Then, for no apparent reason at all, Meursault "fired four shots more into the inert body" (p. 76).

Meursault's Evolution into Consciousness

Before the murder, Meursault was generally at the mercy of outside physical stimuli and his sensuous responses to that stimuli. After the murder, he has gained consciousness of that fact. As he tells the magistrate, "My physical condition at any given moment often influenced my feelings" (p. 80). For much of the investigation and trial, the physical continues to dominate. The heat in the magistrate's office seems to prevent Meursault from realizing the seriousness of his situation. The heat and the flies buzzing around him distract him so that he does not fully hear the magistrate's remarks. The trial, despite its seriousness, often bores him.

Eventually, however, Meursault comes to recognize the significance of having lost his freedom. He also confronts the near certainty that he will lose his life. He begins to cherish his memories of his earlier freedom and to respond to the beauties of life itself. As he is being transported back to jail in a prison van, he becomes aware of the preciousness for him of life outside of prison:

> I recognized, echoing in my tired brain, all the characteristic sounds
> of a town I'd loved, and of a certain hour of the day which I had
> always particularly enjoyed. The shouts of newspaper boys in the
> already languid air, the last calls of birds in the public garden, the
> cries of sandwich vendors, the screech of streetcars at the steep
> corners of the upper town, and that faint rustling overhead as
> darkness sifted down upon the harbor. [p. 122]

This awareness of the life of which he is deprived leads Meursault
temporarily to despair. The sound of an ice cream vendor brings with
it "a rush of memories . . . memories of a life which was mine no longer
and had once provided me with the surest, humblest pleasures: warm
smells of summer, my favorite streets, the sky at evening, Marie's dress,
and her laugh" (p. 132). Such memories bring him to a sense of "the
futility of what was happening," and he wishes to escape into "sleep . . .
and sleep" (p. 132).

After his conviction and during his confrontation with the priest,
Meursault goes beyond despair. His argument with the priest catapults
him first into conscious rebellion and then into a new understanding of
his life and his impending death. He rejects those whom, like the priest,
he numbers among the living dead (p. 151). He argues that he has
accepted society's judgments because he has sinned against society, but
he refuses to view his actions in religious terms. Instead, he agrees with
the priest's distressed assessment that he loves "earthly things" most of
all (p. 149). He even understands why his mother took a fiancé at the
end of her life, believing now that each moment of life should be lived
to the fullest and as though it were the beginning, not the ending of
things.

The difficulty with Meursault's final epiphany, however reassur-
ing it is to Meursault, is that even as he comes to value life, he values
only his own. He does not make the jump from self to others. He
neither regrets any of his actions nor shows remorse about the murder.
Instead, he insists: "I'd been right, I was still right, I was always right.
I'd passed my life in a certain way, and I might have passed it in a
different way, if I felt like it. I'd acted thus, and I hadn't acted otherwise; I hadn't done x, whereas I had done y or z" (p. 151).

Believing now that only one's own life has importance, Meursault
remains indifferent to others. At this moment, in fact, he comes to
celebrate his alienation. Reassured by what he calls "the benign indifference of the universe," Meursault rejoices that the universe is "so like
myself, so brotherly." It is a vision that validates his own life and that
allows him to decide "that I'd been happy—and that I was happy still"
(p. 154). It is in this spirit of revolt against social conventions and in
celebration of his own indifference that Meursault welcomes the

crowd's public declaration of its loathing for him. No longer does he feel even momentary despair at the hatred of others. Now he welcomes their "howls of execration," for those howls reaffirm his estrangement or what he calls his loneliness. Moreover, despite his grief that he will lose his own life, Meursault now defines death as positive, because he believes that it provides individuals with "mournful solace" (p. 18 and p. 154).

The Causes of Meursault's Indifference

The novel provides little insight into Meursault's past. His relationship with his mother seemed predicated on mutual indifference and, as her platitudes reveal, stoicism. Both apparently were alienated from religion. Meursault had "never set eyes on" his father, and his only thought about him in the novel is his mother's account of his father's nausea at seeing the execution of a murderer (p. 138).[5]

In adulthood, Meursault's work provided no genuine nurturing. He has no attachment to his work, and he is totally indifferent that it might take him from Algiers to Paris. The only real information Meursault gives to explain his lack of motivation is that he had been forced to give up his studies, an event that resulted, he explains, in his also giving up all "ambition" and all hope for the future as well (p. 52). But in the end, *The Stranger* is not a psychological study of what brought an individual to believe that all was absurd, that nothing had meaning, as much as it is an exploration of the negative implications of that conviction for the individual who holds it, for those close to such an individual, and for society in general.

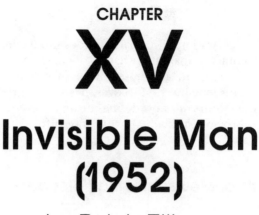

CHAPTER
XV

Invisible Man (1952)
by Ralph Ellison

ON ITS MOST OVERT LEVEL, Ralph Ellison's *Invisible Man* is an account of the struggles of a young black man to achieve visibility (that is, the recognition of his own humanity by others) in an American society that all too often has treated black people as objects. On a more universal level, the novel dramatizes the process by which an individual comes to consciousness of both the possibilities and limitations of life and then takes the next step into a commitment to playing what the invisible man calls "a socially responsible role."[1]

In many ways, *Invisible Man* is a fictional exploration of many of the social and political options historically open to American blacks, particularly black men. Specifically, the narrator's experiences seem to encompass black American history from the end of slavery to the beginning of the black nationalism movement. Because Ellison's method here is to telescope that history and at times to exaggerate its negative aspects, the invisible man encounters, in a short period of time, many negatively drawn stereotypes and equally negative caricatures of historical figures.

The novel's setting, its emphasis on racial issues, and its ultimate celebration of America's principles of diversity, liberty, and justice for all (pp. 561–64) make it very much an American novel. At the same time, however, Ellison has succeeded in universalizing the invisible man's search for self-definition and for meaning. Unnamed, he becomes everyman, and his search becomes a metaphor for the struggle of the moral individual to gain understanding and to find purpose and fulfillment in a dehumanizing, intolerant, and frequently unjust modern world.

The invisible man's own journey from blindness to sight and from moments of alienation to a commitment to responsible action is a painful one. Repeatedly, in his quest for meaning, he embraces identities and a sense of purpose that others offer him. Repeatedly, he recognizes that he has been blinded to those whom he trusts and that his mentors have exploited him and others about whom he cares. Ironically, in his search for humanity, he has become a cog in his mentors' machines and thus has been further dehumanized. Eventually, he recognizes that visibility is in the eyes of the beholder and that he cannot will others to see him. With this perception, he understands that it is his own sight that he must find and value. Even if he is invisible, he realizes, he does not need to be blind.

Crucial to his growing consciousness is his new ability to accept uncertainty. No longer fearing ambivalence, the invisible man now accepts the notion that life is flux, that individuals always change, that success is not guaranteed, and that in fact defeat is almost inevitable. But with this new perspective, he is also able to take more risks and to celebrate the fact that his "world has become one of infinite possibilities" (p. 563). As he explains it, "life is to be lived, not controlled; and humanity is won by continuing to play in the face of certain defeat" (p. 565).

Although Ellison has been criticized for not offering concrete solutions to the social injustices he depicts,[2] the power of the novel in great part is due to its rejection of any one ideological stance. On the one hand, much as did Twain, Fitzgerald, and Faulkner before him, Ellison dramatizes the dangers for both individuals and society when people unreflectively define themselves in terms of externally imposed values or structures. At the same time, he repeatedly insists that life is possibility and that various options exist for the conscious, responsible individual. Ultimately, the novel is existential in its stance that each person must redefine himself or herself in each moment of time.

Ellison was explicit in essays and interviews that his presentation of the American black experience in the novel be read as a metaphor for a more universal, human experience.[3] Such a position is in keeping with his belief that the artist ought to fulfill what he called the moral role of "preserving in art those human values [implicit in specific situations] which can endure by confronting change."[4] The artist must, Ellison explained to John Hersey, "translate" his anger about social injustices "through his craft into consciousness, and thus into understanding, into insight, perceptions. Perhaps, that's where the morality of fiction lies."[5]

Ellison was as emphatic about the moral function of art in his essay, "The Seer and the Seen, Twentieth-Century Fiction." There, he argued that "for all its technical experimentation [twentieth-century American fiction] is nevertheless an ethical instrument, and, as such, it might well exercise some choice in the kind of ethic it prefers to support."[6] Ellison was especially critical of modern artists who do not take an ethical stance, artists "such as Hemingway [who] were seeking a technical perfection rather than moral insight" and who were concerned only with elaborating a "personal myth" rather than "recreating and extending the national myth."[7]

Ellison infuses the novel with references to a wide range of mythological, Biblical, literary, philosophical, historical, and psychological sources. This technique further universalizes the invisible man's experiences. It also demonstrates how an understanding of the past can help illuminate the present. As Ellison argued in *Shadow and Act*, knowledge and acceptance of one's heritage are crucial to self-knowledge. In discussing the importance to his own development of the writings of such figures as Marx, Freud, Pound, Eliot, Stein, and Hemingway, Ellison wrote:

> These were works which, by fulfilling themselves as works of art, by being satisfied to deal with life in terms of their own sources of power, were able to give me a broader sense of life and possibility. Indeed, I understand a bit more about myself as Negro because literature has taught me something of my identity as Western man, as political being. It has also taught me something of the cost of being an individual who aspires to conscious eloquence.[8]

Both within the novel, in essays, and in interviews, Ellison also saluted Homer, Joyce's *Ulysses, Oedipus Rex,* the Bible, Dante, Gorky, Conrad, Melville, Twain, James, the existentialists, and Wright. He further identified Eliot, Hemingway, Malraux, Dostoevsky, and Faulkner as his "ancestors."[9] And in fact, the invisible man's journey within the novel takes on new dimensions when it is understood to be an odyssey in which the narrator has "descended, like Dante, into the depths" (p. 9) in order to find himself. He is also like Jonah, who has plunged into the belly of the whale before being "regurgitated" back into the world (p. 156). Like Oedipus, he has been blinded to the truth and must be stripped of his illusions before he can genuinely see. Like the narrator in Dostoevsky's *Notes from Underground,* he will confess his tale as he attempts to make sense of his place in a world that he sometimes defines as a wasteland. Like Twain's Huck, he is susceptible to being "adopted" by others but eventually he will choose exile. On the other hand, like Conrad's Marlow, he will attempt to reintegrate with society and like Joyce's Stephen, with an existential sense of possibility, he will choose to create art.

Moral and Values Questions

General Questions: Guide to Reading

1. How possible is it for individuals to transcend their personal and cultural histories? To what degree do those histories blind them to the realities of the present and thus make them unable to "see" or even to define the moral choices available to them?
2. Do people genuinely have the free will to act on the moral choices that they make?
3. What in fact is moral choice? What is a "socially responsible" role?
4. Even assuming that a given individual has sight, free will, and a commitment to acting in a socially responsible way, how much can any individual affect either the social order or social values?
5. What is the appropriate balance between an individual's personal needs and that individual's obligation to society or to groups within society?
6. Does power corrupt?
7. Is personal exile an appropriate response to social injustice?
8. What is the relationship between oppression and violence?[10]
9. Is the creation of a work of art a sufficiently social responsible act? In discussing this question, consider the impact on history of both Thoreau's refusal to pay his poll tax and his writing "Civil Disobedience."
10. Is *Invisible Man* a superior work of art, as many of its readers argue, because it has universal implications, or is it flawed, as others insist, because it is not specifically enough either what has been called a "protest novel" or a novel that does justice to the "Afro-American experience"?[11]

Questions for Discussions, Papers, Exams

1. Has the invisible man evolved to a new moral consciousness throughout the novel? What is the significance of his refusal to embrace a specific plan of action? Pay particular attention here to the prologue and the epilogue.
2. How does the blindness/sight imagery function in terms of the invisibility/visibility motif?
3. What is the function of the references to Eden and to the many serpentine images in the novel?
4. Discuss Ellison's debt to Freud, to the existentialists, and to Marx. In this connection, note the references to the invisible man as part of a machine, as mechanical and robot-like.
5. In some ways, *Invisible Man* parodies aspects of Booker T. Washington's *Up from Slavery*. Discuss.
6. Discuss the thematic significance of the various surrealistic scenes, such as the episode in the Golden Day and the Harlem riots, in terms of the invisible man's growing self-knowledge.
7. What are the ingredients of political satire, in terms of both imagery and action, in the Liberty Paint Factory episode?

The American Black Experience

Ellison's fictional treatment of the social and political options open to blacks does not generally do justice to the historical figures upon whom his characters are modeled. Ellison rather harshly caricatures Booker T. Washington and Marcus Garvey. He also presents devastating portrayals of blacks who played a subservient role in relationship to whites but who, when given the power, exploited other blacks. Each character offers the narrator an option that the invisible man initially embraces. In time, however, he comes to see the false underside of the option, only to select another equally self-denying, illusory role.

Grandfather in many ways is the most powerful figure in his life. He exemplifies the "Uncle Tom" stereotype, adopting a subservient mask in order to survive. On his death bed, however, Grandfather reveals that he had assumed that mask as a revolutionary gesture. As he tells the invisible man's father:

> Some, after I'm gone I want you to keep up the good fight. I never told you, but our life is a war and I have been a traitor all my born

days, a spy in the enemy's country ever since I give up the gun back in the reconstruction. Live with your head in the lion's mouth. I want you to overcome 'em with grins, agree 'em to death and destruction, let 'em swoller you till they vomit and bust wide open. [p. 16]

Grandfather's dying words haunt the narrator throughout the novel. Although he eventually understands that Grandfather was exploiting the blindness of those to whom he was invisible, the invisible man nevertheless is distressed by how dehumanizing the role is. For himself, he decides that it is important to distinguish between the negative and positive aspects of American culture. In time, he does so and is able to "affirm the principle on which the country was built and not the men, or at least not the men who did the violence" (p. 561). He will adhere to that part of Grandfather's lesson that has to do with survival and that evidences loyalty to America's promise of equality, liberty, and justice. But he will take more of an active role than Grandfather did in order to inspire consciousness and to bring about social change.

Trueblood fulfills another sort of stereotype but one that is especially demeaning to black people. Because Trueblood is unemployed and has impregnated both his wife and his daughter, he is seen as a shiftless man driven by primal and tabooed sexual impulses (thus, in part, his name). The invisible man is astonished to learn that whites have rewarded Trueblood for his actions. He, along with other blacks, is appalled. What he does not recognize at this point, in his innocence, is that whites are pleased when blacks fulfill negative stereotypes and, in the process, justify racism and inequality. Norton, for instance, monetarily rewards Trueblood for his incest.

Norton himself represents a negative stereotype. He is a white philanthropist but also a voyeur who is drawn to those who can act out the sexual impulses that he has had to suppress. In this case, Norton has stifled his own apparently incestuous desires for his daughter, and he is fascinated by the fact that Trueblood has "looked upon chaos and [was] not destroyed!" (p. 40).

The veteran doctor and the other inmates of the black mental asylum are in marked contrast to Grandfather and to Trueblood. They have not conformed to a subservient role, and they have tragically suffered enormous physical and psychological damage for their independence. The veteran doctor Burnside had been beaten with whips and driven out of his city by ten masked men because he had used his medical skills to save the life of a white man (p. 92). The other inmates, too, had been achievers. As the invisible man realizes with uneasiness: "Many of the men had been doctors, lawyers, teachers, Civil Service workers; there were several cooks, a preacher, a politician and an artist. One very nutty one had been a psychiatrist" (p. 73).

Despite his moments of insanity, Burnside frequently seems to be Ellison's spokesman, articulating many of the novel's major themes. For instance, he tells Norton that at the college the invisible man has become a "walking zombie" who has "learned to repress not only his emotions but his humanity. He's invisible, a walking personification of the Negative, the most perfect achievement of your dreams . . . the mechanical man" (p. 92). Burnside offers the invisible man the advice that the youth eventually will come to understand and to follow: "Be your own father . . . and remember, the world is possibility if only you'll discover it" (p. 154).

The Founder is a fictional version of Booker T. Washington, founder of Tuskegee Institute and embodiment of the American dream for many blacks. The campus is modeled after Tuskegee, which Ellison attended (the statue of the Founder is a replica of a statue of Washington on Tuskegee's campus).[12] But most significantly, the Founder, like Washington, advocated that blacks needed vocational and technical training rather than a humanistic education.

Bledsoe is a second, even more negative version of Washington. Like Washington, he advocates that blacks should know and accept a second-class place in American society. But Bledsoe's motives are insidious in that he advocates and plays a subservient role in order to gain power for himself. In the process, he bleeds other blacks (including the "Truebloods"). Although Bledsoe insists that his favorite hymn is "Live-a-Humble" (p. 104) and although he counsels young blacks to "live content in our place" (p. 104), he himself is ruthless. In a moment of anger, Bledsoe drops his mask and tells the invisible man:

> You're nobody, son. You don't exist—can't you see that? The white folk tell everybody what to think—except men like me. I tell *them;* that's my life, telling white folks how to think about the things I know about. Shocks you, doesn't it? Well, that's the way it is. It's a nasty deal and I don't always like it myself. But you listen to me: I didn't make it, and I know that I can't change it. But I've made my place in it and I'll have every Negro in the country hanging on tree limbs by morning if it means staying where I am. [p. 141]

The invisible man repeatedly is drawn to the figure of Booker T. Washington. During his high school days, he explains, "In those pre-invisible days I visualized myself as a potential Booker T. Washington" (pp. 17–18). During the battle royal, in which the invisible man and other young blacks are blindfolded and paid to fight one another before a white audience, he again thinks of Washington. Humiliated and bleeding after the fight, he gives the audience his speech, patterned in part after Washington's Atlanta Exposition Address. Like Washington, the narrator urges other blacks to "cast down your bucket where you are" (pp. 29–30). But unlike Washington, who argued that "agitation for questions of social equality is the extremest folly,"[13] the invisible man—in a Freudian slip of the tongue—urges "social equality" for blacks. When his white listeners become threatening, he reassures them that he meant "social responsibility" and not "social equality" (pp. 29–30). He is rewarded for this adherence to a submissive role with a briefcase containing a scholarship to the black state college.

At the college, the narrator continues to nurture the dream of becoming like Washington. His description of the Founder's statue, particularly its blindness/sight imagery, anticipates his later ambivalence about Washington:

> In my mind's eye I see the bronze statue of the college Founder, the cold Father symbol, his hands outstretched in the breathtaking gesture of lifting a veil that flutters in hard, metallic folds above the face of a kneeling slave; and *I am standing puzzled unable to decide whether the veil is really being lifted or lowered more firmly in place; whether I am witnessing a revelation or a more efficient blinding.* [p. 36, my emphasis]

After the invisible man is expelled from college for not playing the role demanded of him and after he learns the extent of Bledsoe's malevolence, there are still times that he is tempted by the promise of the Washington dream. Although at one point in his New York odyssey he decides that he will reject the opportunity to become the "resurrected" Washington (p. 300), in what can only be a joke on Ellison's part, the invisible man decides he will pattern himself after the Founder instead (p. 304).

Lucius Brockway (whose first name suggests Lucifer and who is king of the underworld of the ironically named Liberty Paint Factory) is another Bledsoe-like figure. He, too, has adopted a submissive pose in order to gain power and status. He, too, has become as corrupt as those who originally oppressed him. And he, too, is willing to sacrifice other blacks in order to maintain his power and status.

At this point, the invisible man does understand Brockway's need for the "Uncle Tom" mask: "Maybe he was dissimulating, like some of the teachers at the college, who, in order to avoid trouble when driving through the small surrounding towns, wore chauffeur caps and pretended their cars belonged to white men" (p. 208). But what the narrator does not understand is why Brockway would play that role with him. And as with Bledsoe, the invisible man's innocence blinds him to the danger of these sometimes fatherly black men.

Mary Rambo, as her first name suggest, is a mothering or nurturing figure, generous and warm. She offers the invisible man security and a home. Nevertheless, Mary is no more able to see and accept the invisible man's humanity and individuality than were Bledsoe, Brockway, or Norton. Determined to make him a "race leader" (p. 308), Mary thinks in terms of "we" not "I." The narrator is also distressed that Mary possesses a bank with the "self-mocking image" of "a very black, red-lipped and wide-mouthed Negro, whose white eyes stared up at me from the floor, his face an enormous grin" (p. 311). It is a bank that the invisible man breaks but is unsuccessful at throwing away. The implication is that he must still grow a good deal before he is able to rid himself of that negative aspect, the "Uncle Tom" mask, of his past.

The invisible man leaves Mary's home determined to find his own identity but ironically joins the Brotherhood, an organization that chooses for him a new identity, stresses discipline, and instructs him that he is a "soldier" (p. 351). The narrator's experiences with the Brotherhood suggest Ellison's own disenchantment with the American Communist party and also calls to mind Richard Wright's eventual disillusionment with that group.[14]

Ellison's critique of the Brotherhood actually extends beyond the specifics of the American experience. He also objects to two key Marxist tenets: the concept of collectivity and the belief that there is a historical inevitability to events. In contrast, the invisible man comes to believe that individual self-definition rather than an externally imposed identity is crucial and is the prerequisite for social responsibility. In time, the narrator rejects the Brotherhood's demand for absolute allegiance. Rejecting the Marxist notion that history will unfold according to a dialectical pattern, the invisible man decides that all such structures are false. But most significantly, he comes to recognize that he had embraced the structure of the Brotherhood in order to avoid facing the chaos that seemed life.

Brother Tod Clifton, whose first name in German means "death," is psychologically destroyed when he understands that he is invisible. His realization that the Brotherhood is exploiting him and the people of Harlem leads him to self-denying and then suicidal actions. He first sells Sambo dolls on the street. The dolls, which the invisible man defines as "an obscene flouting of everything human" (p. 424), suggest the degree to which Clifton believes he has been abused. His subsequent defiance of the police leads to his being shot to death.

Clifton's death provokes the invisible man to a new introspection. He identifies himself with Clifton but at first is appalled by his friend's self-degrading and suicidal actions. He questions why Clifton left the Brotherhood and chose "to plunge into nothingness, into the void of faceless faces, of soundless voices, lying outside history" (p. 428).[15] Later, when he learns of the Brotherhood's malevolence and hypocrisy, the invisible man is dispirited that he had been "a tool just at the very moment I had thought myself free" (p. 541). Like Clifton, he becomes inclined to self-destructive behavior but overcomes that temptation and commits himself to positive action.

Rinehart, another black who exploits the blindness of others for personal gain, plays a variety of roles: "Rine the runner and Rine the gambler and Rine the briber and Rine the lover and Rinehart the Reverend" (pp. 486–87). When the invisible man puts on sunglasses and a white hat, he is mistaken for Rinehart. The ease with which he can assume a new identity teaches him that "The world in which we lived was without boundaries. A vast, seething, hot world of fluidity" (p. 487). He decides that it is possible to "actually make yourself anew."

Although the narrator initially finds his awareness of possibility frightening (p. 488), he soon celebrates it and commits himself to defining his own identity. Although he rejects Rinehart's cynicism (p. 493), he becomes determined to use what he has learned from Rinehart to try to destroy the Brotherhood's power in Harlem. In deciding to act, he also accepts his past, dedicating himself to Clifton's memory, to Brother Tarp, to the blacks of Harlem, and to himself.

Ras the Exhorter, who becomes Ras the Destroyer, seems an extremely harsh portrait of Marcus Garvey. Although Ellison denied the likeness,[16] the parallels are substantial. Both are West Indian; both organized a black nationalism movement; both were charismatic figures. The invisible man also makes several references to Garvey within the novel (p. 266 and p. 356, for instance). Because Ras eventually turns his violence against other blacks and because, by contributing to social chaos, he unwittingly serves the Brotherhood's interests, the invisible man rejects him. He decides

> that I, a little black man with an assumed name should die because a big black man in his hatred and confusion over the nature of a reality that seemed controlled solely by white men whom I knew to be as blind as he, was just too much, too outrageously absurd. And I knew that it was better to live out one's own absurdity than to die for that of others, whether for Ras's or Jack's. [p. 577]

In self-defense, the invisible man throws a spear at Ras. The spear locks Ras's jaws together, destroying his most powerful weapon, his speech.

By the end of the novel, the invisible man had rejected all the alternatives offered him, except that of the orator and abolitionist, Frederick Douglass. He welcomes Tarp's present, a picture of Douglass, although he wonders whether he, like Douglass, wasn't merely an accident of history who "should have disappeared around the first part of the nineteenth century, rationalized out of existence" (p. 432). Nevertheless, he continues to emulate Douglass in his commitment to freedom and in his use of language as a political tool.

White Stereotypes

The white figures whom the invisible man encounters are as stereotypical as the blacks he meets. Norton (whose name suggests Charles Eliot Norton) is a self-serving philanthropist. His goal is to preserve the social and racial order as it has been. Young Emerson, whose name calls to mind Ralph Waldo Emerson,[17] is far from self-reliant. Like the invisible man, he is dependent on father figures for approval and for his identity. Brother Jack, the leader of the Brotherhood, like Norton, pretends to altruism in regard to blacks but in the end uses black people for his own purposes. A dictatorial man, he sees blacks as "*one* of the raw materials" to be exploited by the Brotherhood. When agitated, Jack begins "spluttering and lapsing into a foreign language" (p. 462), a moment that suggests he may be a foreign agent and not American at all.

Both white women with whom the invisible man is involved fulfill a negative stereotype, that of the white woman who fantasizes about the reputed sexual prowess of black men. The first woman tells the narrator that he is "primitive" and at times has "tom-tom's beating in your voice" (p. 403). Sybil is equally overt, and with her, the invisible man feels as though he is "Brother-Taboo-with-whom-all-things-are-possible" (p. 506).

In each instance, the invisible man eventually gains sight and evolves. He learns that Norton and Jack, much like Bledsoe and Brockway, were false father figures for him and that he must, as the veteran doctor advised him, become his own father. With Sybil, he moves a step closer to achieving his own humanity as he begins to recognize the humanity of others. Although he begins the evening intending to exploit Sybil, he ends it by feeling pity for her and self-disgust that he had failed to assume responsibility (p. 514). He proves that the veteran doctor has been wrong that white women would be his "symbol of freedom" (p. 151). Rather, feeling no desire for Sybil, he understands that she and, by implication, other white women were not the objects of his quest. Of Sybil he realizes, "her navel [was] no goblet" (p. 511).

Cultural Heritage and Individual Choice

The question of how much individuals can and should transcend personal and cultural heritages is one that dominates the novel. Throughout, Ellison dramatizes how much individuals are often unconsciously products of their pasts. He also shows how painful it is for people to accept the negative aspects of their heritage.

The invisible man is first faced with this dilemma shortly after he arrives in New York. Wishing to avoid being identified as a "green" Southern black, he refuses a counterman's suggestion that he order the breakfast special of pork chops and grits. After this assertion of independence, he is surprised and then angered to observe a white man served the same special (pp. 174–76). The moment begins the process by which he tries to make choices in terms of his own preferences rather than basing his actions on the expectations of others. When he is able to indulge himself by eating yams on the street, he celebrates joyfully, "They're my birthmark . . . I yam what I yam"[18] (p. 260). He now can ask himself, "what and how much had I lost by trying to do only what was expected of me instead of what I myself had wished" (p. 260).

He again deals with the issue of expectations at the Brotherhood party at the Chtonian.[19] When a drunken white man asks the invisible man to sing because "*all* colored people sing," the narrator is baffled by his own feelings. On the one hand, he wishes to avoid stereotypical behavior. On the other hand, he wonders, "Shouldn't there be some way for us to be asked to sing?" (p. 307).

After the invisible man has retreated into his underground hole, he attempts to burn the contents of his briefcase in order to provide light with which to see. The gesture is both symbolic and literal. But just as he had earlier found it almost impossible to throw away Mary's Sambo bank, he now finds it difficult to burn Clifton's Sambo doll. He is, in such moments, beginning to accept that he will necessarily carry with him some of the burdens of his past and that he will have to balance his aspirations with the limitations that his social context and his personal heritage place on him.

The Invisible Man as Everyman

When the invisible man concludes his tale by addressing the reader, "Who knows but that, on the lower frequencies, I speak for you" (p.

568), he is making explicit his own sense that his experience has universal implications. The fabric of the novel, interwoven as it is with references to other literature and modes of thought, reinforces this sense of universality. Ellison's description of jazz in *Shadow and Act* particularly illuminates his literary method in this regard. As he wrote:

> true jazz is an art of individual assertion within and against the group. Each true jazz moment . . . springs from a contest in which each artist challenges all the rest; each solo flight, or improvisation, represents (like the successive canvases of a painter) a definition of his identity: as individual, as member of the collectivity and as a link in the chain of tradition. Thus, because jazz finds its very life in an endless improvisation upon traditional materials, the jazzman must lose his identity even as he finds it.[20]

Ellison does, throughout *Invisible Man,* improvise upon traditional materials. Thus, the novel itself becomes a new "link in the chain of tradition." As importantly, it also demonstrates for its readers the ways in which tradition itself can illuminate the present. Although Ellison invites his readers to turn to a wide array of other writers, it is Genesis, Sophocles, Freud, Twain, Eliot, Joyce, and the existentialists to whom he seems most indebted.

Invisible Man, Eden, and The Waste Land

The narrator's evolution from innocence to consciousness is enriched by the Edenic imagery, which accompanies each of his moments of insight. Repeatedly, when he gains the knowledge that he has been blind, he either is expelled from or chooses to exile himself from what he mistakenly has assumed was Eden. Snakes or serpentine shapes frequently punctuate his gaining of knowledge and his expulsions. Unhappily, after the invisible man gains sight, he often blindly embraces another myth, once again deluding himself that he has found Eden.

The novel's first snake image occurs during the battle royal. Blind-folded and in a "sudden fit of blind terror" because of the darkness, the narrator feels "as though I had suddenly found myself in a dark room filled with poisonous cottonmouths" (p. 21). He ignores his instincts however, participates in the fight, and then gives his speech.

Edenic imagery becomes mixed with wasteland imagery at the college. In retrospect, the narrator asks himself: "Why is it that I can recall in all that island of greenness no fountain but one that was broken, corroded and dry? . . . Why do I recall, instead of the odor of seed bursting in springtime, only the yellow contents of the cistern spread over the lawn's dead grass?" (p. 36). Eventually, he decides that "it was the product of a subtle magic, the alchemy of moonlight" that converted the wasteland that was the college into a seemingly Edenic place.

Expelled from the college because of his new knowledge of Bledsoe, the invisible man believes he is leaving "the spot of earth which I identified with the best of all possible worlds." On the bus to New York, he sees a snake, "a moccasin wiggle swiftly along the grey concrete, vanishing into a length of iron pipe that lay beside the road" (p. 154). But because the invisible man wants to remain innocent to Bledsoe's evil and to the illusory nature of the college, he is open to entering another false Eden. He takes a room at the Men's House but remains indifferent to the symbolism he encounters there. The only familiar object in the room is a Gideon Bible with "blood-red-edge pages." In an ironic moment, the invisible man turns to Genesis, with its story of the snake's temptation and Adam and Eve's gaining knowledge of good and evil. But because he is homesick, he "could not read" (p. 159).

He eventually takes a job at the ironically named Liberty Paint Factory. Here there is nothing Edenic. Rather, the factory is a hell-like place, and Lucius Brockway its Lucifer. This episode is symbolically rich in other ways as well. For instance, the company, which supplies the white paint for national monuments, exploits blacks. It is appropriate, therefore, that drops of black paint "dope" are necessary to whiten the paint. Then, after the invisible man is injured owing to Brockway's malevolence, the company doctors subject him to an experimental lobotomy, but their efforts to bring him to a state of indifference fail. Released from the false womb of the lobotomy machine, the invisible man plunges underground again, this time on the subway. Here, too, he observes but does not understand Edenic symbolism in the form of the "young platinum blonde [who] nibbled at a red Delicious apple" (p. 244). Once more he remains innocent to the negative temptations that his world offers him. As he emerges into the world, he thinks of himself as looking "with wild infant's eyes" (p. 245).

This innocence, however, is short-lived, for almost immediately the invisible man comes upon an eviction, grows emotionally distraught, and thinks: "My hands were trembling, my breath rasping as if I had run a long distance or come upon a coiled snake in a busy street" (p. 266). Believing himself "dispossessed of some painful yet precious thing" (p. 266), he gives the speech that prompts the Brotherhood's interest. Although he thinks the Brotherhood is a place of safety, in time he receives an anonymous letter warning him that he may be rising "too fast" in the organization and that he is therefore alienating the white leadership. He thinks of the letter as "rattling poisonously in my hands" (p. 374), but only much later does he understand its real evil, that it was sent by his supposed mentor, Brother Jack.

On the final page of the novel, Ellison uses Edenic imagery one last time. This time, however, it is positive. The invisible man now identifies himself with the snake in that sense that he plans, like a snake, to come out of hibernation, "shaking off the old skin." The moment signals the narrator's commitment to his own rebirth and to his reintegration with the world.

Invisible Man, Oedipus Rex, and the Oedipal Complex

The novel is saturated with references to Sophocles' play, *Oedipus Rex*, and to Freud's use of the Oedipus story to demonstrate the father/son dynamic. The place on the campus "where three roads converge" (p. 35) is an allusion to the crossroads in *Oedipus Rex* where Oedipus kills King Laius without realizing that the king was his father. Like much of the Edenic imagery, the allusion is both serious and ironic. On the one hand, the invisible man, like Oedipus, turns to the blind for guidance and only gains metaphorical sight when he has become physically "blinded" himself (by Rinehart's sunglasses, for instance). On the other hand, whereas the blind Tiresias tells Oedipus the truth, the invisible man is generally deceived by those from whom he seeks guidance. Moreover, whereas Oedipus's murder of his real father brought a plague to Thebes, the invisible man's drive to overthrow his false father figures is positive. This assertion of self becomes his first step in ridding himself and others of the kinds of oppressions that plague black people.

Ellison's allusions to Freud are even more overt. Young Emerson, who is being symbolically castrated by his father, keeps a copy of Freud's *Totem and Taboo* on the coffee table of his father's outer office. Again, Ellison inverts the parallel. Whereas Freud's notion is that sons fear to overthrow their fathers because of the fear of castration, the invisible man comes to see that the symbolic castration that his father figures have performed on him is positive. Specifically, he sees Jack, old Emerson, Bledsoe, Norton, Ras, his school superintendent, and others as having cut away his illusions so that in time he can become his own father.

The novel in fact contains innumerable references to characters who assume symbolic father roles. The college Founder is "the cold Father symbol" (p. 36). The invisible man wants to beg Norton's "pardon for what he had seen; to plead and show him tears, unashamed tears like those of a child before his parents" (p. 97). Bledsoe is "our coal-black daddy of whom we were afraid" (p. 114). Brother Jack first seems "like a bemused father" (p. 332) but later seems like the more negative "great white father" (p. 462). Only Brother Tarp fulfills a genuinely paternal role. He hands down to the invisible man the traditions of the past in order that the narrator can live more fully in the present and have the promise of meaning in the future. When Tarp gives the invisible man the piece of shackle that had kept him in bondage for so many years—a shackle very much in contrast to Bledsoe's polished paperweight—the invisible man accepts it as just such a gift:

> I neither wanted it nor knew what to do with it; although there was no question of keeping it if for no other reason than I felt that Brother Tarp's gesture in offering it was of some deeply felt significance which I was compelled to respect. Something, perhaps, like a man passing on to his son his own father's watch, which the son accepted not because he wanted the old-fashioned time-piece but because the overtones of unstated seriousness and solemnity of the paternal gesture which at once joined him with his ancestors, marked a high point of his present, and promised a concreteness to his nebulous and chaotic future. [p. 380]

The scene in the Golden Day is especially Freudian. Supercargo, the black attendant whose authority depends on his white uniform (pp. 80–81), represents Freud's superego, the "censor," the part of the self that keeps the world in order. Supercargo screams at the inmates, "I want order down there . . . and if there's white folks down there, I wan's *double* order" (p. 81). But because Supercargo, stripped of his uniform, has lost power, the others act out the part of themselves that Freud calls the id. They lose control and attack Supercargo. The narrator is attracted by the irrationality and thinks, "Men were jumping upon Supercargo with both feet now and I felt such an excitement that I wanted to join them" (p. 82). Ellison presents the scene comically, essentially turning it into an extended pun. When the bartender kicks Supercargo, he tells the narrator: "Try it, school-boy, it feels so good. It gives you a relief. . . . Sometimes I get so afraid of him I feel that he's inside my head" (p. 83).

The Freudian motifs, like the references to *Oedipus Rex,* have serious implications in terms of the invisible man's development. Specifically, he begins to confront the less rational, potentially violent side of himself. He also begins to understand that his earlier repression and his being treated like a mechanical man, a cog, a robot, have created in him a deep rage. This rage emerges during the Harlem riots when he is tempted to join in the burning and the looting. Although he does throw the spear at Ras in self-protection, he later internalizes his anger, banging his own head against walls. Eventually, he accepts the violence in himself but decides he must assume responsibility and attempt to bring about social change. He also assigns responsibility for his potential violence to his victimizers, announcing that if they do not act in responsible ways there will be "tragic trouble" (p. 14).

The Invisible Man and Huck Finn

When young Emerson tells the narrator, "with us it's still Jim and Huck Finn," the invisible man cannot "make sense of his ramblings." "Huckleberry?" he thinks to himself, "Why did he keep talking about that kid's story?" (p. 185). Although in this moment Emerson is identifying with Huck, it is in fact the invisible man who is Huck's counterpart. He is the innocent and instinctively moral narrator who reports but does not understand what he sees. Like Huck, he is subject to the attempts of others to adopt him, and, like Huck, he learns the efficacy of role playing.

On the other hand, as with many of Ellison's allusions, the differences are as significant as the similarities. Whereas Huck never recognizes that it is he who is right and society that is wrong, the invisible man comes to that consciousness. And whereas Huck decides to "light out for the Territory ahead of the rest" because he does not want to be "sivilized" again and not because he is making a political gesture,[21] the invisible man concludes that exile is a negation of social responsibility.

Invisible Man and Existentialism

Sartre's introductory essay to *Existentialism and Human Emotions* provides a clear and brief discussion of the brand of existentialism that the narrator eventually embraces. Sartre argues that existence preceeds essence, or that individuals first exist before they create their characters or personalities. He also describes the world as always being in flux and individuals always in a state of becoming. The world therefore offers no absolute values or sense of meaning by which people can legitimately define themselves. Rather, in each moment of time, humans must consciously redefine themselves. Given this freedom, Sartre emphasizes individual responsibility, arguing that by their actions, individuals implicitly reveal the values they wish all people would embrace. Sartre rests his ethical stance on this notion and on the additional belief that it is impossible for anyone to choose evil. Finally, Sartre argues, it is through action and engagement in the world that individuals do reveal themselves.

Invisible Man in some ways seems almost a primer of Sartrean existentialism. At the beginning of the novel, the invisible man is not convinced of his own existence. Bledsoe tells him, "You're nobody son. You don't exist—can't you see that? The white folk tell everybody what to think—except men like me" (p. 141). When the invisible man accepts his invisibility, he also accepts his existence. It is at this point that he decides he can define his own essence. But like Sartre, he comes to view life as ever-changing, and he sees any attempt to impose order as a distortion. As he explains, "the mind that has conceived a plan of living must never lose sight of the chaos against which that pattern was conceived" (p. 567)

He does, however, commit himself to individual action and to social change. He rejects his hibernation, calling it his "greatest social crime" (p. 568). But most importantly, he learns to live with his own uncertainties and his own ambivalences, to affirm life, and to accept the inevitability of death. As he explains:

> So it is now that I denounce and defend, or feel prepared to defend. I condemn and affirm, say no and say yes, say yes and say no. I denounce because though implicated and partially responsible, I have been hurt to the point of abysmal pain, hurt to the point of invisibility. And I defend because in spite of all I find that I love. [p. 566]

He also comes to terms with the violence within him and others, announcing:

> The hibernation is over. I must shake off the old skin and come up for breath. There's a stench in the air, which, from this distance underground, might be the smell either of death or of spring—I hope of spring. But don't let me trick you, there *is* a death in the smell of spring and in the smell of thee as in the smell of me. [p. 566]

Such consciousness and acceptance in turn allows him to see his world as "one of infinite possibilities" (p. 563).

Invisible Man and *Portrait of the Artist as a Young Man*

Ultimately, *Invisible Man* is a portrait of the evolution of the young artist. The narrator decides to model himself after Joyce's Stephen Dedalus in the terms that one of his college professors had outlined:

Stephen's problem, like ours, was not actually one of creating the uncreated conscience of his race, but of creating *the uncreated features of his face*. Our task is that of making ourselves individuals. The conscience of a race is the gift of its individuals who see, evaluate, record. . . . We create the race by creating ourselves and then to our great astonishment we will have created something far more important: We will have created a culture. [p. 346]

Unlike Stephen, the invisible man rejects the exile of his underground world. He chooses instead to reenter the society from which he grew. Also unlike Stephen, he is uncertain about the validity of art, questioning whether the act of writing is not after all the assumption of another role. He also worries that writing in itself negates some of his bitterness and anger at social injustices:

So that even before I finish I've failed (maybe my anger is too heavy; perhaps being a talker, I've used too many words). But I've failed. The very act of putting it all down has confused me and negated some of the anger and some of the bitterness. [p. 566]

But because of his commitment to action and given the realities of his world, the invisible man nevertheless will try. As he puts it, "What else could I do? What else but try to tell you [the reader] what was really happening" (p. 568).

XVI

Catch-22 (1961)

by Joseph Heller

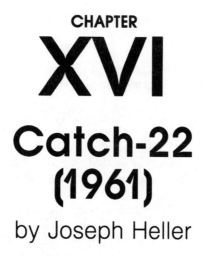

IN A 1962 INTERVIEW WITH PAUL KRASSNER, Joseph Heller discussed the moral and political dimensions of *Catch-22*. To begin with, Heller explained, reader response to the novel had brought him to recognize that the book appealed to certain commonly held moral principles. He told Krassner:

> I learned from Murray Kempton's column also—and this to my surprise—that it's quite an orthodox book in terms of its morality. He referred to its being almost medieval in its moral orthodoxy, which had not occurred to me. But of course as soon as I read his column, I realized he was correct. I suppose just about everybody accepts certain principles of morality. The differences appear in testing certain institutions against those basic principles . . . but—with the exception of a certain appreciation for lechery, which you wouldn't find among the basic virtues; you might find it among the deadly sins—I don't think there's any principle of morality advocated in the book with which most intelligent—even *in*decent—people will disagree.[1]

Despite this insistence that he had learned about many of the book's moral dimensions from its readers, Heller did reveal that the novel's conclusions had seemed inevitable to him for moral reasons.

> I couldn't see any alternative ending. It had a certain amount of integrity, not merely with the action of the book—that could've

permitted anything—but with the moral viewpoint of the book; the heavy suffusion of moral content which is in there, it seemed to me, required a resolution of choice rather than of accident.[2]

Moreover, although Heller insisted that the novel was "not *intended* to be a sociological treatise on anything," he nevertheless described it as "almost an encyclopedia of the current mental atmosphere" and as "a novel of comment." As he elaborated, "there are comments about the loyalty oath, about the free enterprise system, about civil rights, about bureaucracy, about patriotism. . . ."[3]

In addition to its grounding in the American 1950s, *Catch-22* also more generally damns the destruction wrought by any system—be it economic, governmental, bureaucratic, religious, or the military—that dehumanizes those it is meant to serve. The novel judges harshly those who, like Milo, the colonels Korn and Cathcart, and ex-P.F.C. Wintergreen, devalue human life in their quest for profit, status, and power. But despite its bleakness in those ways, *Catch-22* is also a celebration of individual responsibility and of life itelf. For even though the corrupt actually increase their power throughout the course of the novel, *Catch-22* still affirms consciousness and moral choice. As Heller's comment about the novel's final pages suggest, he does value "resolutions of choice rather than of accident."

The novel essentially is structured on Yossarian's evolution, first to a knowledge of good and evil and then to responsibility and moral action. Whereas initially Yossarian values his personal survival above all else, by the end of the novel he is willing to risk his own life for others. Rather than further jeopardizing the lives of his fellow soldiers and with the hope of saving at least one innocent, Nately's whore's kid sister, Yossarian reneges on his "odious" deal with the colonels, a deal that promises him physical safety.[4] He has decided that he will no longer let the Milos of the world "bind his mind" to their immorality. Instead, he will attempt to confront their evil, at least on a personal level.

Yossarian can now define his choice of exile as an act of responsibility. Even as he agrees with Major Danby that it will be "impossible" for him to find the kid sister in Rome and then to escape with her to Sweden, Yossarian finds meaning in the attempt. He tells Danby, "At least I'll be trying" and reminds him that because he is trying to "save" the twelve-year-old girl, "it isn't all selfish, is it?" (p. 462).

Yossarian is able to make such choices because of his new conviction that adults *are* responsible for the innocents of the world. He has come to this belief after Nately's whore, blaming him for the death of her lover, first tries to kill Yossarian. In that moment, Yossarian acknowledges his own culpability in Nately's death, reasoning:

> It was a man's world and [Nately's whore] and everyone younger had every right to blame him and everyone older for every unnatural tragedy that befell them; just as she, even in her grief, was to blame for every man-made misery that landed on her kid sister and on all other children behind her. *Someone had to do something sometime. Every victim was a culprit, every culprit a victim, and somebody had to stand sometime to try to break the lousy chain of inherited habit that was imperiling them all.* [p. 414, my emphasis]

As significantly, Yossarian comes to believe that physical survival alone is not enough. He understands what he calls Snowden's secret, that without consciousness, sensibility, spirit, and the ability to assume responsibility for others, individual life has no more meaning that it does for the soldier in white. Specifically, he realizes:

> Man was matter, that was Snowden's secret. Drop him out a window and he'll fall. Set fire to him and he'll burn. Bury him and he'll rot like other kinds of garbage. The spirit gone, man is garbage. That was Snowden's secret. Ripeness was all. [p. 450]

But ultimately, understanding is not enough. Snowden, after all, is dead. Nately is dead. Kid Sampson is dead. Nately's whore is still trying to kill Yossarian. Dunbar has been "disappeared." The kid sister is still in danger in Rome. For such reasons, Yossarian decides that he must be one of those willing to say no to the evils of the world. The risks to his own freedom and perhaps to his life now seem irrelevant.

Moral and Values Questions

General Questions: Guide to Reading

1. Under what circumstances should an individual adhere to a personal code of morality even if that code is in opposition to prevailing societal norms? What are the implications for the social order when individuals choose to follow their own consciences, particularly in time of war? On the other hand, what are the implications for justice if individuals abdicate individual responsibility and "follow orders" even if those orders are

immoral ones? As one of the questioners at Captain Black's sessions asks, "When is right?" (p. 35).

2. What is the moral obligation of the individual to others, particularly to those who are innocent or unable to protect themselves? How much should any individual be asked to risk for others?

3. Individuals who find themselves in situations they deem immoral have at least some of the following choices: conformity with enthusiasm, conformity that is accompanied by a refusal to acknowledge the immorality of the situation, defiance of the prevailing norms, and exile. What are the attractions of each of these choices? What are the potential costs of these choices to the individual and to the larger society?

4. When is power corrupt?

5. What gives the individual a sense of meaning in a world that appears to lack order, rationality, justice, and a valuing of human life?

Questions for Discussions, Papers, Exams

1. After Snowden's death, Yossarian perches naked in a tree to watch Snowden's funeral. He identifies the tree as "the tree of life . . . and of knowledge of good and evil too" (p. 269). He rejects the temptation that Milo, wrapped around the tree in a serpentine pose, offers him. Specifically, Yossarian spits out the chocolate-covered cotton that symbolizes Milo's exploitation of the war for economic profit. What is the function of Edenic imagery in this scene and elsewhere in the novel? Note, for example, that Yossarian strips after he aborts the mission to Bologna, that he then imagines he is being pursued by "snake-like mushrooms" (pp. 147–48), and that he tells one of his doctors that he was born in a "state of innocence" (p. 440).[5] Then, in relationship to the Edenic imagery, trace Yossarian's growing awareness of good and evil and his responses to the various temptations that Milo and the colonels offer him.

2. What values does Milo embody? In what ways, given those values, is *Catch-22* a critique of capitalism? Why is it significant that Milo, who brings so much death in his drive for profit, is identified as "the corn god, the rain god, and the rice god" whose "large graven images . . . could be found overlooking primitive stone altars red with human blood" (p. 244)?

3. What are the values of the following characters: Aarfy, the col-

onels, Lieutenant Scheisskopf, and Wintergreen? What is the function of these characters in the novel?

4. What is catch-22 itself, and why does it have so much power?

5. What does it mean to be "crazy" in the world of *Catch-22*? What is the relationship of sanity to morality within the novel?[6]

6. Why do so many of Yossarian's friends have names suggesting youthfulness? Note for example, Nately, which suggests "newborn"; *Kid* Sampson; and Snowden, which suggests purity of innocence. Other of Yossarian's friends seem childlike. Dobbs is only fifteen, and Orr is diminutive, inspiring Yossarian's protectiveness.

7. Discuss the function of the night scene in Rome (pp. 420–25).[7] In particular, note who the victims and the victimizers are. Also discuss the significance of Yossarian's recognition that "nothing warped seemed bizarre any more in his strange, distorted surroundings" (p. 421).

8. Discuss the chaplain's evolution.

9. Discuss Dunbar's evolution.

10. Discuss the thematic significance of the chaplain and Clevinger's trials.

11. What is the thematic significance of the practice that the authorities make of "disappearing" people?

12. Why is it significant that the bureaucracy is able to define an individual's identity and at times to determine his or her very existence? In this regard, discuss Yossarian's assumption of Giuseppe's identity, Doc Daneeka's "death," the dead man in Yossarian's tent, and the A. Fortiori confusion of identities.

13. Discuss the novel's lack of chronology, focusing on the thematic significance of the confused time sequence.

14. When the chaplain goes to Wintergreen for help in his attempt to prevent Nately from flying more missions, Heller writes that "the chaplain's pilgrimage to Wintergreen had proved abortive; another shrine was empty" (p. 338). Discuss the function of the religious language in the novel. In doing so, also take into account Yossarian's discussion of God with Lieutenant Scheisskopf's wife (pp. 184–85).

Sanity and Morality

Character after character is labeled insane and so labels one another. Eventually, however, it becomes clear that Heller is inverting the usual definition of sanity. Specifically, on one level, those who conform to social norms are considered sane and those who defy those norms are judged insane. However, because conformity holds many dangers for the moral person, the weak, and the powerless, on another level, those who adhere to the prevailing norms may be "crazy."

The catch in this particular double-bind or catch-22 situation is that what is considered normal in this world frequently is immoral or amoral. For this reason, those few characters—like Dunbar, the chaplain, and Yossarian—who come to recognize the dangers of conformity and try to thwart the system begin to seem "sane." Nevertheless, because such a stance puts them at great risk, they are, within the context of their worlds, more often seen as "crazy." For example, Dunbar is "disappeared" after he refuses to drop bombs on an unsuspecting civilian village (p. 338) and after he announces that the soldier in white is simply a hollow shell of bandages (p. 374). The chaplain is put on trial essentially because he questions authority. Even Doc Stubbs, who tries to overrule the colonels' unjust requirement of an exhorbitant number of missions, is sent to the Pacific as punishment for his dissent.

In the end, Heller suggests that the dangers to society and to individuals alike of conformity are far greater than those of nonconformity, despite the risks to the individual of defying the norm. Or to put it another way, *Catch-22* eventually argues that the decision to act responsibly, whatever its dangers, is the ultimate act of sanity.

Critic Vance Ramsey, in his discussion of Heller's use of paradox, explains the dual meanings of insanity in somewhat different but very illuminating terms:

> In the literature of the absurd, the apparently ordered surface of reality is torn away to reveal the chaos and unreason beneath. Paradox, therefore, is the very essence of the technique of literature of the absurd. Traditional reason is revealed as unreason because it supposes an ordered, rational world. Sanity in the traditional sense is really insanity; that is, if sanity is the ability to come to terms with reality, then it is insane to act as if the world is coherent and rational. Loyalty to traditional institutions can be disloyalty to oneself simply because the institutions may threaten the people they are ostensibly designed to serve.[8]

Absurdity in *Catch-22*

Heller presents two kinds of absurdity in the novel. The first is the Kafkaesque absurdity of an irrational, unjust world in which bureaucracies dominate and in which individuality and even human life have little value. The second kind of absurdity is the existential absurdity most often associated with the works of Camus and Sartre. Specifically, the only absolute is that of death, a certainty that is magnified in *Catch-22* because the setting is war. There is no order, no meaning, and no justice other than that which the individual creates.

Heller points directly to Kafka's *The Trial* in two scenes in the novel: Clevinger's trial and that of the chaplain. Both Clevinger and the chaplain have experiences similar to Kafka's Joseph K. They do not know the charges against them or how the system works. Both are considered guilty simply because they have been charged with crimes. "Clevinger was guilty, of course, or he would not have been accused, and since the only way to prove it was to find him guilty, it was [the judges'] patriotic duty to do so." (p. 82). The chaplain's accusers similarly judge him guilty of acts he did not perform and then add, "We accuse you also of the commission of crimes and infractions we don't even know about yet" (p. 395). Moreover, just as Joseph K. did not know whether his lawyers were his allies or his enemies, so Clevinger's judge, prosecutor, and defending officer were all the same person, the parade-loving and ambitious Lieutenant Scheisskopf (p. 77).

Heller's indebtedness to Camus is equally explicit. In particular, he relies on Camus's version of the myth of Sisyphus. Sisyphus was destined eternally to push a boulder to the top of a mountain only to see it roll back down again so that he could push it back up. Despite the emptiness and endlessness of his task, Camus believes that Sisyphus's consciousness made him happy. Heller offers several variations on Sisyphus. Ex-P.F.C. Wintergreen, for instance, repeatedly goes AWOL and upon his arrest is "sentenced to dig and fill up holes six feet deep, wide, and long for a specified length of time." Like Sisyphus, Wintergreen embraces his purposeless role and finds his meaning in it: " 'It's not a bad life,' he would observe philosophically. 'And I guess somebody has to do it' " (p. 108). The fliers, too, face a seemingly Sisyphian situation. They continue to fly their requisite number of missions only to discover that the colonels have raised the number one more time. Perhaps most importantly, Yossarian becomes an existential hero. Despite his sense of estrangement (p. 422) and his sense of the inevitability of death, Yossarian faces the absurd. He gains consciousness, takes a leap of faith into responsibility for others, and becomes one with his struggle, however hopeless it may be.

The Dangers of Immorality

Milo values profit above all else. Because he is both master and perpetuator of the Kafkaesque bureaucracy that characterizes his world, he is able to bomb his own unit, to take carbon dioxide out of the life jackets to make ice cream sodas, and to steal the morphine from the plane's first-aid kits, all in the conviction that "what's good for M & M Enterprises is good for the country."[9] Milo's indifference to human life has devastating results. The bombing mission kills Mudd, who becomes known as the dead man in Yossarian's tent. The theft of the carbon dioxide endangers Orr and his crew. The morphine theft causes Snowden's death to be horrifyingly painful to him and to Yossarian, who without morphine is helpless in the face of Snowden's pain. Milo is also responsible for Nately's death because it was he who encouraged the colonels to assign Nately more missions.

Colonels Korn and Cathcart similarly exemplify the dangers of an all-powerful bureaucracy that serves those in control at the expense of all else. For example, after Yossarian's burst of patriotism leads him to fly over the target at Ferrara twice, a choice that brings about Kraft's death, the colonels do not share Yossarian's "vile, excruciating dilemma of duty and damnation" (p. 141). Instead, Cathcart explains candidly to Yossarian: "It's not that I'm being sentimental or anything. I don't give a damn about the men or the airplanes. It's just that it looks so lousy on the report. How am I going to cover up something like this in the report?" (p. 142). Later in the novel Korn is even willing to bomb a civilian village solely because "Colonel Cathcart wants to come out of this mission with a good clean aerial photograph he won't be ashamed to send through channels" (p. 337).

In time, Yossarian learns that such immorality is universal. He sees that the American public will accept Milo's bombing of his own unit because of the "tremendous profit" Milo has made (p. 266). Although initially newspapers, government officials, mothers, and service organizations denounced Milo's actions, they all are quieted when "he opened his books" and demonstrates that he could "reimburse the government for all the people and property he had destroyed" and still have money left to continue his syndicate operations (p. 266). Yossarian next recognizes that Milo's influence is worldwide. In Malta, Milo "had been knighted, commissioned a major in the Royal Welsh Fusiliers and named Assistant Governor-General of Malta because he had brought the egg trade there" (p. 243). Milo is also

> the Vice-Shah of Oran and his person was sacred . . . also the Caliph of Baghdad, the Imam of Damascus, and the Sheik of Araby. Milo was the corn god, the rain god, and the rice god in backward regions where such crude gods were still worshiped by ignorant and superstitious people, and deep inside the jungles of Africa, he intimated with

becoming modesty, large graven images of his mustached face could be found overlooking primitive stone altars red with human blood. [p. 244]

Milo's brand of immorality and devaluing of human life also characterizes Rome, the Eternal City, home of the Vatican and of some of the most glorious art of Western civilization. In Rome, Yossarian finds that mobs are in control. He also realizes that there is no more compassion, order, or justice in Rome than there had been in Pianosa or with Milo on his travels. The police in this world are now the ones to be feared, and children, animals, and other helpless beings are routinely victimized. Significantly, Yossarian becomes aware that his own "spirit was sick" (p. 426) and that the perversion of values he sees in Rome has come to seem normal to him (p. 421). Yossarian thus "walked in lonely torture, feeling estranged" and for the moment is totally unable to interfere in the violence he sees around him (p. 422).

The culmination of atrocities comes when Yossarian seeks out the simple, virgin maid who had cleaned the officer's quarters. Hoping that her innocence would solace him, Yossarian learns instead that Aarfy, another figure of amorality, has raped and murdered the maid because he didn't want to "let her go around saying bad things about us" (p. 427). Yossarian, in horror at Aarfy's actions, insists to Aarfy that he is insane to believe that he will go unpunished for the murder. Aarfy, who understands the larger insanity of the world better than Yossarian does, insists otherwise, explaining: "She was only a servant girl. I hardly think they're going to make too much of a fuss over one poor Italian servant girl when so many thousands of lives are being lost every day" (p. 328). Tragically, Aarfy is right. The military police arrive and arrest "Yossarian for being in Rome without a pass. They apologize to Aarfy for intruding" (p. 429).

The Question of Identity

The source of much comedy but also of serious satire in *Catch-22* is the fact that the bureaucracy has the power to determine identity and, at least in official terms, the existence of individuals. When the doctors want Yossarian to play the part of the dying Giuseppe, Yossarian does so. Giuseppe's parents never question the fact that this man, whom they've never seen before and who calls himself Yossarian, is their son because the doctors have identified him as their child. When the system chooses to believe that Yossarian is A. Fortiori, Yossarian's protestations of his own identity have no impact. The dead man in Yossarian's tent, Mudd, is not declared officially dead because he had never officially signed in when he arrived at Pianosa. Because he does not exist in terms of the base's records, he cannot be declared dead. In contrast, Doc Daneeka is officially decreed deceased because the records show he was in McWatt's plane, which crashed. Daneeka's personal protests notwithstanding, the bureaucracy rules, paying his wife his life insurance and funeral expense grants from various sources. Mrs. Daneeka, herself another example of immorality, ignores her husband's letters that he is still alive and moves with the insurance money and "her children to Lansing, Michigan, and left no forwarding address" (p. 354).

Catch-22: An Inverted Eden and a Waste Land

It is appropriate that Milo is a fertility god in this world in which death dominates. April, the cruelest month in Eliot's *The Waste Land* for those who have consciousness and a desire for life, is "the best month of all for Milo" (p. 257), the man at whose altar human lives are sacrificed. In addition, in this world in "which everything green looked black and everything else was the color of pus" (p. 147), it is equally fitting that Milo is identified as the serpent.

Indeed, Heller suggests that Pianosa is an inverted Eden. Milo, as the serpent, tempts Yossarian and others not with the apple, which would give them knowledge of good and evil, but with moral blindness. Heller makes the association explicit when Yossarian, stripped in Adamic fashion, perches in a tree to watch the funeral of one of the innocents, Snowden. Milo, dressed in olive green, drapes himself around the tree in serpentine fashion and offers Yossarian a bite of the chocolate-covered cotton. The moment is important in Yossarian's evolution. He recognizes the cotton for what it is and refuses to join forces with Milo to exploit others. As significantly, he attempts to confront Milo with his own evil, reminding Milo that he is responsible for Mudd's death because he organized the air raid and profited from it.

Later, near the end of the novel, his spirit sick from his experiences in Rome, Yossarian temporarily succumbs to temptation. He accepts the deal that the colonels offer him, a deal that would allow him to go home safely and in the guise of a hero. But his acquiescence is short-lived. Attacked once again by Nately's whore, Yossarian realizes that physical survival is meaningless without "spirit." He reneges on the deal. After declaring that he was born "in a state of innocence" (p. 440), he now faces up to his knowledge of good and evil. He will not act in a way that will be harmful to the other men in his unit. He also knows that in this inverted Eden, knowledge of morality and exile offer the only hope of salvation.

Perhaps even more importantly, Yossarian decides that he will assume responsibility for the innocents of the world. He has realized how many of his youthful friends have been killed. He has become aware of "all the poor and stupid and diseased people he had seen in Italy, Egypt and North Africa and knew about in other areas of the world" (p. 414). He has also come to believe that the only good people in the world were "the children . . . Albert Einstein and an old violinist or sculptor somewhere" (p. 422). He decides that in order to "save himself" (p. 456), he will take responsibility for the last innocent in his own personal sphere, Nately's whore's kid sister. As he tells Danby: "There's a young kid in Rome whose life I'd like to save if I can find her. I'll take her to Sweden with me if I can find her, so it isn't all selfish, is it?" (p. 462).

In other words, even though Yossarian knows that he cannot alter the system that dominates his world, he can make personal decisions about how to live his life. At the very least, he can refuse to participate in or help perpetuate the immorality that he sees. He can refuse to be blinded to the evils that Milo and the colonels embody. He may no longer be able to ensure his own survival, his own life, but he will be able to live with the spirit he has so come to value.

Religion and the Presence of Evil

Catch-22 dramatizes one of the most difficult issues that theologians face: the presence of evil in the world. Yossarian in effect asks the key question: How can there be a God when children and others who are vulnerable yet innocent suffer so much? In his conversation with Lieutenant Scheisskopf's wife, he elaborates:

> And don't tell me God works in mysterious ways. . . . There's nothing so mysterious about it. He's not working at all. He's playing. Or else He's forgotten all about us. That's the kind of God you people talk about—a country bumpkin, a clumsy, bungling, brainless, conceited, uncouth hayseed. . . . Why in the world did He ever create pain? [p. 184]

In *Catch-22,* there does not appear to be the sort of good, just, and merciful God in whom Lieutenant Scheisskopf's wife wants to believe. As the chaplain discovers, "shrine after shrine is empty" (p. 339) or, as Yossarian learns, Milo occupies them. Whatever salvation this world offers is secular not religious. At the end of the novel, the chaplain himself comes to believe that the only miracles are human ones. When he learns that Orr has managed to row to Sweden, the chaplain exclaims, "It's . . . a miracle of human intelligence and human endurance." Moments later, he similarly celebrates, "It's a miracle of human perseverance" (pp. 458–59). Yossarian, realizing that his own survival will depend on his own intelligence, endurance, and perseverance, wishes belatedly that he had had "some faith" (p. 459). Once again, the faith being celebrated is human not divine, for Yossarian wishes he had believed more in Orr. Ultimately, Heller suggests that the best alternative (or "or") is that presented by Orr, that of human effort.

Dunbar, the Chaplain, and Responsibility

Dunbar, Yossarian's friend, is a minor but significant character whose evolution precedes Yossarian's. Dunbar, too, originally sought to escape physical danger by going into the hospital. Eventually, recognizing the full horror of the system, he refuses to drop bombs on the civilian village the colonels were destroying simply because they desired a clear aerial photograph. Instead, Dunbar "dropped his bombs hundreds of yards past the village and would face a court-martial if it could ever be shown he had done it deliberately." Yossarian, not yet at the point where he is able to defy the system actively, is unsure whether Dunbar has been "shown the light" or has had his brains scrambled in an earlier fall in the hospital (p. 339). Later, when Dunbar realizes that the soldier in white is nothing more than a symbolic embodiment of just how much individuals are dehumanized, he causes a panic among the other soldiers in the hospital. In return, like others who apparently disrupted the system, he is "disappeared" (p. 376). Nevertheless, his rebellion and disappearance in part inspires Yossarian's defiance.

Yossarian, in his turn, motivates others to stand up to the evil they see. The other men in the unit jump out of the bushes at night secretly to ask his progress. The implication is that if Yossarian's refusal to fly more missions is successful, others will also refuse to serve the corrupt colonels.

It is the chaplain who most evolves under Yossarian's influence. He moves from a stance of acquiescence and timidity to one of determination. He decides to challenge the system, promising himself that he will "persevere" and fight back (p. 462). He also encourages Yossarian to flee to Sweden.

The Glorious Loyalty-Oath Crusade

Heller explained in his interview with Krassner that *Catch-22* is more contemporaneous with the period during which he wrote the book than it is with World War II.[10] And indeed, the novel is often about the cold war and McCarthyism. For example, Captain Black's glorious loyalty-oath crusade satirizes the McCarthy-inspired requirement in the fifties that individuals sign loyalty oaths before assuming jobs in the public and, at times, in the educational sectors. Major Major Major Major suffers through a variation of blacklisting when he is labeled subversive because he does not sign a loyalty oath (even though in his case, in typical *Catch-22* fashion, he is not allowed to do so). Heller in this episode does, however, suggest that individual action can make a difference. In one of the more comic scenes in the novel, Major——de Coverly puts a stop to the crusade by ignoring the requirement that he sign an oath before he eats. ——de Coverly simply asserts, "Gimme eat. . . . Give everybody eat" (p. 120).[11]

Catch-22's Lack of Chronological Order

The novel may be confusing to the first-time reader because it lacks a clear, chronological order and because it abounds with so many characters who themselves are often caricatures. In fact, the distorted time sequence is not especially significant in itself; what is important is that it emphasizes the seeming irrationality that prevails. In addition, as Yossarian comes to a greater understanding, he brings new clarity to the events. As he changes and gains a better perspective, he returns to key events in his mind again and again. For example, although he is obsessed by Snowden's death throughout the novel, it is only at the end of the book that he genuinely understands what he calls Snowden's secret. The effect of this device is that the reader, too, learns to understand the meaning of events as Yossarian does.

Names and Other Miscellany

Heller sometimes uses names for humor, sometimes for more serious purposes. Milo Minderbinder, someone who is able to "see more things than most people but [who] could see none of them too distinctly" (p. 66), is himself blind to morality and binds other people's minds as well. In contrast to the Biblical snake whose apple is forbidden to Adam and Eve because "God does know that in the day ye eat thereof, then your eye shall be opened and ye shall be as gods, knowing good and evil,"[12] Milo wants others to be amoral so that his own evil can go unchallenged. Nately's name suggests "newborn." Kid Sampson's name similarly points to his youth. Snowden's name suggests both his purity and the coldness of his death. Others—like Nately's whore, Nately's whore's kid sister, and Lieutenant Scheisskopf's wife—are identified in terms of others. They exist in the novel only as they are related to other, more significant characters. Yossarian's name rhymes with his nationality so that he becomes Yossarian the Assyrian. As Heller explained to Krassner, he decides to make Yossarian an Assyrian precisely because so few people know anything about Assyria. (No longer existent, Assyria once was one of the four areas bordering Eden in Genesis.) Heller suggested that the chaplain became an Anabaptist for similar reasons because his readers would bring few prior associations to the character. The chaplain's faith also, however, has its ironies because Anabaptists are pacifists who do not believe in bearing arms and who do not serve in government positions.

Yossarian's Desertion: Moral or Immoral

Catch-22 is not a pacifist novel, and Yossarian's desertion is not presented as a model for soldiers under all circumstances. Yossarian's final conversation with Major Danby provides his philosophical justification for his decision to flee the army. First, he argues that he has already performed his duty, flying many more missions than usually required. Second, he argues that the war is nearly over. He tells Danby, "The country's not in danger any more, but I am" (p. 455). But most of all, Yossarian believes that he is no longer serving his ideals or any other ideals but rather that he is serving only those who are profiting from the war. As he explains it: "When I look up, I see people cashing in. I don't see heaven or saints or angels. I see people cashing in on every decent impulse and every human tragedy" (p. 455).

Given these beliefs, Yossarian's decision becomes an existential leap of faith into individual responsibility despite all odds. Yossarian believes that he is embracing his own responsibilities now, despite his expectation that his plan to reach Sweden via Rome is, as Danby explains, "impossible. It's almost a geographical impossibility to get there from here" (p. 462). Nevertheless, Yossarian makes his leap, both metaphorically and physically, as he "jumped" one more time out of the reach of Nately's whore's knife (p. 463).

CHAPTER

XVII

The Bell Jar
(1963)

by Sylvia Plath

LIKE *Adventures of Huckleberry Finn, The Great Gatsby,* AND *Invisible Man,*
Sylvia Plath's *The Bell Jar* dramatizes the power of social values to shape
individual perceptions, goals, and eventually choices. Indeed, in many
ways, Plath's autobiographical heroine, Esther Greenwood, is a female
version of Huck, Gatsby, and the invisible man. The adults in her world
similarly attempt to "adopt" her so that she will live according to their
values. But whereas her male predecessors are products of a value
system that rewards male individuality even as it requires a good deal
of conformity, Esther has to contend with far more stringent conventions. It is her struggle to come to terms with these conventions so that
she can make her own choices that the novel dramatizes.

Esther's initial attempts to define herself are limited by her experience of society's narrow expectations for women. In contrast to men
who have the option to marry, have children, and pursue a career,
Esther believes she must choose between family and profession. Her
mother, her boyfriend, and her potential mentors all insist that she
choose only one role for herself. Because Esther has so absorbed this
value, she believes that her desire to preserve all possibilities is a sign of
neurosis. Poetry, an academic life, and marriage and children seem to
her to be "mutually exclusive things."[1] As she tells Buddy Willard when

180

she rejects his proposal of marriage: "If neurotic is wanting two mutually exclusive things at one and the same time, then I'm neurotic as hell. I'll be flying back and forth between one mutually exclusive thing and another for the rest of my days" (p. 76).

In time, Esther's torment over her inability to embrace only one role leads her to a mental breakdown. She first becomes alienated from others and from herself, then she tries to commit suicide. Only after shock treatment and extensive therapy does Esther regain her mental health. The therapy is especially crucial, for Esther's doctor encourages the girl to defy constraining conventions. As significantly, Dr. Nolan serves as a role model for Esther in that she has become a successful professional who is also warm, generous, and attractive. Eventually, as Esther comes to recognize society's limitations, she begins to value her own instincts. Like the invisible man, she intends to reenter society. With some optimism, she plans to return to college, describing herself as having been "born twice—patched, retreaded, and approved for the road" (p. 199).

Plath does attribute Esther's breakdown primarily to negative social values. In Laingian terms, Esther is driven crazy by her inability to conform to social conventions that are essentially dehumanizing and therefore themselves insane.[2] At the same time, Plath also roots Esther's mental problems in the specifics of her childhood. The death of her father, her mother's anger at having to support her two children, and Esther's own talents as a student and a poet all contribute to her alienation. On the other hand, the novel's conclusion is essentially optimistic. As Esther encounters a positive role model and gains consciousness of her self and her history, she begins to make her own choices. Most significantly, believing that she can take responsibility, she does so in a variety of situations.

Although it has been documented that much of *The Bell Jar* is autobiographical, it is also clear that Plath has fictionalized many aspects of her own life.[3] It is therefore important to make a separation between author and heroine, particularly in terms of the novel's conclusion. Although Sylvia Plath did commit suicide a month after *The Bell Jar* was published (under the pseudonym Victoria Lucas), Esther Greenwood does not kill herself. The distinction between Plath and Esther is also important if Plath's craft as a novelist is to be acknowledged. Her presentation of Esther's breakdown is particularly worthy of attention. Here, Esther's language, her negative self-image, and the language she uses to communicate her perceptions reveal her growing psychological distress and loss of control.

Moral and Values Questions

General Questions: Guide to Reading

1. What were the differing versions of the American dream for men and women in the fifties and early sixties? Has the nature of the dream changed in any substantial way since *The Bell Jar* was published?
2. What forces generally shape an individual's values and goals?
3. How do individuals judge the validity of their own values when those values come into conflict with social standards and expectations? By what criteria should individuals choose to defy convention?
4. What is the potential impact of social censure on the nonconformist?

Questions for Discussions, Papers, Exams

1. What does the bell jar stand for? What is the origin of that image for Esther?
2. Each of the minor characters has a symbolic function within the novel in terms of Esther's choices. What is the symbolic function of at least the following characters: the woman poet at Esther's college? Philomena Guinea? Mrs. Willard? Dodo Conway? Betsy? Doreen? Mrs. Greenwood? Dr. Nolan? Joan?
3. Discuss the images with which Esther describes herself prior to her breakdown.
4. The novel begins with a reference to the Rosenbergs' execution. Why?
5. Discuss Esther's attitudes toward children. In particular, note the frequency with which her imagery includes infants. Then, discuss the importance of Esther's reference, early in the novel, to her own baby (p. 3).
6. Esther develops a double for herself, Elly Higgenbottom. She also sees Betsy, Doreen, and Joan as her alter egos at different points. Her senior's thesis is on doubling or twins in Joyce's fiction. Discuss the thematic function of such allusions to doubling in the novel.

Esther and the American Dream

When Esther describes her experiences as a summer editor on a national magazine, she emphasizes the rags-to-riches aspect of her apparent success: "Look what can happen in this country. . . . A girl lives in some out-of-the-way town for nineteen years, so poor that she can't afford a magazine, and then she gets a scholarship to college and wins a prize here and a prize there and ends up steering New York like her own private car" (p. 2).

Esther's reality is, however, far different from her public image. As she puts it, "I wasn't steering anything, not even myself" (p. 2). To begin with, Esther feels betrayed by her expectation that her academic successes would bring her happiness and professional success. In New York, she begins to realize that her intelligence and academic skills probably will be of little use in securing for her the life she seeks: "I felt like a racehorse in a world without racetracks or a champion college footballer suddenly confronted by Wall Street and a business suit, his days of glory shrunk to a gold cup on his mantel with a date engraved on it like the date on a tombstone" (p. 62).

Even more significantly, almost everyone important in Esther's life is pressuring her to choose a role for herself. On the one hand, there are those who insist that she choose a role in which she would be "serving men" (p. 62). Her mother wants her to learn shorthand so she could "get a good job after college" and "would be in demand among all the up-and-coming young men" (p. 61). Buddy wants her to marry him and give up her desire to write poetry. He tells Esther that a poem is a "piece of dust" (p. 45) and insists that once she marries and has children, she will lose the desire to write. Esther believes that he might even be accurate, and she thinks: "maybe it was true that when you were married and had children it was like being brainwashed and afterward you went about numb as a slave in some private, totalitarian state" (p. 69).

Buddy's mother has been equally adamant that women really desired marriage and children above all else. Buddy assumes that his mother was right: "He was always saying how his mother said, 'What a man wants is a mate and what a woman wants is infinite security,' and 'What a man is is an arrow into the future and what a woman is is the place the arrow shoots off from'" (p. 58).

Esther's contemporaries also give her the message that romance and marriage are the only valid goals. The girls in her college dorm accept her only when she begins dating Buddy. After her suicide attempt, when she fears that she is blind, a nurse attempts to reassure her about her future by telling her, "There are lots of blind people in the world. You'll marry a nice blind man someday" (p. 140). And even after Esther turns down Buddy's proposal by telling him that she never wants to get married (p. 76), he assumes that marriage still has priority in her life. For example, in retaliation for her independence, he later taunts her, "I wonder who you'll marry now, Esther. Now you've been in a mental hospital" (p. 197).

In contrast, Esther is also pulled by women who have turned away from children, femininity, and often from marriage in favor of careers. The famous woman poet at Esther's college "lived with another woman—a stumpy old Classical scholar with a cropped Dutch cut." When Esther tells her that she "might well get married and have a pack of children someday," the poet responds with horror, crying out, "But what about your *career?*" (p. 180). JayCee, Esther's editor, is successful but childless, married to an unattractive man, and is herself unfeminine. She pushes Esther to choose a career, telling her that with her ambivalence, "you'll never get anywhere" (p. 27). Philomena Guinea, the novelist who endows Esther's scholarship, is successful too, but unmarried and childless. She similarly wants Esther to abandon relationships with men, telling Mrs. Greenwood that she would not pay for Esther's hospitalization "if there was a boy in the case" (p. 151). When Mrs. Greenwood assures her that Esther's problem is her writing and not a boy, Philomena Guinea pays for Esther's treatment.

Esther eventually rejects these models, much as she rejects Mrs. Willard, her own mother, and Dodo Conway, the neighbor pregnant with her seventh child. She wonders: "Why did I attract these weird old women. There was the famous poet, and Philomena Guinea, and JayCee, and the Christian Scientist lady and lord knows who, and they all wanted to adopt me in some way, and, for the price of their care and influence, have me resemble them" (p. 180).

But Esther continues to have ambivalences, particularly about children. At times, she totally rejects the possibility of marriage and a family. When she sees Dodo Conway, she thinks, "Children make me sick" (p. 26). Before she's fitted for a diaphragm, she decides, "If I had to wait on a baby all day, I would go mad" (p. 182). Nevertheless, there are other moments when Esther desires children. When she fantasizes about becoming Elly Higgenbottom, the orphan, she thinks, "And one day I might just marry a virile, but tender garage mechanic and have a big cowy family, like Dodo Conway" (p. 108). When she tries to visit her father's grave, she has a similar fantasy about life with the prison guard she meets:

I was thinking that if I'd had the sense to go on living in that old town I might just have met this prison guard in school and married him and had a parcel of little kids by now. It would be nice, living by the sea with piles of little kids and pigs and chickens, wearing what my grandmother called wash dresses, and sitting around in some kitchen with bright linoleum and fat arms, drinking pots of coffee. [p. 123]

Esther also associates infants with purity. After her insulin reaction, she tastes milk "luxuriously, the way a baby tastes its mother" (p. 164). When she takes a bath that makes her "feel so much myself," she thinks of herself as renewed, as "pure and sweet as a new baby" (p. 17). Moreover, it is the vision of stillborn babies in glass bottles that is the origin of Esther's vision of the bell jar (p. 51). When she is feeling totally detached from her world, she thinks of herself as being like those fetuses, "sitting under the same glass bell jar, stewing in my own sour air" (p. 152).

Esther's inability to choose one role for herself paralyzes her and then later contributes to her breakdown. When she envisions herself as sitting in a fig tree, confronted with a myriad of possibilities, she thinks:

From the tip of every branch, like a fat purple fig, a wonderful future beckoned and winked. One fig was a husband and a happy home and children, and another fig was a famous poet and another fig was a brilliant professor, and another fig was EeGee, the amazing editor, and another fig was Constantin and Socrates and Attila and a pack of other lovers with queer names and offbeat professions, and another fig was an Olympic lady crew champion, and beyond and above these figs were many more figs I couldn't quite make out. [p. 62]

Such paralysis ultimately leads Esther to try to commit suicide. Her imagery suggests her own sense of impending death:

I saw myself sitting in the crotch of this fig tree, starving to death, just because I couldn't make up my mind which of the figs I would choose. I wanted each and every one of them, but choosing one meant losing all the rest, and, as I sat there, unable to decide, the figs began to wrinkle and go black, and one by one, they plopped to the ground at my feet. [p. 63]

After Dr. Nolan convinces Esther that she can defy such conventions and can live with her own ambivalence, Esther regains her mental health. She is finally able to accept her uncertainty about her future, able to live with the fact that her future is one of "question marks" (p. 199).

The Double Standard

Esther has also been inculcated with the double standard for male and female sexual behavior. She has been influenced by the article her mother sent her entitled, "In Defense of Chastity." As Esther describes the piece:

> The main point of the article was that a man's world is different from a woman's world and a man's emotions are different from a woman's emotions and only marriage can bring the two worlds and the two different sets of emotions together properly. My mother said this was something a girl didn't know about till it was too late, so she had to take the advice of people who were already experts like a married woman. [pp. 65–66]

The movie that Esther sees reinforces the notion that women must be celibate until marriage. In that movie:

> the nice girl was going to end up with the nice football hero and the sexy girl was going to end up with nobody, because the man named Gil had only wanted a mistress and not a wife all along and was now packing off to Europe on a single ticket. [p. 34]

Esther applies the same standards to her friends and to herself. Betsy and Doreen seem embodiments to Esther of a "nice girl" and a "sexy girl," respectively. Betsy is from Kansas and associated with innocence. In contrast, Doreen seems sophisticated and "suggests a whole life of marvelous, elaborate decadence" that attracts Esther "like a magnet" (p. 4). Esther initially gravitates toward Doreen because "Doreen had intuition. Everything she said was like a secret voice speaking straight out of my own bones" (p. 6). Later, however, Esther chooses "to be loyal to Betsy and her innocent friends, deciding, 'It was Betsy I resembled at heart' " (p. 19). In fact, when Esther rejects Doreen, she reveals both her desire to see herself as innocent and the degree to which she has accepted society's judgments. She begins to think of Doreen as "an ugly concrete testimony to my own dirty nature" (p. 7).

Even as Esther has absorbed the values of the double standard, she rails against it. She is particularly enraged that Buddy and others have been hypocritical about male sexual behavior. Her mother and grandmother had "started hinting around to me a lot lately about what a fine, clean boy Buddy Willard was, coming from such a fine, clean family." In fact, Esther realizes, "All I'd heard about really was how fine and clean Buddy was and how he was the kind of person a girl should stay fine and clean for" (p. 55). Buddy has also made Esther feel that she "was so sexy and he was so pure" (p. 56). He attributes his sexual interest in her to his feelings of caring about her (p. 57). Thus, when Esther learns that Buddy has had an affair, she is appalled because, as she comes to realize in time, "I couldn't stand the idea of a woman having to have a single pure life and a man being able to have a double life, one pure and one not" (p. 66).

Dr. Nolan scoffs at the power of the double standard and encourages Esther to assume for herself the same sexual freedom that Buddy and other men had. She sends Esther to be fitted for a diaphragm so that the girl will be free from the fear of pregnancy. As Esther describes the moment:

> I climbed up on the examination table, thinking: "I am climbing to freedom, freedom from fear, freedom from marrying the wrong person, like Buddy Willard, just because of sex, freedom from the Florence Crittenden Homes where all the poor girls go who should have been fitted out like me, because what they did, they would do anyway, regardless." [p. 182]

Dr. Nolan also helps Esther come to terms with some of her earlier expectations. She helps Esther believe that she can be her "own woman" and can take control of her life in new ways. In concrete terms. Esther begins to distance herself from her mother and her mother's values. She now chooses to take a lover on her own terms, to assert herself with Buddy, and to handle such difficult situations as Joan's funeral. She comes to some new understanding that Joan's lesbianism was the result of a desire for tenderness. But most significantly, Esther comes to some acceptance of the negativity of her past, rejecting forgetfulness because her earlier difficult moments "were part of me. They were my landscape" (p. 194).

Esther's Breakdown: Images of Self-Negation

As Esther loses control of herself and moves closer to her suicide attempt, her narrative is permeated with negative self-images. For instance, she describes herself in New York as being out of control and at the mercy of an inner sense of emptiness and inadequacy:

> I wasn't steering anything, not even myself. I just bumped from my hotel to work and to parties and from parties to my hotel and back to work like a numb trolleybus. I guess I should have been excited the way most of the other girls were, but I couldn't get myself to react. I

felt very still and very empty, the way the eye of a tornado must feel, moving dully along in the middle of the surrounding hullabaloo. [p. 2]

Later, in the bar with Doreen, Esther feels "myself melting away in the shadows like the negative of a person I'd never seen before in my life" (p. 8). Then, as she watches Doreen and Lenny dance, she thinks of herself as "shrinking to a small black dot against all those red and white rugs and that pine panelling. I felt like a hole in the ground" (p. 14). As Lenny and Doreen "get more and more crazy about each other," Esther's sense of herself diminishes, and she explains:

It's like watching Paris from an express caboose heading in the opposite direction—every second the city gets smaller and smaller and lonelier and lonelier, rushing away from all those lights and that excitement at about a million miles an hour. [p. 14]

Images of death appear. Esther sees her telephone as "dumb as a death's head" (p. 16). She thinks of bathtubs as being "coffin-shaped" (p. 16). The letters of the German alphabet make her think of the Nazi concentration camps, and she describes them as being "dense, black, barbed-wire letters" (p. 27). Even earlier, when she was in college, her physics class "was death" to her (p. 28), and she saw physics formulas as "hideous, cramped, scorpion-lettered" (p. 29). The conference room at the magazine has a "tomblike morning gloom" for Esther (p. 82). Esther describes her last night in New York in similar language. She sees the city's "buildings blackened, as if for a funeral." She throws her new wardrobe out the window, explaining, "I fed my wardrobe to the night wind, and flutteringly, like a loved one's ashes, the gray scraps were ferried off . . . in the dark heart of New York" (p. 91).

Esther's tendency to seek alter egos also reveals her sense of alienation. At various times, she allies herself with Doreen, Betsy, and later Joan. In each case, she rejects these women for very different reasons. She turns away from Doreen because of her impurity, from Betsy because of her innocence, and Joan because of her lesbianism. Esther also seeks fictional counterparts. She at times assumes the role of Elly Higgenbottom from Chicago. She names the heroine of the novel she cannot write "Elaine," thinking that the name had the same number of letters as Esther did. Even her interest in the images of twins in Joyce suggests Esther's split self.

When Esther attends Joan's funeral, she wonders "what I thought I was burying" (p. 198). The sense is that she may be burying her old suicidal self. Although she is aware that the bell jar of insanity may again descend (p. 197), Esther essentially has come to accept herself and to value her own life. She now has confidence in her own values, perceptions, and choices. Moreover, in contrast to the scene in which she had attempted to drown herself but had been defeated by her heart beating, "I am I am I am" (p. 129), Esther now accepts her sense of her existence as "the old brag of my heart." She now accepts the "I am, I am, I am" (p. 199).[4]

The Rosenbergs' Execution and Esther's Shock Treatments

Ethel and Julius Rosenberg were executed on June 19, 1953, after being convicted of espionage. Esther begins her narrative by locating it in the "summer they electrocuted the Rosenbergs" (p. 1). The thought of their execution makes her sick. She becomes appalled that her coeditor Hilda is "glad they're going to die" (p. 81). Although Esther insists to herself that the Rosenbergs' execution "had nothing to do with me" (p. 1), she has a deeply felt connection to it. First of all, Esther apparently identifies with the view that the Rosenbergs were the victims of a judgment against the nonconforming views they held. Second, she identifies her very damaging initial set of shock treatments with the execution. The implication of the connection for Esther is that society does punish those who do not conform fully to its dictates. Later, as Esther comes to be more sure of herself, she at least is able to find ways to avoid her earlier victim role.

XVIII

Sula
(1973)
by Toni Morrison

Toni Morrison's *Sula* dramatizes the tension inherent in the individual's quest for independence and self-realization in a society that values conformity and offers limited opportunities for personal fulfillment. Specifically, many of her characters find it difficult to balance their own needs, desires, and expectations with those of family, friends, and community. At the same time, the novel emphasizes how compelling the desire for security and a sense of order can be. Even those characters who are the most independent seek to impose an order on their lives. But as *Sula* makes clear—and often in brutal ways—such order often is either illusory or temporary. Indeed, life in Morrison's world is characterized by unexpected changes over which the individual has little or no control.

The problem of achieving self-realization is magnified in the novel by the social context. As blacks in a small Ohio town in the first decades of the twentieth century, the male characters typically are denied jobs that would provide them with economic security and dignity. The women, who are expected to marry and have children, often are abandoned by their discontented husbands and must raise their children in poverty. Only menial jobs are available for men and women alike.

Only Sula, the title character, genuinely attempts to transcend convention, to change, and to accept change in others. She refuses the conventionally feminine role and remains true to the vision she and

Nel had created as they approached adolescence: "Because each had discovered years before that they were neither white nor male, and that all freedom and triumph were forbidden to them, they had set about creating something else to be."[1] In time, Sula leaves Medallion. Determined to "live in this world" on her own terms (p. 123), without seeking or needing security, she attends college, travels from city to city, and takes a series of lovers whom she has no intention of marrying. But although Sula's courage in remaining true to herself seems admirable within the novel, Morrison suggests that Sula carries her concern with self too far. Like Camus's Meursault, she lacks all "moral sense." Because she believes that she can count neither on herself nor on others, she fails to assume responsibility of any sort. The result is that, like Meursault, she brings a great deal of hurt and damage to the lives of others and she herself dies alienated and alone.

In contrast, Nel comes to conform fully. Swayed by her mother's hopes and Jude's apparent need for her, Nel gives up her childhood dream of travel and independence in favor of marriage. For her mother, Helene, Nel's wedding is "the culmination of all she had been, thought, or done in the world" (p. 68). Nel's life becomes contented if unexciting. She and Jude have three children, and Jude works as a waiter in the hotel.

After Sula casually seduces Jude, Nel is devastated. At this point their now very different value systems clash. Nel cannot understand how her best friend could destroy her marriage and the structure of her life. Sula, incapable of understanding possessive love at this point in her life, is angered by Nel's response. She feels betrayed by what she sees as Nel's conformity and her need for security:

> Now Nel was one of *them.* One of the spiders whose only thought was the next rung of the web, who dangled in dark dry places suspended by their own spittle, more terrified of the free fall than the snake's breath below.... But alive was what they, and now Nel, did not want to be. Too dangerous. Now Nel belonged to the town and all of its ways. She had given herself over to them, and the flick of their tongues would drive her back into her little dry corner where she would cling to her spittle high above the breath of the snake and the fall. [pp. 103–104]

Ironically, it is Nel not Sula who eventually evolves the most. By the end of the novel, Nel gains consciousness and more fully accepts responsibility for her earlier actions. Implicitly, she is able to forgive Sula as she understands their likenesses. In this way, the novel becomes Nel's book at least as much as Sula's, although in a larger sense it is about the complexities of friendship most of all.

Many of the other characters are as alienated as Sula. But unlike Sula, many of them did not make conscious choices. Instead, like Nel, they were at various times victims of circumstances over which they had little or no control. With these characters, Morrison explores the impact of a lack of choice. Her conclusion, like that of such writers as Twain, Faulkner, and Camus before her, is that oppression and powerlessness often lead to violence directed either against the self or others.

Moral and Values Questions

General Questions: Guide to Reading

1. What is the source of an individual's values?
2. What are the limitations that being part of a community necessarily imposes on the individual? What are the dangers for both the individual and the community if an individual attempts to live totally outside its moral boundaries?
3. What factors conspire to make people conform? What is the price of nonconformity?
4. What factors go into making someone fulfilled? What is the effect on the individual who is denied outlets for expression and opportunities for self-realization? for fulfilling work? for self-respect? What happens to people who are not given love?
5. What opportunities for fulfilling work, respect, and self-realization existed for black people in a town like Medallion, Ohio, in the first four decades of this century?
6. What is the relationship between oppression and violence?
7. Repeatedly, Morrison suggests, people need to have a sense of control over their lives. What do people conventionally do to achieve this sense of control? How do people typically attempt to create order if their lives promise none?
8. How do people live with the knowledge of death's inevitability?

Questions for Discussions, Papers, Exams

1. What is the function of National Suicide Day?
2. Discuss the events leading to Chicken Little's death. In particular, take into account the impact for Sula of overhearing her mother's

remark to her friends, "I love Sula. I just don't like her. That's the difference" (p. 49). Also take into account the symbolic implications and sexual language of the long passage describing Nel and Sula's play with the twigs preceding Chicken Little's appearance (pp. 49–50).

3. What does Eva mean when she accuses Nel of killing Chicken Little, telling her: "You. Sula. What's the difference. You was there. You watched, didn't you" (p. 145).
4. What does Nel mean when she fears that she will become like custard?
5. Does Sula betray her own values when she falls in love with Ajax?
6. What are the implications of Sula's affair with Jude and of her putting Eva in a nursing home?
7. Why does Sula's nonconformity arouse so much ire in the community but have such a salutary effect on the actions of her neighbors?
8. What is the function of the Deweys?
9. What is the significance of Sula's birthmark? Why does it mean different things to different people?[2]

The Need to Order Experience

After Shadrack's experience in the war, he loses all memory of his past. Because he is totally without roots and without values derived from "tribe" or "source," he must define himself. As Morrison characterizes him:

> Twenty-two years old, weak, hot, frightened, not daring to acknowledge the fact that he didn't even know who or what he was . . . with no past, no language, no tribe, no source, no address book, no comb, no pencil, no clock, no pocket handkerchief, no rug, no bed, no can opener, no faded postcard, no soap, no key, no tobacco pouch, no soiled underwear and nothing nothing nothing to do. [p. 10]

What Shadrack is aware of is the horror and unexpected nature of death. Because he needs a way "to order and focus experience" and to make "a place for fear as well as a way of controlling it," Shadrack invents National Suicide Day. His hope is "that if one day a year were devoted to [death], everybody could get it out of the way and the rest of the year would be safe and free" (p. 12).

Others in the community similarly attempt to order experience. Like Shadrack, if they can incorporate the unexpected or the unusual into "the fabric of life" (p. 14), they can live with it. For instance, although initially they feared Shadrack, "once the people understood the boundaries and the nature of his madness, they could fit him, so to speak, into the scheme of things" (p. 13). They assimilate National Suicide Day in much the same way: "In fact they had simply stopped remarking on the holiday because they had absorbed it into their thoughts, into their language, into their lives" (p. 13). Sula they accommodate by defining as a "roach" and a "bitch" (p. 97). In fact, they go another step. Believing Sula to be evil, the townspeople embrace the good in order to separate themselves from her. Teapot's once negligent mother, for example, becomes devoted to her son because she believes Sula intended to harm him. The wives in the town similarly begin to cherish their husbands after Sula discards them.

Eva is perhaps the most conscious of how a negative force can bring a positive order to life. When she begins to feel hatred for her former husband BoyBoy, her life takes on a new meaning:

> Knowing that she would hate him long and well filled her with pleasant anticipation, like when you know you are going to fall in love with someone and you wait for the happy signs. Hating BoyBoy, she could get on with it, and have the safety, the thrill, the consistency of that hatred as long as she wanted or needed it to define and strengthen her or protect her from routine vulnerabilities. [p. 31]

Nel, too, seeks order in her life, a need she first recognizes on her train journey to New Orleans with her mother. Until that moment, Nel had seen Helene as a genuinely solid person because she had earned the respect of her community and always behaved with dignity. But when the white conductor insults Helene for entering the wrong train car, Helene acts in a demeaning way. She becomes obsequious and smiles "dazzlingly and coquettishly at the salmon-colored face of the conductor" who had just told her, "We don't 'low no mistakes on this train. Now git your butt on in there" (p. 18). Nel's response is terror for she believes that her mother has become "custard," without substance at all. And, Nel reasons, if her mother "were really custard, then there was the chance that Nel was too" (p. 19).

In time, Nel learns with even more pain that there is no way to ensure that life will not bring changes. When she discovers Sula and Jude making love, she is reminded of the scene on the train. With anguish, she decides that Jude's "eyes looked like the soldiers' that time on the train when my mother turned to custard" (p. 91). Nel now rejects Sula's belief that "the real hell of Hell is that it is forever" (p. 92). Rather, she is convinced: "Sula was wrong. Hell ain't things lasting forever. Hell is change. Not only did men leave and children grow up and die, but even the misery didn't last. One day she wouldn't even have that. This very grief that had twisted her into a curve on the floor and flayed her would be gone. She would lose that too" (p. 93).

Sula: The Need for Change

Sula represents a very different stance. Determined to embrace change, she sees her own inconsistency as a virtue. She also refuses to assume responsibility for the impact of her actions on others. Specifically: "She lived out her days exploring her own thoughts and emotions, giving them full reign, feeling no obligation to please anybody unless their pleasure pleased her. As willing to feel pain as to give pain, to feel pleasure as to give pleasure, hers was an experimental life" (p. 102).

Sula even denies the validity of Nel's hurt. She explains to her best friend that she slept with her husband because "there was this space in front of me, behind me, in my head. Some space. And Jude filled it up. That's all. He just filled up the space" (p. 124). When Nel, whose life has been altered irrevocably by Sula's whim, protests, Sula is adamant: "It matters, Nel, but only to you. Not to anybody else. Being good to somebody is just like being mean to somebody. Risky. You don't get nothing for it" (pp. 124–25).

Only with Ajax does Sula experience possessive love. Only with him is she tempted to conform to the conventionally feminine role. She puts a green ribbon in her hair, wears perfume, and cleans her house. But because Ajax, too, values change and rejects security, he leaves her. The relationship and its ending make Sula decide that she has now experienced everything life offers. Determined to take control of her own life, she justifies her actions to Nel by insisting, "My lonely is *mine*" (p. 123). Morrison also suggests that Sula wills her own death. After her affair with Ajax, Sula decides, "There aren't any more new songs and I have sung all the ones there are" (p. 118). Shortly after that, Sula Peace, at the age of thirty, dies.

It is clear within the novel that Sula's amorality stems from the fact that her childhood gave her "no center, no speck around which to grow" (pp. 102–103). Like Shadrack, Sula had no source of values. In addition, she had been devastated by two experiences: her mother's comment that she loved her but didn't like her, and her responsibility for Chicken Little's death.[3] Since those episodes, Sula had done only what she herself desired:

ever since her mother's remarks sent her flying up those stairs, ever since her one major feeling of responsibility had been exorcised on the bank of a river with a closed place in the middle. The first experience taught her there was no other that you could count on; the second that there was no self to count on either. [pp. 102–103]

In addition, Sula's life offered her no outlets for her "idle imagination":

Had she paints, or clay, or knew the discipline of the dance, or strings; had she anything to engage her tremendous curiosity and her gift for metaphor, she might have exchanged the restlessness and preoccupation with whim for an activity that provided her with all she yearned for. And like any artist with no art form, she became dangerous. [p. 105]

It is for these reasons that Sula was able to find pleasure in moments of pain for others and was able to assert herself despite the cost to those who cared about her. She thus watched her mother burn to death because she "was thrilled" (p. 127). She was able to put the healthy, alert Eva in a dreadful nursing home without regret. She could break up Nel's marriage without empathy. She even realized that she might have hurt Ajax simply out of curiosity.

Sula's moment of death, however, suggests that the human connection is far more important to her than she realized. Although she earlier refused to apologize to Nel, she thinks with apparent regret that Nel will "never remember the days when we were two throats and one eye and we had no price" (p. 126). And as she dies, soothed by the thought that death would bring her "a sleep of water always,"[4] Sula thinks of Nel one more time, wanting to communicate with her: "'Well, I'll be damned,' she thought, 'it didn't even hurt. Wait'll I tell Nel' " (p. 128).

Sula is wrong that Nel will not remember their closeness. Twenty-five years later, Nel recognizes that she was very much like Sula. When Eva confronts Nel with her knowledge that Nel, too, "watched" Chicken Little's drowning, Nel for the first time faces her own responsibility in that episode. She recognizes that it had been she and not Sula who had made the decision not to go for help and not to tell anyone later. She also recognizes that she had found an almost sexual pleasure in watching the death. Like Sula, who had been thrilled watching Hannah burn to death, Nel realizes that Chicken's death brought her "the tranquillity that follows a joyful stimulation" (p. 146). For the first time, the gray ball that has been haunting Nel since she found Sula and Jude together dissipates. Even more significantly, Nel understands that it has been the end of her friendship with Sula, even more than her loss of Jude, that she has been mourning.

Racism, Alienation, and Violence

The imagery of the novel's opening paragraph suggests just how much the lives of the black people of Medallion have been thwarted by the actions of the whites: "In that place where they tore the nightshade and blackberry patches from their roots to make room for the Medallion City Golf Course, there was once a neighborhood. . . . It is called the suburbs now, but when black people lived there it was called the Bottom" (p. 3).

The dangers of being black are evident throughout the novel. Helene's vulnerability on the train reveals that her standing in the black community has no relevance to how she is treated by whites. The response of the white bargeman to Chicken Little's body, the police treatment of Ajax and his friends when they visit the jailed Tar Baby, and the refusal of whites to hire blacks for hard labor all point to ways in which blacks were denied their humanity.

Several of the men are destroyed because life in Medallion denies them dignity and self-worth. Jude is refused fulfilling work because of his blackness. Thus, he marries Nel believing that a family will give his life some value. He decides that without Nel "he was a waiter hanging around a kitchen like a woman. With her he was head of a household pinned to an unsatisfactory job out of necessity. The two of them together would make one Jude" (p. 71).

Later, however, still bitter about his demeaning work life, Jude leaves Nel and their children for Sula. Then, when she discards him, he flees Medallion for Detroit, where he buys but never sends birthday cards to his sons. BoyBoy, Eva's husband, years earlier had accepted his own "defeat" and left his family for women who "reminded Eva of Chicago" (p. 131).

Such impotence often leads to alienation. For instance, Shadrack and Plum are both psychologically destroyed by World War I. Shadrack is "blasted and permanently astonished" by the horror of the unexpected and violent deaths occurring around him. He retreats into his own shack, entering the world only for National Suicide Day and his twice-weekly effort to sell fish. The rest of the time "he was drunk, loud, obscene, funny and outrageous. But he never touched anybody, never fought, never caressed" (p. 13). In other words, with the exception of his devotion to his memory of Sula on the day of Chicken Little's death, Shadrack has no genuine human contact. Plum similarly returns home from the war disturbed and a heroin addict. He spends most of his time alone in his room. Tar Baby, for reasons no one knows, similarly has retreated to his room in order to drink himself to death.

Others translate their impotence and alienation to violence, sometimes directed at themselves and sometimes at others. Eva is reputed to have amputated her own leg in order to gain the insurance money that would feed and shelter her children. Sula cuts off her own fingertip when she and Nel are threatened with physical danger from some white boys. Eva sets Plum on fire in response to her sense of helplessness at his drug addiction. Sula and Nel make no effort to save Chicken Little when Sula throws the child into the water. Indeed, as noted earlier and as both Nel and Sula recognize, in this world violence sometimes even brings pleasure.[5]

Morrison presents such violence with almost chilling matter-of-factness. Although she does not condone it, she suggests that in a world where poverty prevails and few genuine options for a fulfilled life exist, violence and pain are almost inevitable. Certainly the black people who live in the Bottom of Medallion believe that their negative lot in life is "God's will." In fact, many of them are convinced "that the only way to avoid the Hand of God is to get in it" (p. 56). This belief in turn prompts them to let evil "run its course." As Morrison explains,

> What was taken by outsiders to be slackness, slovenliness or even generosity was in fact a full recognition of the legitimacy of forces other than good ones. They did not believe doctors could heal—for them, none ever had done so. They did not believe death was accidental—life might be, but death was deliberate. They did not believe Nature was ever askew—only inconvenient. . . . The purpose of evil was to survive it and they determined (without ever knowing they had made up their minds to do it) to survive floods, white people, tuberculosis, famine and ignorance. They knew anger well but not despair, and they didn't stone sinners for the same reason they didn't commit suicide—it was beneath them. [p. 78]

It is not surprising then that the black people of Medallion become victims of their own pent-up rage. At the end of the novel, they attempt to destroy the tunnel to the New River Road, on which the men were not allowed to work. Indeed, the tunnel represented to them all their poverty and pain:

> Their hooded eyes swept over the place where their hope had lain since 1927. There was the promise: leaf-dead. The teeth unrepaired, the coal credit cut off, the chest pains unattended, the school shoes

unbought, the rush-stuffed mattresses, the broken toilets, the lean-
ing porches, the slurred remarks and the staggering childish malevolence of their employers. . . . Old and young, women and children,
lame and hearty, they killed as best they could, the tunnel they were
forbidden to build. [p. 138]

In the process, many of them died as well. Nevertheless, it should be
stressed that despite its bleakness, *Sula* in many ways is a celebration of
love and responsibility. Eva's love for her children, Hannah's love for
men, Nel's ultimate ability to love Sula and to come to terms with
herself, all are presented as affirmative and sustaining. In contrast, it is
the absence of love and the failure of responsibility that so often bring
devastation.

The Deweys and Sula's Birthmark

The Deweys become literal manifestations of the ways in which what
Ralph Ellison calls invisibility determines an individual's sense of self
and place in the world. Because Eva sees the Deweys as being alike and
gives them the same name, they begin to perceive themselves as one.
Although they are of different ages, coloring, and physical characteris-
tics, others eventually cannot tell them apart either.

Sula's birthmark similarly suggests how visibility is in the eye of the
beholder. When she is a child and unthreatening to family, friends, or
community, the birthmark on her eye seems "shaped something like a
stemmed rose" (p. 45). When Jude finds her seductive, the birthmark
reminds him of a "copperhead" (p. 89). For the town, however, the
birthmark has a negative cast, and after Sula alienates the community,
it clears up "the meaning of the birthmark over her eye; it was not a
stemmed rose, or a snake, it was Hannah's ashes marking her from the
very beginning" (p. 99). Only Shadrack continues to see the birthmark
as positive, thinking, "She had a tadpole over her eye, that was how he
knew she was a friend—she had the mark of the fish he loved" (p. 134).

Appendix
Notes
Bibliography
Index

APPENDIX
Suggested Course Themes

THE COURSE THEMES LISTED BELOW all lend themselves to a consideration of moral and values questions. I have included in each of them
both works discussed in this volume and others which I have found
effective in my own classrooms. Quite obviously, neither the topics I
suggest nor the books I recommend are definitive in any way. An
extraordinary number of other works might be chosen instead of or in
addition to these works. By the same token, many of the works listed
could be taught under many and sometimes all of the other themes.

I. Civilization versus Wilderness
   a. *Walden,* Henry David Thoreau
   b. *The Scarlet Letter,* Nathaniel Hawthorne
   c. "Young Goodman Brown," Nathaniel Hawthorne
   d. *Adventures of Huckleberry Finn,* Mark Twain
   e. *Heart of Darkness,* Joseph Conrad
   f. *The Trial,* Franz Kafka
   g. *In Our Time* (especially "Big Two-Hearted River"),
      Ernest Hemingway
   h. *Death of a Salesman,* Arthur Miller
   i. *Lord of the Flies,* William Golding

j. *Deliverance,* James Dickey

k. *Surfacing,* Margaret Atwood

II. Individual versus Society
   a. *Pride and Prejudice,* Jane Austen
   b. "Civil Disobedience," Henry David Thoreau
   c. *The Scarlet Letter,* Nathaniel Hawthorne
   d. *The Yellow Wallpaper,* Charlotte Perkins Gilman
   e. "Rocking Horse Winner," D. H. Lawrence
   f. *Portrait of the Artist as a Young Man,* James Joyce
   g. *Light in August,* William Faulkner
   h. *The Stranger,* Albert Camus
   i. *Native Son,* Richard Wright
   j. *The Bell Jar,* Sylvia Plath
   k. *One Flew Over the Cuckoo's Nest,* Ken Kesey
   l. *Sula,* Toni Morrison

III. Search for Self
   a. *Death of Ivan Ilych,* Leo Tolstoy
   b. *Madame Bovary,* Gustave Flaubert
   c. *The Awakening,* Kate Chopin
   d. *A Doll's House,* Henrik Ibsen
   e. *The Metamorphosis,* Franz Kafka
   f. *The Dubliners,* James Joyce
   g. *To the Lighthouse,* Virginia Woolf
   h. *The Great Gatsby,* F. Scott Fitzgerald
   i. "Barn Burning," William Faulkner
   j. *Go Tell It on the Mountain,* James Baldwin
   k. "Everything That Rises Must Converge," Flannery O'Connor
   l. *The Bluest Eye,* Toni Morrison
   m. *Raisin in the Sun,* Lorraine Hansberry
   n. *The Woman Warrior,* Maxine Hong Kingston

IV. Responsibility
   a. *The Scarlet Letter,* Nathaniel Hawthorne
   b. "Bartleby the Scrivener," Herman Melville
   c. *Billy Budd,* Herman Melville
   d. *The Turn of the Screw,* Henry James
   e. *Daisy Miller,* Henry James
   f. *Heart of Darkness,* Joseph Conrad
   g. *The Awakening,* Kate Chopin
   h. *Mrs. Dalloway,* Virginia Woolf

i. "Barn Burning" and "Dry September," William Faulkner
j. *A Streetcar Named Desire,* Tennessee Williams
k. *Catch-22,* Joseph Heller
l. *Invisible Man,* Ralph Ellison
m. *Song of Solomon,* Toni Morrison
n. *Sophie's Choice,* William Styron

V. Consciousness
   a. *Death of Ivan Ilych,* Leo Tolstoy
   b. *Notes from Underground,* Fedor Dostoevsky
   c. *The Metamorphosis,* Franz Kafka
   d. *In Our Time,* Ernest Hemingway
   e. *Portrait of the Artist as a Young Man,* James Joyce
   f. *The Stranger,* Albert Camus
   g. *Waiting for Godot,* Samuel Beckett
   h. *The Crucible,* Arthur Miller
   i. *Invisible Man,* Ralph Ellison
   j. *Who's Afraid of Virginia Woolf,* Edward Albee
   k. *The Golden Notebook,* Doris Lessing
   l. *Something Happened,* Joseph Heller

VI. Literature of Madness
   a. *Hamlet,* William Shakespeare
   b. *King Lear,* William Shakespeare
   c. *The Turn of the Screw,* Henry James
   d. *The Yellow Wallpaper,* Charlotte Perkins Gilman
   e. "A Rose for Emily," William Faulkner
   f. "The Man Who Lived Underground," Richard Wright
   g. *A Streetcar Named Desire,* Tennessee Williams
   h. *The Bell Jar,* Sylvia Plath
   i. *One Flew Over the Cuckoo's Nest,* Ken Kesey
   j. *Pale Fire,* Vladimir Nabokov

VII. Black American Individual
   a. *Adventures of Huckleberry Finn,* Mark Twain
   b. *Their Eyes Were Watching God,* Zora Neale Hurston
   c. "Dry September," William Faulkner
   d. *Native Son,* Richard Wright
   e. "The Man Who Lived Underground," Richard Wright
   f. *Go Down, Moses,* William Faulkner
   g. *Invisible Man,* Ralph Ellison
   h. *Go Tell It on the Mountain,* James Baldwin

    i.   *Raisin in the Sun,* Lorraine Hansberry

    j.   *Sula,* Toni Morrison

VIII. Images of Women

    a.   *Pride and Prejudice,* Jane Austen

    b.   *The Scarlet Letter,* Nathaniel Hawthorne

    c.   *Daisy Miller,* Henry James

    d.   *Madame Bovary,* Gustave Flaubert

    e.   *A Doll's House,* Henrik Ibsen

    f.   *The Awakening,* Kate Chopin

    g.   *The Yellow Wallpaper,* Charlotte Perkins Gilman

    h.   *To the Lighthouse,* Virginia Woolf

    i.   *Mrs. Dalloway,* Virginia Woolf

    j.   *A Streetcar Named Desire,* Tennessee Williams

    k.   *Raisin in the Sun,* Lorraine Hansberry

    l.   *The Bell Jar,* Sylvia Plath

    m. *Sula,* Toni Morrison

Notes

Preface

1. For a detailed discussion of national surveys, see chapter one of this book and also: Arthur Levine, *When Dreams and Heroes Died: A Portrait of Today's College Student* (San Francisco: Jossey-Bass, 1980). Much of my information about faculty opinion has come to me directly, either in personal conversations or in written correspondence after I published an essay expressing my concern that students were indifferent to moral and values questions ("All's Not Well Aboard the 'Indomitable,' " *Chronicle of Higher Education,* October 3, 1977) and after I moderated a panel, "Literature and Values," at the December 1978 Modern Language Association Convention, New York. I talked to or heard from several hundred teachers.

2. See Levine, *When Dreams and Heroes Died;* also Christopher Lasch, *The Culture of Narcissism* (New York: Warner Books, 1979); Peter Marin, "The New Narcissism," *Harpers,* October 1975, pp. 45–46; and Tom Wolfe, "The 'Me' Decade and the Third Great Awakening," *New York,* August 1976, pp. 26–40.

3. Levine, *When Dreams and Heroes Died,* pp. 60–66.

4. Jack Magarrell, "Colleges Offered 15 Pct. More Courses This Year, Survey Finds: Remedial Classes Increase 22 Pct.," *Chronicle of Higher Education,* June 1, 1981, p. 1 and p. 8. I am not suggesting that teaching basic skills is not a necessity but rather that it has, in many situations, become the goal of education rather than the foundation for it.

Chapter I: Values and American Education

1. Joseph Heller, *Catch-22* (New York: Dell Publishing Co., 1962), p. 455.

2. I also discuss Weiss's course, student reaction to *Seven Beauties*, and Richard Hunt's essay on no-fault history in: Susan Resneck Parr, "The Teaching of Ethics in Undergraduate Nonethics Courses," in both *Ethics Teaching in Higher Education*, Daniel Callahan and Sissela Bok, eds. (New York: Plenum, 1980), and *Liberal Education*, 66, no. 1 (Spring 1980), pp. 51–66.

3. Richard M. Hunt, "No-Fault, Guilt-Free History," *The New York Times*, February 16, 1976, p. 19.

4. Levine, *When Dreams and Heroes Died*, p. 131.

5. Ibid., p. 103.

6. Ibid., p. 22.

7. Ibid., p. 113.

8. Arthur Levine, "Today's College Students: Going First Class on the Titanic," *Change*, March 1981, p. 17.

9. Thomas S. Barrows, Stephen F. Klein, and John L. D. Clark, eds., *What College Students Know and Believe about Their World* (New Rochelle, N.Y.: Change Magazine Press, 1981), p. 38.

10. Ibid., p. 39.

11. Levine, *When Dreams and Heroes Died*, p. 61.

12. Ibid., p. 64.

13. Levine, *When Dreams and Heroes Died*, pp. 60–62. Also see Magarrell, "Colleges Offered 15 pct. More Courses," p. 1 and p. 8.

14. Levine, *When Dreams and Heroes Died*, p. 112.

15. Once again, either after reading my *Chronicle* piece or attending the MLA "Literature and Values" special session, faculty members communicated these concerns to me either directly or in writing.

16. Erwin Chargaff, "Knowledge Without Wisdom," *Harpers*, May 1980, p. 47.

17. Paul Copperman, for example, makes this argument in *The Literacy Hoax: The Decline of Reading, Writing, and Learning in the Public Schools and What We Can Do About It* (New York: William Morrow, 1978).

18. Walter Kaufmann, *The Future of the Humanities* (New York: Readers Digest Press, 1977), p. xix.

19. See, for example, Frederick Rudolph, *Curriculum* (San Francisco: Jossey-Bass Publishers, 1978), pp. 250–64, and Council on Learning, *The Role of the Scholarly Disciplines* (New Rochelle, N.Y.: Change Magazine Press, 1980).

20. For example, see Sidney B. Simon, Leland W. Howe, and Howard Kirschenbaum, *Values Clarification: A Handbook of Practical Strategies for Teachers and Students* (New York: Hart Publishing Company, 1972).

21. *The Teaching of Ethics in Higher Education,* The Hastings Center (Hastings-on-Hudson, N.Y.: Institute of Society, Ethics, and Life Sciences, 1980), p. 22.

22. Dena Kleiman, "Parents' Groups Purging Schools of 'Humanist' Books and Classes," *New York Times,* May 17, 1981, p. 1 and p. 52. Also, see *American Educator,* American Federation of Teachers (Winter 1979) for examples of efforts in this direction. In an unpublished proposal, "Educating for Responsible Citizenship in a Democratic Society: An Interdisciplinary Approach to Teaching Traditional Values in the Public Schools," the AFT outlines its goal as indoctrinating students in what it refers to as "real morality."

23. Rudolph, *Curriculum,* passim.

24. Elizabeth Coleman, dean of the undergraduate division of the New School for Social Research, makes this point in " 'More' Has Not Meant 'Better' in the Organization of Academe," *Chronicle of Higher Education,* June 1, 1981, p. 48.

25. Diane Ravitch, *The Great School Wars: New York City, 1805–1973: A History of the Public Schools as Battlefield of Social Change* (New York: Basic Books, 1974), p. 404.

26. Rudolph, *Curriculum,* passim.

27. For a particularly vehement attack on this trend, see Mark Harris, "What Creative Writing Creates Is Students," *New York Times Book Review,* July 27, 1980, p. 25.

28. Frances FitzGerald, *America Revised: History Schoolbooks in the Twentieth Century* (Boston: An Atlantic Monthly Press Book, Little, Brown & Co., 1979), p. 46.

29. Beverly T. Watkins, "More Decisions on Purchasing Textbooks Now Made by Committees, Survey Shows," *Chronicle of Higher Education,* April 28, 1980, p. 1 and p. 4.

30. Ivan Illich, *Deschooling Society* (New York: Harper & Row 1971).

31. Jan Beyea, "Nuclear Reactors: How Safe Are They?," The Forum of the National Academy of Sciences, May 5, 1980, Washington, D.C.

Chapter II: Literature, Values, and Moral Choice

1. Recent work in moral development has raised an additional question: At what stage in a student's growth are certain issues appropriate and understandable? For a discussion of this question, see, e.g.: W. G. Perry, Jr., *Forms of Intellectual and Ethical Development in the College Years: A Scheme* (New York: Holt, Rinehart & Winston, 1970), and the work of Lawrence Kohlberg (e.g., "Education for Justice: A Modern Statement of the Platonic View," in N. F. Sizer and T. R. Sizer eds., *Moral Education: Five Lectures* [Cambridge, Mass.: Harvard University Press, 1970]; "Stages of Moral Development as a Basis for Moral Education," in C. M. Beck, B. S. Crittenden, and E. V. Sullivan, eds., *Moral*

Education [New York: Newman Press, 1971]; and "Moral States and Moralization," in T. Lickona ed., *Moral Development and Behavior* [New York: Holt, Rinehart and Winston, 1976]).

2. Erich Fromm, *Escape from Freedom* (New York: Avon Books, 1965).

3. Jean-Paul Sartre, *Existentialism and Human Emotions* (New York: The Wisdom Library, Philosophical Library, 1957).

4. Henry David Thoreau, "Civil Disobedience," in *Walden and Civil Disobedience* (Boston: Riverside Edition, Houghton Mifflin Co., 1960).

5. Rollo May, *Power and Innocence: A Search for the Sources of Violence* (New York: Delta Books, Dell Publishing Co., 1972) and *Love and Will* (New York: Laurel Edition, Dell Publishing Co., 1969).

6. Michael Novak, *The Experience of Nothingness* (New York: Harper Torchbooks, Harper & Row, 1970), p. 66 and *passim*.

7. Stanley Milgram, *Obedience to Authority* (New York: Harper Colophon Books, Harper & Row, 1975).

8. Novak, *The Experience of Nothingness*, p. 58.

9. Victor E. Frankl, *Man's Search for Meaning: An Introduction to Logotherapy* (New York: Pocket Books, Simon & Schuster, 1963).

10. Sigmund Freud, *Civilization and Its Discontents*, trans. James Strachey (New York: W. W. Norton & Co., 1961).

11. Reinhold Niebuhr, *Moral Man and Immoral Society* (New York: Charles Scribner's Sons, 1960).

12. Richard L. Rubenstein, *The Cunning of History: The Holocaust and the American Future* (New York: Harper Colophon Books, Harper & Row, 1978).

13. R. D. Laing, *The Politics of Experience* (New York: Ballantine Books, 1967).

14. May, *Power and Innocence*.

15. Like so much else, the question of how much teachers should make direct connections between the literature and contemporary life will vary from situation to situation. Certainly, I agree with Jean Smith, an Upper Darby, Pennsylvania, high school English teacher, that students "need practice in being reflective" about such connections and "need practice in applying abstract ideas to real life situations." The issue then becomes one of degree, and each teacher will have to make that judgment in terms of the needs of each particular group of students.

Chapter III: *The Scarlet Letter*

1. Nathaniel Hawthorne, *The Scarlet Letter and Selected Tales* (New York: Penguin Books, 1979), p. 75. All subsequent references to *The Scarlet Letter* will be incorporated in the body of the text.

Chapter IV: *Adventures of Huckleberry Finn (Tom Sawyer's Comrade)*

1. Mark Twain, *Adventures of Huckleberry Finn (Tom Sawyer's Comrade)*, (Boston: The Riverside Press, Houghton Mifflin Co., 1958), p. 2. All subsequent references to the novel will be incorporated in the body of the text.

2. Walter Blair, "The Composition of *Huckleberry Finn*," in *The Art of Huckleberry Finn*, ed. Hamlin Hill and Walter Blair (Scranton, Pa.: Chandler Publishing Co., 1969), pp. 1, 7.

3. Niebuhr, *Moral Man and Immoral Society*, p. xii.

4. May, *Power and Innocence;* Hannah Arendt, *On Violence* (New York: Harcourt Brace Jovanovich, 1969).

5. For a discussion of Huck's disguises and his "rebirth" as Tom Sawyer, see James M. Cox, "Remarks on the Sad Initiation of Huckleberry Finn," *The Sewanee Review*, 62 (1954), pp. 389–405, reprinted in *Interpretations of American Literature*, ed. Charles Feidelson, Jr., and Paul Brodtkorb, Jr. (New York: Oxford University Press, 1959), pp. 229–43.

6. Leo Marx, *The Machine in the Garden: Technology and the Pastoral Ideal in America* (New York: Oxford University Press, 1964), p. 340.

7. Leslie Fiedler argues that Huck and Jim approach a marital relationship rather than a child-parent one. See *Love and Death in the American Novel* (New York: Dell Publishing Co., 1966), pp. 352–54.

8. For discussions of the complexities of the ending of *Huckleberry Finn*, see, e.g., in Hill and Blair, eds., *The Art of Huckleberry Finn:* Lionel Trilling, "Introduction to *Huckleberry Finn*," pp. 501–11; William Van O'Connor, "Why *Huckleberry Finn* Is Not the Great American Novel," pp. 512–19; Frank Baladanza, "The Structure of *Huckleberry Finn*," pp. 520–28; and James M. Cox, "The Ending of *Huckleberry Finn*," pp. 547–54. Also see Leo Marx, "Mr. Eliot, Mr. Trilling, and Huckleberry Finn," *American Scholar*, 22 (Autumn 1953), pp. 423–40.

Chapter V: *The Death of Ivan Ilych*

1. Leo Tolstoy, *The Death of Ivan Ilych*, in *The Death of Ivan Ilych and Other Stories*, trans. Aylmer Maude (New York: A Signet Classic, The New American Library of World Literature, 1960), pp. 154–56. All subsequent references to the story will be incorporated in the body of the text.

2. William Barrett so describes Kierkegaard's tale in *Irrational Man: A Study in Existential Philosophy* (Garden City, N.Y.: Doubleday Anchor Books, Doubleday & Co., 1962), p. 4.

3. See Novak, *The Experience of Nothingness;* Fromm, *Escape from Freedom;* and Frankl, *Man's Search for Meaning.*

4. Elisabeth Kübler-Ross, *On Death and Dying* (New York: Macmillan Publishing Co., 1969).

Chapter VI: *The Yellow Wallpaper*

1. Charlotte Perkins Gilman, *The Yellow Wallpaper* (Old Westbury, N.Y.: The Feminist Press, 1973), p. 10. All subsequent references to the story will be incorporated in the body of the text.

2. For a full discussion of Charlotte Perkins Gilman's life, see "Private Woman, Public Woman: The Contradictions of Charlotte Perkins Gilman," by Carol Ruth Berkin, in Mary Beth Norton and Carol Ruth Berkin, *Women of America: A History* (Boston: Houghton Mifflin Co., 1979), pp. 150–79.

3. See the afterword to *The Yellow Wallpaper* by Elaine R. Hedges, pp. 37–41.

4. R. D. Laing, *The Politics of Experience.* It might also be useful in this regard to discuss Thoreau's assertion "If a man does not keep pace with his companions, perhaps it is because he hears a different drummer. Let him step to the music which he hears, however measured or far away." See Thoreau, *Walden and Civil Disobedience,* p. 222.

5. See Berkin and Norton, *Women of America: A History.*

6. See Phyllis Chesler, *Women and Madness* (New York: Avon Books, 1972).

7. I am indebted to Jean Smith for the insight that the wallpaper's contradictions mirror that of the narrator's.

8. Erich Fromm's distinction in *Escape from Freedom* of "freedom from" and "freedom to" may be useful here. The narrator in her insanity is freed *from* her past situation. However, she does not have any more freedom *to* express or be herself.

Chapter VII: *The Turn of the Screw*

1. Henry James, *The Turn of the Screw* in *The Turn of the Screw and Other Stories* (New York: A Signet Classic, New American Library, 1962), p. 380. All subsequent references to the novella will be incorporated in the body of the text.

2. See Martina Slaughter, "Edmund Wilson and *The Turn of the Screw,*" in Robert Kimbrough, ed., *The Turn of the Screw* (New York: W. W. Norton & Co., 1966), pp. 211–14.

3. Edna Kenton, "Henry James to the Ruminant Reader: *The Turn of the Screw*" in Kimbrough, ed., *Turn of the Screw*, pp. 209–11.

4. Slaughter, in Kimbrough, ed., *Turn of the Screw*, p. 210.

5. Ibid., p. 213.

6. Eric Solomon, "The Return of the Screw," in Kimbrough, ed, *Turn of the Screw*, pp. 237–45.

7. The governess's use of the word *blind* in this passage is typical of her ambiguous language and the ways in which James uses that language to suggest her possible unreliability as a narrator.

8. Once again, note the implications of the governess's language, particularly her reference to the word *grossness* and the possible play on language with the phrase *beautiful intercourse*. For a discussion of the ways the governess's background shapes her perceptions, see Leon Edel, "The Point of View," in Kimbrough, ed., *Turn of the Screw*, pp. 228–34.

9. Harold C. Goddard, "A Pre-Freudian Reading of *The Turn of the Screw*" in Kimbrough, ed., *Turn of the Screw* pp. 181–209.

Chapter VIII: *Heart of Darkness*

1. Joseph Conrad, *Heart of Darkness: An Authoritative Text, Backgrounds and Sources, Essays in Criticism,* ed. Robert Kimbrough (New York: W. W. Norton & Co. 1963), p. 59. All subsequent references to this work will be incorporated in the body of the text.

2. See Novak, *The Experience of Nothingness;* Fromm, *Escape From Freedom;* and Frankl, *Man's Search for Meaning.*

3. For a theoretical discussion of the complexities of truth telling and lying, see Sissela Bok, *Lying: Moral Choice in Public and Private Life* (New York: Pantheon Books, 1978).

4. For a discussion of the relationship of politics and language, see George Orwell, "Politics and the English Language," in *The Orwell Reader* (New York: Harcourt, Brace & Co., 1948).

Chapter IX: *The Awakening*

1. Kate Chopin, *The Awakening* (New York: Avon Books, 1972), p. 140. All subsequent references to this novel will be incorporated in the body of the text.

2. Per Seyersted, *Kate Chopin: A Critical Biography* (Baton Rouge: Louisiana State University Press, 1969), pp. 173–81.

3. Ibid., p. 178.

4. Seyersted, ed., *The Complete Works of Kate Chopin* (Baton Rouge: Louisiana State University Press, 1969), p. 14.

5. For example, see Kenneth Eble, "A Forgotten Novel," in *The Awakening: An Authoritative Text, Contexts, Criticism,* ed. Margaret Culley (New York: W. W. Norton & Co., 1976), pp. 165–70.

6. A. Alvarez. *The Savage God: A Study of Suicide* (New York: Bantam Books, 1972).

7. For a discussion of this moment, see Seyersted, *Kate Chopin,* p. 156.

8. See Culley, ed., *The Awakening: An Authoritative Text,* pp. 177–78.

9. In this conjunction, see Gilman, *The Yellow Wallpaper,* and Chesler *Women and Madness* (New York: Avon Books, 1973).

10. Culley, ed., *The Awakening: An Authoritative Text,* p. 118.

11. Evelyn Underhill, *Practical Mysticism* (New York: E. P. Dutton, 1915).

12. Ibid., p. 69.

13. Ibid., p. 169.

14. Ibid.

15. George Arms, "Contrasting Forces in the Novel," in Culley, ed., *The Awakening: An Authoritative Text,* p. 128.

16. Underhill, *Practical Mysticism,* p. 170.

17. James E. Miller, Jr., *A Critical Guide to "Leaves of Grass"* (Chicago: University of Chicago Press, 1957).

18. Chopin almost certainly was also influenced by Flaubert's *Madame Bovary,* and the two works might effectively be taught in conjunction with one another.

Chapter X: *The Metamorphosis*

1. Franz Kafka, *The Metamorphosis,* trans. Stanley Corngold (New York: Bantam Books, 1972), p. 3. All subsequent references to the story will be incorporated in the body of the text.

2. See Alvarez, *The Savage God,* and Albert Camus, *The Myth of Sisyphus and Other Essays* (New York: Vintage Books, 1955).

3. Camus, *The Myth of Sisyphus,* p. 5.

Chapter XI: *The Great Gatsby*

1. F. Scott Fitzgerald, *The Great Gatsby* (New York: Charles Scribner's Sons, 1953), p. 2. All subsequent references to the novel will be incorporated in the body of the text.

2. T. S. Eliot, *The Waste Land*, in *Selected Poems* (New York: Harbrace Paperback Library, 1964).

3. See Lawrence Chenoweth, *The American Dream of Success: The Search for Self in the Twentieth Century* (North Scituate, Mass.: Duxbury Press, 1974).

4. For a discussion of *Waste Land* imagery, see, e.g., John W. Bicknell, "The Waste Land of F. Scott Fitzgerald," *The Virginia Quarterly Review*, 30 (Autumn 1954), 556–72; reprinted in Kenneth Eble, ed., *F. Scott Fitzgerald* (New York: McGraw-Hill, 1973).

5. Eliot, *The Waste Land*, lines 131–34.

6. Gary J. Scrimgeour, "Against *The Great Gatsby*," in *Twentieth Century Interpretations of The Great Gatsby*, ed. Ernest Lockridge (Englewood Cliffs, N.J.: Prentice-Hall, 1968), p. 76.

7. In this passage, Fitzgerald seems to be playing with the concept of the transitoriness of nature, of "roses" in this instance, as well as of Daisy herself.

8. Walt Whitman, *Song of Myself*, in *Complete Poetry and Selected Prose*, ed. James E. Miller, Jr. (Boston: Houghton Mifflin Co., 1959), section 4.

Chapter XII: "Dry September"

1. William Faulkner, "Dry September," in *Selected Short Stories of William Faulkner* (New York: The Modern Library, 1961), p. 75. All subsequent references to the story will be incorporated in the body of the text.

2. For a discussion of violence, see May, *Power and Innocence*. For a discussion of the relationship of racism to repressed sexuality and violence, see Calvin C. Hernton, *Sex and Racism in America* (New York: Grove Press, 1965), and Eldridge Cleaver, *Soul on Ice* (New York: A Delta Book, Dell Publishing Co., 1968).

3. See, e.g., Niebuhr, *Moral Man and Immoral Society*, and Milgram, *Obedience to Authority*.

4. See W. J. Cash, *The Mind of the South* (New York: Vintage Books, 1941).

5. It is likely that Faulkner is punning in this passage in his use of "dark world." On the one hand, the blacks of Jefferson have been stricken. On the other hand, the world itself is a darker, bleaker place because of the horror and injustice of Will's murder.

6. T. S. Eliot, *The Waste Land*.

7. It might be useful to read "Dry September" in conjunction with "Barn Burning" (the next work to be discussed), "A Rose for Emily," and "That Evening Sun." Each deals in different ways with the question of how much responsibility any individual can and should assume for others. "A Rose for Emily" also explores the question of community responsibility.

Chapter XIII: "Barn Burning"

1. "Barn Burning," in William Faulkner, *Selected Short Stories*, p. 3. All subsequent references to the story will be incorporated in the body of the text.

2. Although Sarty himself is not consciously performing an act of civil disobedience or choosing violence over legal methods, the story does point to the complexities of such choices. It might be useful in this regard to discuss advocates of civil disobedience, on the one hand (e.g., Thoreau, Gandhi, and Martin Luther King), and those who believe violence is acceptable as a political act.

Chapter XIV: *The Stranger*

1. Conor Cruise O'Brien, *Albert Camus of Europe and Africa* (New York: The Viking Press, 1979), p. 19.

2. Albert Camus, *The Stranger,* trans. Stuart Gilbert (New York: The Viking Press, 1954), p. 120. All subsequent references to the novel will be incorporated in the body of the text.

3. O'Brien, *Albert Camus,* p. 19.

4. Richard Wright explores the same issue in *Native Son* and Norman Mailer does so in his portrayal of Gary Gilmore, *Executioner's Song* (Boston: Little, Brown & Co., 1980).

5. Camus may be suggesting here that Meursault's memory may on a deeply subconscious level have motivated him to act so that he himself would be executed. But Camus does nothing else in the novel to encourage this sort of psychoanalytic reading.

Chapter XV: *Invisible Man*

1. Ralph Ellison, *Invisible Man* (New York: Vintage Books, 1972), p. 567. All subsequent references to this novel will be incorporated in the body of the text.

2. See Irving Howe, "Black Boys and Native Sons," in *A World More Attractive* (New York: Horizon Press, 1963), pp. 98–122. Ellison's response appears in *Shadow and Act* (New York: Vintage Books, 1964), pp. 107–43. Also see the essays in *Ralph Ellison: A Collection of Critical Essays,* ed. John Hersey (Englewood Cliffs, N.J.: Prentice-Hall, 1974).

3. Ellison, *Shadow and Act,* Introduction.

4. Ibid., p. 21.

5. Hersey, *Ralph Ellison,* p. 18.

6. Ellison, *Shadow and Act,* p. 44.

7. Ibid., p. 38.

8. Ibid., p. 117.

9. Ibid., p. 140.

10. See, e.g., Rollo May, *Power and Innocence.*

11. See Howe, "Black Boys and Native Sons," and Ellison, *Shadow and Act,* pp. 107–43.

12. Ralph Ellison attended Tuskegee Institute with aspirations of becoming a symphonic composer. He was also a jazz musician. By his own account, reading *The Waste Land* during his sophomore year brought about his "real transition" (*Shadow and Act,* p. 159). At the end of his junior year, he voluntarily left Tuskegee, moved to New York, met Richard Wright, who became his literary mentor, and began his career as a writer.

13. Booker T. Washington, *Up from Slavery* (New York: Bantam Books, 1959), p. 159.

14. Ellison's depiction of the American Communist party in some ways reflects Richard Wright's disillusionment with the group, a disillusionment Wright suggests in *Native Son.*

15. Ellison uses the word *history* here in a dual sense meaning both a record of events and suggesting the Marxist concept of historical inevitability.

16. Ellison, *Shadow and Act,* p. 181. Ras's name suggests both "race" and the Rastaferians, a group of West Indians who believe that Haile Selassie was god and that, as one of the inmates explains in the Golden Day episode, Ethiopia would rule the world.

17. It is interesting to note that Ellison's full name is Ralph Waldo Ellison. When Emerson, in a reference to Whitman's Calamus poems, asks the invisible man to go to the Club Calamus with him, Ellison is suggesting young Emerson's homosexuality.

18. The phrase "I yam what I yam" is a pun on the translation of the Hebrew word for God, Yahweh, which means "I am what I am."

19. The Chtonian itself is a mythical name, referring to the underworld home of the gods. Note also other mythological allusions: to Sybil (the prophetess) and to Brother Jack as being like a Cyclops.

20. Ellison, *Shadow and Act,* p. 234.

21. Mark Twain, *Adventures of Huckleberry Finn,* p. 245. The catalog of possessions of the evicted couple is reminiscent of Twain's cataloging the Grangerford's possessions. The details reveal the characters' history and their values.

Chapter XVI: *Catch-22*

1. "An Impolite Interview with Joseph Heller," with Paul Krassner, *The Realist,* November 1962, pp. 18–31; reprinted in *Joseph Heller's Catch-22: A*

Critical Edition, ed. Robert M. Scotto (New York: A Delta Book, Dell Publishing Co., 1973), pp. 456–78. All future references to the Krassner interview will be to the Scotto edition. Heller's remarks about the morality of the novel can be found in ibid., p. 457.

2. Scotto, *Joseph Heller's Catch-22,* pp. 471–472.

3. Ibid., p. 458.

4. Joseph Heller, *Catch-22* (New York: Dell Publishing Co., 1962), p. 444. All subsequent references to the novel will be incorporated in the body of the text.

5. For a fuller discussion of the Eden imagery and its relationship to Heller's use of *Waste Land* imagery, see Susan Resneck Parr, "Everything Green Looked Black: *Catch-22* as an Inverted Eden," *Notes on Modern American Literature,* 4, no. 4 (Fall 1980), 7–10.

6. For a discussion of the relationship of sanity to morality, see R. D. Laing, *The Politics of Experience.*

7. Minna Doskow, "The Night Journey in *Catch-22," Twentieth Century Literature,* 12 (January 1967), 186–93; reprinted in Scotto, *Joseph Heller's Catch-22,* pp. 491–501.

8. Vance Ramsey, "From Here to Absurdity: Heller's *Catch-22,"* in *Seven Contemporary Authors: Essays on Cozzens, Miller, West, Golding, Heller, Albee, and Powers* (Austin: Univeristy of Texas Press, 1968), pp. 99–118; reprinted in *A "Catch-22" Casebook,* ed. Frederick Kiley and Walter McDonald (New York: Thomas Y. Crowell Co., 1973), pp. 228–29.

9. Heller here is satirizing Secretary of Defense Charles E. Wilson's statement during his confirmation hearings for his position in the Eisenhower administration that what was good for General Motors was good for the country.

10. Scotto, *Joseph Heller's Catch-22,* p. 459.

11. For a detailed picture of the blacklisting that occurred during the fifties, see Victor Navasky, *Naming Names* (New York: The Viking Press, 1980).

12. Genesis 3:5.

Chapter XVII: *The Bell Jar*

1. Sylvia Plath, *The Bell Jar* (New York: Bantam Books, 1972), p. 76. All subsequent references to the novel will be incorporated in the body of the text.

2. Laing, *The Politics of Experience.* For a discussion of Plath's own breakdown in similar terms, see Chesler, *Women and Madness.*

3. For a discussion of Plath's life, see Eileen Arid, *Sylvia Plath: Her Life and Work* (New York: Perennial Library, Harper & Row, 1973), and Nancy Hunter Steiner, *A Closer Look at Ariel: A Memory of Sylvia Plath* (New York: Popular Library, 1974). For a discussion of Plath's suicide, see A. Alvarez, *The Savage God.* Anne Sexton's tribute to Plath also would be illuminating in her

poem "Sylvia's Death" in *Live or Die* (Boston: Houghton Mifflin Co., 1966), as would Plath's own poetry.

4. Esther's reference to her own baby earlier in the novel (p. 3) suggests that in time she made the choice to be a mother. This is the only instance in the novel where Plath hints at Esther's future, but the moment may be meant to suggest that Esther has been able to integrate her writing and her wish for motherhood.

Chapter XVIII: *Sula*

1. Toni Morrison, *Sula* (New York: Bantam Books, 1973), p. 44. All subsequent references to the novel will be incorporated in the body of the text.

2. The novel is infused with Biblical symbolism. Although it is not pertinent to Morrison's exploration of moral and values questions, the novel is enriched by it. In particular, Morrison draws on the book of Daniel and the story of Shadrack, Daniel, and Nebuchadnezzar. Sula's birthmark puts her in contrast to Daniel, who was brought to Jerusalem because he was a child without blemish.

3. It is also likely that Plum's death affected Sula. Her voice apparently is the child's voice Eva hears on the staircase after she has set the fire (p. 41), and Sula notes the incident when she discusses Eva with Nel.

4. The word *always* is a significant one in the novel. When Sula and Nel fear that Shadrack has seen Chicken Little drown, Sula runs to his cabin. Shadrack, trying to tell her he will love her eternally, tells her "always." Sula apparently believes that he means he will always remember the drowning. After Sula's death, Shadrack realizes that his promise of eternity to Sula, like his hopes for National Suicide Day as a way of controlling death, was a misperception: "So he had been wrong. Terribly wrong. No 'always' at all. Another dying away of someone whose face he knew" (p. 135).

5. Throughout the novel, Morrison allies sexual language with violence and death. See the passages describing Nel and Sula's play before Chicken Little's death (pp. 49–50), Sula's sense of her lovemaking (pp. 105–106), and the recognition on Nel's part of the pleasure Chicken Little's drowning brought her.

Bibliography

ALVAREZ, A. *The Savage God: A Study of Suicide.* New York: Bantam Books, 1972.

AMERICAN FEDERATION OF TEACHERS. *American Educator* (Winter 1979).

ARENDT, HANNAH. *Eichmann in Jerusalem: A Report on the Banality of Evil.* New York: The Viking Press, 1963.

———. *On Violence.* New York: Harcourt Brace Jovanovich, 1969.

ARID, EILEEN. *Sylvia Plath: Her Life and Work.* New York: Perennial Library, Harper & Row, 1973.

BARRETT, WILLIAM. *Irrational Man: A Study in Existential Philosophy.* Garden City, N.Y.: Doubleday Anchor Books, Doubleday & Co., 1962.

BARROWS, THOMAS S., KLEIN, STEPHEN F., AND CLARK, JOHN L. D.; WITH NATHANIEL HARTSHORNE. *What College Students Know and Believe about Their World,* Education and the World View Series, V. New Rochelle, N.Y.: Change Magazine Press, 1981.

BERKIN, CAROL RUTH. "Private Woman, Public Woman: The Contradictions of Charlotte Perkins Gilman." In *Women of America: A History* by Mary Beth Norton and Carol Ruth Berkin. Boston: Houghton Mifflin Co., 1979.

BEYEA, JAN. "Nuclear Reactors: How Safe Are They?" The Forum of the National Academy of Sciences, Washington, D.C., May 5, 1980.

BICKNELL, JOHN W. "The Waste Land of F. Scott Fitzgerald." *The Virginia Quarterly Review,* 30 (Autumn 1954), pp. 556–72; reprinted in Eble, ED. *F. Scott Fitzgerald.*

BOK, DEREK. "Can Ethics Be Taught?" *Change* October 1976, pp. 26–30.

BOK, SISSELA. *Lying: Moral Choice in Public and Private Life.* New York: Pantheon Books, 1978.

BONHAM, GEORGE. "Education and the World View." *Change,* May–June 1980, pp. 2–7.

BREE, GERMAINE. ED. *Camus,* Twentieth Century Views. Englewood Cliffs, N.J.: Prentice-Hall, 1962.

CALLAHAN, DANIEL, AND BOK, SISSELA. *Ethics Teaching in Higher Education.* New York: Plenum, 1980.

———. "The Role of Applied Ethics in Learning." *Change,* September 1979, pp. 23–27.

CAMUS, ALBERT. *The Myth of Sisyphus and Other Essays,* trans. Justin O'Brien. New York: Vintage Books, 1955.

———. *The Stranger,* trans. Stuart Gilbert. New York: The Viking Press, 1954.

CASH, W. J. *The Mind of the South.* New York: Vintage Books, 1941.

CHARGAFF, ERWIN. "Knowledge Without Wisdom." *Harpers,* May 1980, pp. 4–48.

CHASE, ALSTON. *Group Memory: A Guide to College and Student Survival in the 1980s.* Boston: an Atlantic Monthly Press Book, Little, Brown & Co., 1980.

CHENOWETH, LAWRENCE. *The American Dream of Success: The Search for Self in The Twentieth Century.* North Scituate, Mass.: Duxbury Press, 1974.

CHESLER, PHYLLIS. *Women and Madness.* New York: Avon Books, 1973.

CHOPIN, KATE. *The Awakening.* New York: Avon Books, 1972.

CLEAVER, ELDRIDGE. *Soul on Ice.* New York: A Delta Book, Dell Publishing Co., 1968.

COLEMAN, ELIZABETH. " 'More' Has Not Meant 'Better' in the Organization of Academe." *Chronicle of Higher Education,* June 1, 1981, p. 48.

CONRAD, JOSEPH. *Heart of Darkness.* In *Heart of Darkness: An Authoritative Text, Backgrounds and Sources, Essays in Criticism,* ed. Robert Kimbrough. New York: W. W. Norton & Co., 1963.

COOKE, M. G. ED. *Modern Black Novelists,* Twentieth Century Views. Englewood Cliffs, N.J.: Prentice-Hall, 1971.

COPPERMAN, PAUL. *The Literacy Hoax: The Decline of Reading, Writing, and Learning in the Public Schools and What We Can Do About It.* New York: William Morrow & Co., 1978.

COUNCIL ON LEARNING. *The Role of the Scholarly Disciplines.* New Rochelle, N.Y.: Change Magazine Press, 1980.

COX, JAMES. "Remarks on the Sad Initiation of Huckleberry Finn." *The Sewanee Review,* 62 (1954), pp. 389–405; reprinted in Feidelson and Brodtkorb, *Interpretations of American Literature.*

CROWLEY, DONALD J., ED. *Nathaniel Hawthorne.* New York: McGraw-Hill, 1975.

CULLEY, MARGARET, ED. *The Awakening: An Authoritative Text, Contexts, Criticism.* New York: W. W. Norton & Co., 1976.

DELATTRE, D. J., AND BENNETT, W. J. "Where the Values Movement Goes Wrong." *Change,* February 1979, pp. 38–43.

DOSKOW, MINNA. "The Night Journey in *Catch-22.*" *Twentieth Century Literature,* 12 (January 1967), 186–93; reprinted in Scotto, ed. *Joseph Heller's Catch-22: A Critical Edition.*

EBLE, KENNETH. "A Forgotten Novel." In Culley, ed., *The Awakening: An Authoritative Text, Contexts, Criticism,* pp. 165–70.

————, ED. *F. Scott Fitzgerald.* New York: McGraw-Hill, 1973.

EDEL, LEON. "The Point of View." In Kimbrough, *The Turn of the Screw,* pp. 228–34.

ELIOT, T. S. *The Waste Land.* In *Selected Poems.* New York: Harbrace Paperback Library, 1964.

ELLISON, RALPH. *Invisible Man.* New York: Vintage Books, 1972.

————. *Shadow and Act.* New York: Vintage Books, 1964.

ERIKSON, E. H. *Childhood and Society.* New York: W. W. Norton & Co., 1963.

FAULKNER, WILLIAM. *Selected Short Stories of William Faulkner.* New York: The Modern Library, 1961.

FEIDELSON, CHARLES, JR., AND BRODTKORB, PAUL, JR., EDS. *Interpretations of American Literature.* New York: Oxford University Press, 1959.

FIEDLER, LESLIE. *Love and Death in the American Novel.* New York: Dell Publishing Co., 1966.

FITZGERALD, F. SCOTT. *The Great Gatsby.* New York: Charles Scribner's Sons, 1953.

FITZGERALD, FRANCES. *America Revised: History Schoolbooks in the Twentieth Century.* Boston: An Atlantic Monthly Press Book, Little, Brown & Co., 1979.

FRANKL, VICTOR E. *Man's Search for Meaning: An Introduction to Logotherapy.* New York: Pocket Books, Simon & Schuster, 1963.

FREUD, SIGMUND. *Civilization and Its Discontents,* trans. James Strachey. New York: W. W. Norton & Company, 1961.

FRIERE, PAULO. *Pedagogy of the Oppressed.* New York: Herder & Herder, 1970.

FROMM, ERICH. *Escape from Freedom.* New York: Avon Books, 1965.

GARDNER, JOHN. *On Moral Fiction.* New York: Basic Books, 1978.

GILMAN, CHARLOTTE PERKINS. *The Yellow Wallpaper,* afterword by Elaine R. Hedges. Old Westbury, N.Y.: The Feminist Press, 1973.

GODDARD, HAROLD C. "A Pre-Freudian Reading of *The Turn of the Screw.*" In Kimbrough, ed. *The Turn of the Screw,* pp. 181–209.

HAMALIAN, LEO, ED. *Franz Kafka.* New York: McGraw-Hill, n.d.

HARRIS, MARK. "What Creative Writing Creates Is Students." *New York Times Book Review,* July 27, 1980, p. 25.

THE HASTINGS CENTER. *The Teaching of Ethics in Higher Education.* Hastings-on-Hudson, N.Y.: Institute of Society, Ethics, and Life Sciences, 1980.

HAWTHORNE, NATHANIEL. *The Scarlet Letter and Selected Tales.* New York: Penguin Books, 1979.

HELLER, JOSEPH. *Catch-22.* New York: Dell Publishing Co., 1955.

HERNTON, CALVIN. *Sex and Racism in America.* New York: Grove Press, 1965.

HERSEY, JOHN, ED. *Ralph Ellison: A Collection of Critical Essays,* Twentieth Century Views. Englewood Cliffs, N.J.: Prentice-Hall, 1974.

HILL, HAMLIN, AND BLAIR, WALTER, EDS. *The Art of Huckleberry Finn.* Scranton, Pa.: Chandler Publishing Co., 1969.

HOFFMAN, DANIEL. *Form and Fable in American Fiction*. New York: Oxford University Press, 1965.

HOWE, IRVING. "Black Boys and Native Sons." In *A World More Attractive*. New York: Horizon Press, 1963, pp. 98–122.

HUNT, RICHARD. "No-Fault, Guilt-Free History." *The New York Times*, February 16, 1976, p. 19.

ILLICH, IVAN. *Deschooling Society*. New York: Harper & Row, 1971.

JAMES, HENRY. *The Turn of the Screw*. In *The Turn of the Screw and Other Stories*. New York: A Signet Classic, New American Library, 1962.

KAFKA, FRANZ. *The Metamorphosis*, trans. Stanley Corngold. New York: Bantam Books, 1972.

KAUFMANN, WALTER. *The Future of the Humanities*. New York: Readers Digest Press, 1977.

KAUL, A. N., ED. *Hawthorne*, Twentieth Century Views. Englewood Cliffs, N.J.: Prentice-Hall, 1966.

KENTON, EDNA. "Henry James to the Ruminant Reader: *The Turn of the Screw*." In Kimbrough, ed., *The Turn of the Screw*, pp. 209–11.

KILEY, FREDERICK, AND MCDONALD, WALTER, EDS. *A "Catch-22" Casebook*. New York: Thomas Y. Crowell Co., 1973.

KIMBROUGH, ROBERT, ED. *The Turn of the Screw*. New York: W. W. Norton & Co., 1966.

KIRSCHENBAUM, H., AND SIMON, S. B. *Readings in Values Clarification*. Minneapolis: Vinston Press, 1973.

KLEIMAN, DENA. "Parents' Groups Purging Schools of 'Humanist' Books and Classes." *New York Times*, May 17, 1981, p. 1 and p. 52.

KOHLBERG, L. "Education for Justice: A Modern Statement of the Platonic View." In N. F. Sizer and T. R. Sizer, eds., *Moral Education: Five Lectures*. Cambridge, Mass.: Harvard University Press, 1970.

———. "Moral States and Moralization." In *Moral Development and Behavior*. New York: Holt, Rinehart & Winston, 1976.

———. "Stages of Moral Development as a Basis for Moral Education." In C. M. Beck, B. S. Crittenden, and E. V. Sullivan, eds. *Moral Education*. New York: Newman Press, 1971.

KRASSNER, PAUL. "An Impolite Interview with Joseph Heller." *The Realist*, November 1962, pp. 18–31; reprinted in Scotto, ed., *Joseph Heller's Catch-22: A Critical Edition*.

KÜBLER-ROSS, ELISABETH. *On Death and Dying*. New York: Macmillan Co., 1969.

LAING, R. D. *The Politics of Experience*. New York: Ballantine Books, 1967.

LASCH, CHRISTOPHER. *The Culture of Narcissism: American Life in an Age of Diminishing Expectations*. New York: Warner Books, 1979.

LEVINE, ARTHUR. "Today's College Students: Going First Class on the Titanic." *Change*, March 1981, pp. 16–23.

————. *When Dreams and Heroes Died: A Portrait of Today's College Student.* San Francisco: Jossey-Bass, 1980.

LOCKRIDGE, ERNEST, ED. *Twentieth Century Interpretations of The Great Gatsby.* Englewood Cliffs, N.J.: Prentice-Hall, 1968.

MARGARRELL, JACK. "Colleges Offered 15 Pct. More Courses This Year, Survey Finds: Remedial Classes Increase 22 Pct." *Chronicle of Higher Education,* 1 June 1981, p. 1 and p. 8.

MARIN, PETER. "The New Narcissism." *Harpers Magazine,* October 1975, pp. 45–46.

MARX, LEO. *The Machine in the Garden: Technology and the Pastoral Ideal in America.* New York: Oxford University Press, 1964.

————. "Mr. Eliot, Mr. Trilling, and Huckleberry Finn." *American Scholar,* 22 (Autumn 1953), 423–40.

MAY, ROLLO. *Love and Will.* New York: Laurel Edition, Dell Publishing Co., 1969.

————. *Power and Innocence: A Search for the Sources of Violence.* New York: Delta Books, Dell Publishing Co., 1972.

MILGRAM, STANLEY. *Obedience to Authority.* New York: Harper Colophon Books, Harper & Row, 1975.

MILLER, JAMES E., JR. *A Critical Guide to "Leaves of Grass."* Chicago: University of Chicago Press, 1957.

MODERN LANGUAGE ASSOCIATION. *Options for the Teaching of English: The Undergraduate Curriculum.* New York: Modern Language Association, 1975.

MORRISON, TONI. *Sula.* New York: Bantam Books, 1973.

NAVASKY, VICTOR S. *Naming Names.* New York: The Viking Press, 1980.

NIEBUHR, REINHOLD. *Moral Man and Immoral Society.* New York: Charles Scribner's Sons, 1960.

NOVAK, MICHAEL. *The Experience of Nothingness.* New York: Harper Torchbooks, Harper & Row, 1970.

O'BRIEN, CONOR CRUISE. *Albert Camus of Europe and Africa.* New York: The Viking Press, 1979.

O'CONNELL, BARRY. "Where Does Harvard Lead Us?" *Change,* September 1978, pp. 35–40, 61.

ORWELL, GEORGE. "Politics and the English Language." In *The Orwell Reader.* New York: Harcourt, Brace & Co., 1948.

PARR, SUSAN RESNECK. "All's Not Well Aboard the 'Indomitable.' " *Chronicle of Higher Education* (October 3, 1977).

————. "Everything Green Looked Black: *Catch-22* as an Inverted Eden." *Notes on Modern American Literature,* 4, no. 4 (Fall 1980), 7–10.

————. "The Teaching of Ethics in Undergraduate Nonethics Courses." In *Ethics Teaching in Higher Education,* ed. Daniel Callahan and Sissela Bok.

New York: Plenum, 1980; and in *Liberal Education*, 66, no. 1 (Spring 1980), pp. 51–66.

PERRY, WILLIAM, JR. *Forms of Intellectual and Ethical Development in the College Years: A Scheme.* New York: Holt, Rinehart & Winston, 1970.

PLATH, SYLVIA. *The Bell Jar.* New York: Bantam Books, 1972.

RAMSEY, VANCE. "From Here to Absurdity: Heller's *Catch-22.*" In Kiley and McDonald, eds. *A "Catch-22" Casebook,* pp. 231–36.

RATH, L. E., HARMON, M., AND SIMON, S. B. *Values and Teaching.* Columbus, Ohio: Merrill, 1966.

RAVITCH, DIANE. *The Great School Wars: New York City, 1805–1973. A History of the Public Schools as Battlefield of Social Change.* New York: Basic Books, 1974.

REPORT OF THE COMMISSION ON THE HUMANITIES. *The Humanities in American Life.* Berkeley: University of California Press, 1980.

THE ROCKEFELLER FOUNDATION. *Working Papers: Toward the Restoration of the Liberal Arts Curriculum.* New York: The Rockefeller Foundation, June 1979.

RUBENSTEIN, RICHARD L. *The Cunning of History: The Holocaust and the American Future.* New York: Harper Colophon Books, Harper & Row, 1978.

RUDOLPH, FREDERICK. *Curriculum.* San Francisco: Jossey-Bass, 1978.

SANFORD, JOHN. *The Invisible Partners: How the Male and Female in Each of Us Affects our Relationships.* New York: Paulist Press, 1980.

SARTRE, JEAN-PAUL. *Existentialism and Human Emotions.* New York: The Wisdom Library, Philosophical Library, 1957.

SCIMGEOUR, GARY J. "Against *The Great Gatsby.*" In *Twentieth Century Interpretations of The Great Gatsby,* ed. Ernest Lockridge. Englewood Cliffs, N.J.: Prentice-Hall, 1968.

SCOTTO, ROBERT M., ED. *Joseph Heller's Catch-22: A Critical Edition.* New York: A Delta Book, Dell Publishing Co., 1973.

SCULLY, MALCOLM G. "Taking Foreign Languages Out of the Classroom." *Chronicle of Higher Education,* September 22, 1980, p. 9.

SEXTON, ANNE. *Live or Die.* Boston: Houghton Mifflin Co., 1966.

SEYERSTED, PER, ED. *The Complete Works of Kate Chopin.* Baton Rouge: Louisiana State University Press, 1969.

———. *Kate Chopin: A Critical Biography.* Baton Rouge: Louisiana State University Press, 1969.

SIMON, SIDNEY B., HOWE, LELAND W., AND KIRSCHENBAUM, HOWARD. *Values Clarification: A Handbook of Practical Strategies for Teachers and Students.* New York: Hart Publishing Co., 1972.

SLATER, PHILIP. *The Pursuit of Loneliness: American Culture at the Breaking Point.* Boston: Beacon Press, 1976.

SLAUGHTER, MARTINA. "Edmund Wilson and The Turn of the Screw." In Kimbrough, ed. *The Turn of the Screw,* pp. 211–14.

SLOAN, DOUGLAS, ED. *Education and Values*. New York: Teachers College Press, 1980.

SMITH, HENRY NASH. *Virgin Land: The American West as Symbol and Myth*. Cambridge, Mass.: Harvard University Press, 1970.

SOLOMON, ERIC. "The Return of the Screw." In Kimbrough, ed. *The Turn of the Screw*, pp. 237–45.

SOLZHENITSYN, ALEXANDER. "The Exhausted West." *Harvard Magazine*, July/August 1978.

STEINER, NANCY HUNTER. *A Closer Look at Ariel: A Memory of Sylvia Plath*. New York: Popular Library, 1974.

THOREAU, HENRY DAVID. "Civil Disobedience." In *Walden and Civil Disobedience*. Boston: Riverside Edition, Houghton Mifflin Co., 1960.

TOLSTOY, LEO. *The Death of Ivan Ilych and Other Stories*. trans. Aylmer Maude. New York: The New American Library of World Literature, 1960.

TOMPKINS, JAN P., ED. *Twentieth Century Interpretations of The Turn of the Screw and Other Tales*. Englewood Cliffs, N.J.: Prentice-Hall, 1970.

TONKIN, HUMPHREY, AND EDWARDS, JANE. "Curricular Strategies for the 21st Century." In *The World in the Curriculum*, Education and the World View Series, II. New Rochelle, N.Y.: Change Magazine Press, 1981.

TROW, MARTIN. "Higher Education and Moral Development." *AAUP Bulletin*, 62 (1976), 20–27.

TWAIN, MARK. *Adventures of Huckleberry Finn (Tom Sawyer's Comrade)*. Boston: Houghton Mifflin Co., 1958.

UNDERHILL, EVELYN. *Practical Mysticism*. New York: E. P. Dutton, 1915.

WASHINGTON, BOOKER T. *Up From Slavery*. New York: Bantam Books, 1959.

WATKINS, BEVERLY T. "More Decisions on Purchasing Textbooks Now Made by Committees, Survey Shows." *Chronicle of Higher Education*, April 28, 1980, p. 1 and p. 4.

WHITMAN, WALT. *Complete Poetry and Selected Prose*, ed. James E. Miller, Jr. Boston: Houghton Mifflin Co., 1959.

WILSON, JAMES Q. "Harvard's Core Curriculum: A View from the Inside." *Change*, 10 (November 1978), pp. 40–43.

WOLFE, TOM. *Mauve Gloves and Madmen, Clutter and Vine*. New York: Bantam Books, 1977.

———. "The 'Me' Decade and the Third Great Awakening." *New York*, August 1976, pp. 26–40.

WRIGHT, RICHARD. *Native Son*. New York: Harper & Row, 1966.

YANKELOVICH, DANIEL. *The Changing Values on Campus: Political and Personal Attitudes of Today's College Students*. New York: Washington Square Press, 1972.

Index